Touching All the Bases

Baseball in 101 Fascinating Stories

Thomas D. Phillips

THE SCARECROW PRESS, INC.
Lanham • Toronto • Plymouth, UK
2012

Published by Scarecrow Press, Inc.
A wholly owned subsidiary of The Rowman & Littlefield Publishing Group, Inc.
4501 Forbes Boulevard, Suite 200, Lanham, Maryland 20706
www.rowman.com

10 Thornbury Road, Plymouth PL6 7PP, United Kingdom

British Library Cataloguing in Publication Information Available

Library of Congress Cataloging-in-Publication Data

Phillips, Thomas D.
Touching all the bases : baseball in 101 fascinating stories / Thomas D. Phillips.
  p. cm.
Includes bibliographical references and index.
ISBN 978-0-8108-8552-3 (cloth : alk. paper) — ISBN 978-0-8108-8553-0 (ebook)
1. Baseball—Anecdotes. I. Title.
GV873.P53 2012
796.357—dc23
2012017248

Printed in the United States of America

Contents

Introduction

The goal of *Touching All the Bases* is to tell the whole story of baseball—its evolution as a sport, its defining moments on the field, and the external forces that shaped its history.

The book evolved from events many years ago when a friend and I, both young officers, volunteered to coach youth baseball at a small city near the military post. We were first told that the town's two teams had already been selected, but a few days later, just before the season started, the league decided to form a third team composed of youngsters who had been cut from the two established clubs. At best, the town's approach was a questionable way of addressing the real need to provide additional chances to play. Nonetheless, we were eager to coach, and we were quickly assigned the kids who had not made the other teams.

It was clear from the first practice that the kids knew little of the basics and that, fundamentals aside, most could not run as fast, throw as far, or catch as well as the youngsters who had made the other teams—and they knew it. Perhaps worse, most knew little about the game itself.

My friend and I decided that we would simply try to teach them to understand and enjoy the game, starting with the fundamentals and adding bit by bit as the season went along. But equally as important, we hoped to not only improve their skills but get them to appreciate the game and its magic.

We began each practice with a story about the game or its history: Joe DiMaggio's hitting streak, Johnny Vander Meer's back-to-back no-hitters, Bill Wambsganss's unassisted triple play—a small vignette each day. Above all, we wanted the youngsters to enjoy the game and savor it for a lifetime.

Those stories succeeded beyond our fondest expectations. As a coach, I found that the stories provided an extra benefit: when practices began, they were a great way of getting kids settled and focused. As I coached different age groups around the country and around the world, I discovered that it was not just that first group of kids who were intrigued by the stories; *everyone* seemed to be fascinated by them: the parents who attended the practices, my own teammates, friends and acquaintances who loved the sport—all were engrossed by the tales. Interested bystanders almost always joined the conversation after questions like . . .

- Who threw the first curve?
- How do you figure earned run average?
- What was the best team?
- What was the longest game?
- Why are the bases 90 feet apart?
- Seventeen runs in one inning—you're kidding, right?
- Who gets the money from World Series games?
- What does "free agency" mean, anyway?

Accounts of Mays's catch at the Polo Grounds, Ruth's "called shot," Larsen's perfect game, and the "Homer in the Gloamin'" seemed to be of interest to fans of all ages. More recently, topics such as interleague play and the "steroids issue" increasingly sparked discussion.

Beginning with those first teaching moments many summers ago, it became evident that the stories fascinated a much broader audience—not just players but fans both dedicated and casual, grandparents as well as grandchildren. As time went by, I expanded the story base to cover all aspects of the sport: the most famous games, teams, and plays; the greatest individual achievements; how the game began; how the equipment developed; notable firsts; ballparks; nicknames; and many other facets of the game that convey a sense of its magic.

As the scope of the stories evolved, it seemed useful to also develop a cultural history of baseball that would complement descriptions of its physical components and draw together the major aspects of the game in a single, comprehensive work. Hopefully, the results of that process in the pages that follow will entertain, interest, and inform casual fans as well as those most intensely committed to the sport.

The book is dedicated to all those who reserve a special place in their lives for the game of baseball.

Chapter One

In the Beginning . . .

. . . there was a diamond, a team, and a set of rules.

1. THE DIAMOND, THE TEAM, AND THE SET OF RULES

The Diamond

If the exact date is ever discovered, many who love the game of baseball believe that it should be celebrated as a national holiday. As baseball legend has it, on one spring or summer day—probably in 1845, although some sentiment places it earlier—a young man named Alexander Cartwright went to a meadow in Manhattan and laid out a diamond-shaped playing area with bases 90 feet apart.

If fans of the game wished to commemorate the site, many historians would say the plaque should be set near the corner of Twenty-Seventh Street and Fourth Avenue. Other researchers identify the tract as "a meadow on the slope of Murray Hill near Fourth Avenue." It seems clear that both descriptions refer to the same general location.

Unfortunately, no sketch of the diamond or copies of the rules (if any were written down) have survived from Cartwright's time at the Manhattan site, which he and a group of friends had been using since about 1842 to play a version of a bat-and-ball game.

Things became a little clearer when Cartwright and his group had to find another place to play. In 1845, they moved across the Hudson River and began playing at a "picturesque and delightful" location in Hoboken, New Jersey. There, at what many would argue was the first true baseball field, the group rented a section of ground at a site called Elysian Fields, a term that has come down through baseball history conjuring up visions of a wondrous game played in idyllic settings.

The Team

Possibly to help pay rental fees for use of the Elysian Fields grounds, Cartwright formed the Knickerbocker Ball Club. The name "Knickerbocker" came from the fire station in which Cartwright worked when he and his friends began playing ball on the Manhattan meadow. At the Elysian Fields on June 19, 1846, the Knickerbockers played a well-documented first game against an outside team.

Some have noted that the Knickerbockers were probably not the nation's first baseball club; indeed, there are occasional references to earlier contests between teams playing variants of bat-and-ball games. However, unlike the Knickerbocker Ball Club, which existed as an organization for several years, other teams were short-lived and soon dropped from view.

The Rules

At about the same time that Alexander Cartwright formed the Knickerbocker Ball Club, he set down rules for the game. The year most often cited is 1845, but there remains some dispute. The 20 written rules issued by Cartwright were the first to codify instructions for the sport that has evolved into the present-day game.

Variations of bat-and-ball games were being played long before Cartwright put his rules on paper or went to the meadow in Manhattan, and other popular versions existed during his time. Cartwright, though, was the first to prescribe distances and guidelines for what was initially called "base ball." Over the years, "base ball" morphed into "baseball" as the game became ingrained in the nation's fabric.

While the sport defined by Cartwright's rules differed in some aspects from its modern-day counterpart, present-day fans would recognize major components of today's game in them: the field was diamond shaped; three missed swings retired a batter; outs were also made by catching a ball in the air, throwing to first base to beat a runner, or tagging a base runner; and three outs constituted a team's at bat during an inning.

How the most magical part of Cartwright's game came about remains a mystery. Ninety feet between bases turned out to be *just right*. Had the dimensions been set even a bit longer, almost every ground ball would result in an out. Any closer and most batters would be safe. Ninety feet is just right.

As baseball legend goes, when Cartwright went to the meadow, he carried a chart with him. The dimensions of the ball diamond he sketched that June day may have been determined simply by the size of the meadow. Or, he may have stepped off about 30 paces and decided the distance was right. No one knows.

However it came about, as the great baseball writer Red Smith noted, "The world's fastest runner cannot run to first base ahead of a sharply hit ball that is cleanly handled by an infielder. . . . Let the fielder juggle the ball for one moment or delay his throw an instant and the runner will be safe. Ninety feet demands perfection. . . . That single dimension makes baseball a fine art—and nobody knows for sure how it came to be."

Chapter Two

Firsts

Over the long history of baseball, the more than a century and a half from the forming of the first team to the 30 major league franchises playing 162 games a year, the number of first-time events associated with the sport would likely fill the memory capacity of a modern computer. The stories in this chapter shine the spotlight on those notable firsts that set precedents or changed the sport so significantly that they have remained permanent fixtures.

2. FIRST ALL-SALARIED PROFESSIONAL TEAM

The 1869 Cincinnati Red Stockings were the first team in baseball to have all players on salary. The Red Stockings were led by Harry Wright, a former cricket player. In return for the $1,200 the club paid him, Wright served the team as captain, player, recruiter, and publicity agent. Other players on the team received a total of $9,300 in salaries. The pay scale ranged from $1,400 (paid to Harry Wright's brother George, a star of the team) to $600 (for a player named Richard Hurley, the team's only substitute).[1]

The Red Stockings went through the entire 1869 season undefeated (among the 70 or so wins, there was 1 tie game) and were acknowledged for their excellent play by President Ulysses S. Grant, who personally met with the players when the team made a special postseason trip to Washington, DC.

In February 2009, a baseball card depicting the 1869 Red Stockings team sold on eBay for $64,073. The price for what is believed to be one of history's first baseball cards was more than six times the total salary paid to the entire 1869 team.

3. THE PIONEERS

The Curve Ball

It is quite likely that the first curve ball was a clamshell! The exact timing is a little murky, but it appears that sometime in 1863, William "Candy" Cummings, a 120-pound pitcher, discovered that he could make clamshells turn to the left or right depending on how he released them. In one of history's great leaps of logic, Cummings transferred that skill to throwing a baseball.

Though the claim is disputed, many sources credit Cummings, who played with the New York Excelsiors club, with throwing the first curve in a game. The date most often cited is 1864, but for sure he was throwing curves in 1867 when the Excelsiors played Harvard.

Bobby Mathews, who pitched at about the same time for the Fort Wayne Kekiongas, was also reportedly one of the early "inventors" of the curve ball.

Ironically, skeptics at first dismissed the curve ball as an "optical illusion." It was not until August 16, 1870, at a game at Capitoline Grounds, home of the Brooklyn Atlantics, that a pitcher named Fred Goldsmith conclusively ended the "optical illusion" argument by throwing an "inshoot curve" between two stakes: one positioned between the pitcher's box and home plate, the other placed to the right of home plate.

The Relay Throw and Cutoff Play

As the game took hold and its popularity increased, innovations began almost immediately. Indeed, Harry Wright, manager of that first professional team, the 1869 Cincinnati Red Stockings, is sometimes credited with developing the relay throw from the outfield, using the shortstop or the second baseman to intercept the ball and propel it more quickly to the appropriate base. Other sources believe that the play evolved even earlier, when games were played on larger or completely open fields. In those conditions, relays occurred spontaneously or as part of a practiced routine when outfielders tracked down balls hit to the far edges of the playing area. In 1868, Henry Chadwick, an early baseball writer and statistician, suggested a variation using outfielders as the relay players. Cutoff plays aimed at preventing runners from taking extra bases on hits to the outfield came soon after, although the play may not have been used systematically until the 1890s. John McGraw and Hughie Jennings, then players with the Baltimore Orioles, are sometimes cited as the inventors of the cutoff play, but there are other claimants, and widespread use by a number of teams may have occurred almost simultaneously as knowledge of the play spread and its value became evident.

Batting Practice and Fungo Flies

In the 1880s, Harry Wright, then managing the Philadelphia Phillies, began the regimen of having his team take batting practice before each game. Wright was also apparently the first to hit fungo fly balls to prepare his team for a game.

The Wheel Play

Although the first instance of the shortstop covering third base while the third baseman charged toward home plate to field a bunt is not certain, a documented occurrence took place as early as the 1903 World Series. In a game against the American League champion Boston Pilgrims, Pittsburgh Pirate third baseman Jimmy Leach threw to shortstop Honus Wagner to foil a sacrifice attempt.

The Hit and Run

Many features of what is now sometimes called "inside baseball" or "small ball"—moving runners from base to base, playing for one run at a time—evolved surprisingly early in the game's history. While there is no way of determining exactly when the hit-and-run play was first used in a major league game, there is evidence in the form of an essay that describes the play explicitly—identifying Tom McCarthy, manager of the Boston ball club, as already using it by 1893.

In later years, Cap Anson of the Chicago White Stockings and John McGraw of the Baltimore Orioles would claim credit for introducing the play, but McCarthy's use remains the first written evidence. Regardless of the official inventor, by the mid-1890s some teams had refined the play and were using it as a standard feature of their offenses.

Spring Training

Cap Anson is thought to be the first to conduct a spring training session for his team. In 1887, Anson took the White Stockings to Hot Springs, Arkansas, to prepare the club for a series of preseason games. The Stockings' Hot Springs sojourn is regarded by many as being the first spring training for a major league organization. (Present-day spring training sites are shown at Appendix A.)

Instructional Films and Other Firsts

John McGraw was the first manager to film players during spring training for instructional purposes. Although films had been taken of baseball activities since the turn of the century, McGraw was the first to film portions of his

New York Giants' spring training sessions, doing so circa 1915. In addition to his film innovations and early hit-and-run involvement, McGraw is thought by many to have been the inventor of both the squeeze play and the "Baltimore chop"—driving the ball hard into the ground or off the plate so that the resulting high bounce would allow the batter time to beat the fielder's throw to first base.

Playing Off the Bag at First Base

Joe Start, a first baseman who played for National League teams in New York and Hartford in the mid- to late 1870s, is cited by many as being the first to play off the bag when no runners were on base.

The First Professional Umpire

There remains some question, but perhaps the first full-time professional umpire was John "Honest John" Gaffney. Gaffney was paid $2,500 plus expenses to officiate the 1888 season. Previously, umpires had been hired and reimbursed game by game. Gaffney's other related claim to fame is that he is thought to be the first umpire to call pitches from behind the plate when the bases were empty.

The Box Score and Statistical Records

The box score was devised by Henry Chadwick, a journalist and baseball devotee who wrote about the sport for several New York City publications. Patterned after a cricket scorecard, the format and substance of Chadwick's invention have changed little over the years. Even use of the *K* to denote a strikeout—as taken from the last letter of *struck* (out)—is found in early published box scores. Chadwick is also credited with devising early statistical measures, such as batting average and earned run average. As early as 1861, he began recording and publishing statistics on games played, outs, runs, home runs, and strikeouts, creating the sport's first-of-its-kind database. Chadwick's early work as a baseball writer and statistician is sometimes credited with influencing the development of sports journalism as a unique discipline.

4. FIRST WORLD SERIES

In 1903, a national agreement among club owners established the American and National leagues as coequal major leagues. The agreement brought relative stability to the game after years of turmoil. While the pact did not specifically call for a postseason championship series, the stage was set for one, and Boston (American League) and Pittsburgh (National League) agreed to play a nine-game series after the 1903 season. Boston won that first series five games to three.

The next year, 1904, the owner of the National League champion New York Giants refused to play the Boston team in a championship event, but beginning in 1905 the games became established as an annual postseason competition. Within a decade the games, soon christened the "World Series," became a national event.

Best-of-nine game series were played only during that 1903 contest and again briefly from 1919 to 1921. All other World Series matches have been best-of-seven competitions.

From the time of that first World Series in 1903 through 1968, the league champion and World Series representative was the team with the best won-lost record at the end of the season. In 1969, when both leagues expanded to 12 teams and divided into two divisions, best-of-five playoffs were instituted to determine league champions. In 1985, the League Championship Series was changed to a best-of-seven format.

Ten years later, with further expansion, the playoff system was revised to include four teams in each league, three division champions plus an additional "wild card" entry (the nondivision winning team with the best record). Since that time, the two sets of division-level playoffs have been best-of-five competitions. League champions—the clubs that represent each league in the World Series—are determined by best-of-seven League Championship Series.

Effective with the 2012 season, the playoff pool was expanded from four to five teams in each league, creating a one-game playoff between each league's pair of wild card winners. In each league, the two nondivision winning teams with the best won-lost records meet in a single "play-in" game to determine which club advances to the division playoff round. (Appendix B shows World Series results and describes how World Series and League Championship bonus shares are determined.)

5. FIRST NIGHT GAME

The first night game played in the major leagues—May 24, 1935, at Crosley Field in Cincinnati—was a red-letter event in baseball history. Surprisingly, perhaps, the occasion did not come about easily.

Despite the success of several minor leagues that began playing night baseball in 1930,[2] the major leagues continued to ban teams from playing under the lights. Finally, in 1934, the Cincinnati Reds, a team facing serious financial difficulties, petitioned the National League for permission to play

games at night. The Reds' presentation focused almost entirely on econom-
ics, pointing out that 70 percent of the team's 1934 gross revenue had come
from 15 playing dates, only one of which—opening day—had not occurred
on a Sunday or holiday. In a decision that outraged some owners and critics,
the league agreed to allow the Reds to play seven night games beginning in
1935.

To get ready to play ball at night, the Reds installed eight 130-foot light
towers with 641 fifteen hundred-watt bulbs, which at the time cost $4.75
each. Understandably, the team made a production out of the occasion. At
precisely 8:30 pm, President Franklin D. Roosevelt pressed a button in the
White House that turned on the lights at Crosley Field.

Although played on a bitterly cold evening, the night game was an instant
success: the 20,422 fans who attended were 10 times the average number
who normally saw the team play a day game on a workday. Equally as
important to the critics was the fact that neither the players nor the fans had
any trouble seeing the ball.

Still, night baseball did not spread quickly. Other than the Reds, no other
team installed lights until 1938. Several remained without lights until 1941,
and teams were limited to seven night games per season until 1942 when
those restrictions were loosened to accommodate wartime work hours.

In that first game under the lights, the Reds bested the Phillies 2–1.

Thirty-seven more years would elapse before the first World Series game
was played at night. On October 13, 1971, at Three Rivers Stadium in Pittsburgh, the Pirates beat the Baltimore Orioles 4–3.

6. FIRST FARM SYSTEM

Perhaps best known as the general manager who brought Jackie Robinson to
the big leagues, Branch Rickey had a long and storied career in baseball.
Among other innovations, he started a preseason "Baseball College" to teach
fundamentals, and he introduced training devices such as sliding pits and
batting tees. In the 1920s, Rickey, then general manager of the St. Louis
Cardinals, was responsible for one of the most significant changes to the
baseball establishment.

Before Rickey, major league teams sometimes signed prospects and op-
tioned them to minor league teams for additional seasoning. On some occasions, major league teams actually owned or contracted with minor league
teams. Rickey, however, was the first to construct an entire system of "farm
teams"—one or more teams in every minor league classification—for the
purpose of identifying and building a pool of talent to support the major
league franchise.

Earlier conventional wisdom was that an entire structure of minor league teams would not be cost-effective for the major league club; it was easier and cheaper, many thought, to simply buy the contracts of players who had proven track records or had shown potential in the minors.

Changes to the draft rule altered that calculation. The new rules not only limited the number of players that could be drafted but also increased the price for those who were. Rickey recognized the impact of the changes but at first moved cautiously: As late as 1929, the Cardinal farm system consisted of only five teams.

Then, beginning in 1930, two new factors caused Rickey to greatly expand the Cardinal system. First, additional limits were placed on drafting players. Second, the Great Depression caused minor league salaries to plummet, allowing Cardinal scouts to sign far more players. By 1936, Rickey had 28 minor league teams in the Cardinal system.

Rickey's innovation was wildly successful, producing a flow of productive new talent for the big club. In fact, the farm system produced more major league–caliber players than the Cardinals could absorb, allowing the team to sell prospects to other clubs or replace their own established or aging stars with quality products from the farm system.

Big league clubs continue to have farm teams today, although the system devised by Branch Rickey has been greatly reduced and modified by changes to player acquisition rules and the demise of many minor league operations.

7. FIRST RADIO AND TELEVISION BROADCASTS

On August 5, 1921, radio station KDKA in Pittsburgh aired the first broadcast of a major league game. Pittsburgh's Forbes Field was the site of the broadcast. Harold Arlin was the announcer for the game that day between the Pirates and the Philadelphia Phillies, won by the Pirates 8–5.

Despite the success of the initial broadcast, many club owners were reluctant to broadcast games, fearing that fans would stay at home and listen to games rather than travel to ballparks to see them. In the 1920s, the Chicago Cubs franchise was the only one that broadcast all of the team's games. The onset of the Great Depression in the 1930s brought additional financial strains and increased many owners' fears of radio. On several occasions, owners discussed a complete ban of radio broadcasts. In 1934, the three New York teams—the Yankees, Dodgers, and Giants—instituted a ban that continued for five years. Slowly, the trend turned toward additional broadcasts, as owners realized that the turnstile evidence showed that broadcasts helped create interest and actually brought more fans to the park.

To legendary sportscaster Red Barber went the honor of announcing the first baseball game shown on television. On August 26, 1939, Barber handled the broadcast of a game between the Cincinnati Reds and the Brooklyn Dodgers from Ebbets Field in Brooklyn. Barber's first words were "This is Red Barber speaking. Let me say hello to you all." Billy Werber of the Reds was the first major league hitter to bat on television.

8. FIRST DESIGNATED HITTER . . . AND ITS ANCESTOR

Seeking primarily to add offensive punch to the game, the American League approved the designated hitter (DH) rule—allowing a player in the lineup to bat who did not play in the field—beginning with the 1973 season. On April 5, Ron Blomberg of the New York Yankees became the first DH. Ironically, Blomberg did not hit; he walked.

The following day, on opening day in Oakland, Tony Oliva of the Minnesota Twins became the first DH to hit a home run. Oliva homered in the first inning off A's pitcher Catfish Hunter.

The DH's lineal ancestor, the pinch hitter, was probably first used on May 6, 1889, when the Philadelphia Phillies' Kid Gleason batted for a noninjured teammate. Before Gleason's at bat, in the years before the introduction of the "free substitute" rule in 1891, there were other instances where substitute batters were inserted to take the places of injured players. It is believed that the first successful pinch hitter in that circumstance was Jim Devlin, a player for the Philadelphia Whites of the National Association. Devlin singled as a substitute batter on October 2, 1873.

NOTES

1. There is a bit of contention about the salary numbers. One recent source cites Harry and George Wright's salaries as $1,800 each and a total team payroll of $9,400.
2. On April 28, 1930, Independence, Kansas, and Muskogee, Oklahoma, of the Class C Western Association played the first official professional night baseball game.

Chapter Three

The Most Famous Plays

One of the surest ways to spark a discussion—or produce an argument—among baseball fans is to start a conversation about baseball's greatest plays. Realistically, there is no sure way of identifying the "best" plays made over the past 100-plus years of modern major league baseball, and this section makes no attempt to do so. Rather, it recounts some of the most famous (if not the best). Some of the plays were indeed spectacular, but the selection criterion that all of them share is that they came at critical moments on baseball's largest and brightest stages: tight pennant races, playoff games, and the World Series. Even with that qualification, the list is not all-inclusive. Stories in later chapters describe plays that, while remarkable, occurred within the context of some even larger action. (See, for example, "The Garbled Phone Calls Game: 'Can You Hear Me Now?'" and "September 28, 2011: Hours and Hours of Excitement" both in chapter 9.)

9. BILL WAMBSGANSS: UNASSISTED TRIPLE PLAY

Only 15 have occurred in all of baseball history.[1] The unassisted triple play is rarer even than a perfect game. Few other plays are as dependent on game situation, circumstance, skill, and luck.

The unassisted triple play that Cleveland second baseman Bill Wambsganss made on October 10, 1920, remains unique, however, because it happened at a key point during a World Series game.

The Indians and the Brooklyn Robins, as the team was then called, were tied at two games apiece going into game 5 of the World Series. Trailing in the game, Brooklyn had two runners on with none out in the fifth inning. With Pete Kilduff on second and Otto Miller on first, Cleveland pitcher Jim

Bagby delivered a pitch to left-handed hitter Clarence Mitchell. Mitchell hit a line-drive bullet toward second base. Wambsganss speared it, stepped on second to retire Kilduff, and then tagged out Miller coming from first. Cleveland went on to win the game 8–1 on the way to taking the nine-game series five games to two. Wambsganss's unassisted triple play remains the only one ever recorded in World Series competition. (A list of unassisted triple plays is shown in Appendix C.)

10. WILLIE MAYS: "THE CATCH"

So remarkable that it is still called "The Catch," the sensational play made by Willie Mays in the 1954 World Series remains at the top of most baseball all-time highlight reels.

History conspired to make an already incredible play loom even larger and more improbable. It came at a crucial point in the game, in a ballpark whose strange dimensions made it possible there and at no other place in baseball. The play showcased Mays's brilliance and started an underdog New York Giants team on the way to a World Series championship.

The 1954 Indians won 111 games in a 154-game season, dethroning the five-time consecutive World Series champion New York Yankees by an impressive eight games. The Indians brought with them to the series one of the great pitching staffs of all time: Bob Lemon, Early Wynn, Mike Garcia, Bob Feller, and a relief corps that was equally as deep. With power hitters Vic Wertz, Al Rosen, Larry Doby (who led the league in home runs and RBI), Bobby Avila (the American League batting champion), and a solid defense, the Indians were loaded.

The first game of the series was played on September 29 at the Polo Grounds in New York City. Built in 1911 and only modestly reconfigured over the years, its playing field was one of the most oddly shaped in all of baseball. While the left- and right-field lines were not much more than Little League distance at 280 and 258 feet, respectively, the center field wall stood a gargantuan 475 feet from home plate. The score was tied in the late innings when the Indians put two runners on base. The Giants countered by bringing in left-hander Don Liddle to pitch to the Indians' power-hitting first baseman Vic Wertz.

Wertz absolutely crushed a Liddle pitch, blasting it to the deepest part of the deepest center field in baseball. Mays, the Giants center fielder, took off at the crack of the bat, losing his cap as he turned his back to the plate and raced toward the wall. Running at full speed, he caught the ball over his shoulder, then spun around, throwing the ball back to the infield to keep the lead runner from scoring. Mays turned Wertz's drive—which would have been a home run in almost every other park and would likely have gone clear out of many of them—into nothing more than a very long out. It is regarded by most as the greatest catch in World Series history.

Mays's play saved the Giants, who went on to win the game in extra innings and sweep the series.

11. BOBBY THOMSON: "THE SHOT HEARD 'ROUND THE WORLD"

It is perhaps the most famous home run in baseball history.

The date: October 3, 1951. The scene: the Polo Grounds in New York City, home of the New York Giants. The situation: the bottom of the ninth inning of the third and final game of the playoff series between the Giants and the Brooklyn Dodgers. At stake: the National League championship and a trip to the World Series.

For the New York Giants, many things about the 1951 season were miraculous. On August 11, the Giants trailed the league-leading Dodgers by 13 1/2 games. The Giants won the next 16 in a row and 37 of their final 44 games, including the last 7. They ended the season tied with the Dodgers.

The teams split the first two games of the series, setting the stage for the climactic third game. The Giants trailed 4–1 going into the bottom of the ninth inning. Hitting against Dodger starting pitcher Don Newcombe (who was pitching on two days' rest), Giants shortstop Alvin Dark led off with a single. Right fielder Don Mueller followed with a single to right, sending Dark to third. Newcombe got the next batter, left fielder Monte Irvin, to pop up, but the next batter, first baseman Whitey Lockman, doubled to left, scoring Dark.

Third baseman Bobby Thomson came to the plate with one out, runners on second and third, and the Giants trailing 4–2. Brooklyn manager Charley Dressen took out the obviously tiring Newcombe and brought in right-hander Ralph Branca to face Thomson. Branca threw a first-pitch fastball for a strike. Then came his second pitch. In baseball lore, it made Thomson immortal.

Intending to set up a breaking ball down and away that he had planned for his third pitch, Branca delivered a fastball up and in to the right-handed Thomson. Thomson swung, pulling a low line drive down the left-field line. The foul lines were invitingly close in the strangely configured Polo Grounds, with the left-field foul pole only 280 feet from home plate. The wall then gradually curved away toward the area where the ball hit by Thomson was headed, a roll-up door in the 17-foot wall marked at 315 feet. Dodger outfielder Andy Pafko raced toward the wall, but Thomson's sinking liner cleared the fence about 40 feet from the foul line.

With dramatic suddenness, Thomson's one swing of the bat turned seeming defeat into a 5–4 victory. More important, the three-run home run gave the playoff series and, with it, the National League pennant to the Giants.

The game is remembered not only for Thomson's home run but also for Giants radio announcer Russ Hodges's "call," which became one of the most famous in history: "Branca throws . . . [*sound of ball meeting bat*]. There's a long drive. . . . It's gonna be, I believe . . . the Giants win the pennant! The Giants win the pennant! The Giants win the pennant! The Giants win the pennant! The Giants win the pennant!"

In later years, modest controversy about the game has arisen with the allegation that using a telescope from their center-field offices, the Giants were stealing signs that day (not in itself a violation of major league rules) and that Thomson might have benefited from it. Thomson denied it.

Controversy or not, the game became an instant classic. The "shot heard 'round the world" appellation was quickly given to it, which was aptly assigned as many have noted, because U.S. military personnel fighting in Korea and on duty at other places around the globe listened to the game on radio.

12. ENOS SLAUGHTER: "THE MAD DASH"

October 15, 1946: With two outs and the score tied 3–3 in the eighth inning of the seventh and deciding game of the World Series, Enos "Country" Slaughter of the St. Louis Cardinals scored all the way from first base on what normally would have been a routine single. Slaughter, who had led off the inning with a base hit, broke from first base on a pitch delivered by Boston Red Sox pitcher Bob Klinger. The Cardinals' batter Harry Walker drove Klinger's pitch over shortstop Johnny Pesky's head into left center field. Sox outfielder Leon Culbertson shakily fielded Walker's hit and threw the ball to Pesky, his relay man. Pesky, thinking that Slaughter would stop at third, held the ball for an instant. Slaughter, though, raced around third and continued toward home plate. Pesky's hurried throw was a little to the left and up the third base line. Slaughter slid across home plate with what turned out to be the winning run, giving the Cardinals the game and the series.

13. GABBY HARTNETT: THE "HOMER IN THE GLOAMIN'"

In the long and storied history of the Chicago Cubs franchise, a home run struck in the gathering twilight of a late September day remains the most famous hit by a Cubs player.

On September 28, 1938, in the throes of a tight pennant race, the Cubs trailed the Pittsburgh Pirates by a half game. With the season finale only three days away, the teams met at Wrigley Field to play the decisive series.

The teams battled through inning after hard-fought inning, eventually going into the bottom of the ninth tied 5–5. As the long game progressed and darkness began to envelop the field (lights didn't come to Wrigley until 50 years later), the umpires were set to call the game at the end of the inning. Under the rules at the time, the game would be replayed from the beginning the next day as part of a doubleheader.

When the Cubs came to bat in the bottom of the ninth, Pirates pitcher Mace Brown took advantage of the near darkness, throwing one fastball after another past Cubs hitters. After the first two Cubs were easily retired, Cubs catcher/manager Gabby Hartnett came to the plate. With two more fastballs, Brown quickly got ahead in the count 0–2. Then, in the dusk of the approaching evening, Hartnett hit the next pitch—another fastball—into the bleachers in left-center field.

Hartnett's home run gave the Cubs a 6–5 victory and put them a half game ahead in the pennant race. They clinched it three days later, finishing two games ahead of the Pirates, culminating a marvelous 19–3–1 stretch that sent them to the World Series.

The name "Homer in the Gloamin'" was coined quickly and has stuck through the following years as an apt description of the ball hit into the approaching darkness.

14. JETER'S MIRACLE

On October 13, 2001, the New York Yankees battled the Oakland A's in the third game of the American League Divisional Series. It was a must-win game for the Yankees, who trailed two games to none in the best-of-five series.

At Oakland Coliseum, the game was deep into the seventh inning; there were two outs, and Oakland had a runner, Jeremy Giambi, on first base. With the Yankees clinging to a 1–0 lead, Oakland batter Terrence Long drilled a long drive deep into right field. Running at the crack of the bat, Giambi

streaked around the bases while Yankee outfielder Shane Spencer retrieved
the ball. When Spencer reached the ball, he fired it toward home plate,
completely overthrowing two cutoff men.

As Giambi rounded third, Derek Jeter raced in from shortstop as Spencer's throw flew toward the plate. Far out of position, Jeter fielded the ball up
the line between home plate and first base and while still running at full
speed flipped it like a shovel pass to catcher Jorge Posada. Posada caught the
backhand toss and made a blindside sweep tag on Giambi coming down the
line from third.

Almost overnight, Jeter's play was recognized as one of the best of all
time.

The Yankees went on to win the game and the next two as well, to take
the series 3–2. A few days later they defeated Seattle four games to one to
win the American League pennant.

15. BILL MAZEROSKI: SEVENTH-GAME WALK-OFF HOME RUN

The walk-off home run struck by the Pittsburgh Pirates' Bill Mazeroski in
the 1960 World Series against the New York Yankees was the first time that
a series had ever been decided by a home run in the bottom of the ninth of the
seventh game.

Mazeroski, the Pirates' second baseman, was far more renowned for his
fielding skills than for his hitting prowess—in fact, some think that he might
have been the best fielding second baseman of all time. Nonetheless, his
home run leading off the bottom of the ninth gave the Pirates an improbable
10–9 victory and the World Series championship.

That it was the slick-fielding Mazeroski who got the decisive hit was only
one of the many unusual aspects of the 1960 series. During the seven games,
the Yankees outscored the Pirates by an incredible 55–27 runs, got 31 more
hits (91–60) than did the Pirates, had a batting average 82 points higher (.338
to .256), and hit 10 home runs to Pittsburgh's 4. Yankee pitcher Whitey Ford
threw two complete-game shutouts. For the only time, a player from the
losing team—Yankee second baseman Bobby Richardson (who hit .367 and
drove in 12 runs)—was named the World Series most valuable player.

The seventh game was a seesaw contest. The Pirates jumped off to an
early 4–1 lead and then trailed 7–4 going into the eighth. With five runs in
the bottom of the inning, Pittsburgh regained the lead, carrying a 9–7 advantage into the ninth. The Yankees promptly tied the score with two runs in the
inning, making it 9–9 and setting the stage for Mazeroski's heroics. With
right-hander Ralph Terry pitching in relief for the Yankees, Mazeroski hit a
one-ball, no-strike fastball far over the left-field wall.

In a series in which they were dominated statistically and probably outplayed overall, the Pirates found a way to win. Mazeroski's home run remains one of a kind: a walk-off shot that won a series in the seventh game. [2]

Yankees Wins

Game 2: 16–3, Forbes Field
Game 3: 10–0, Yankee Stadium
Game 6: 12–0, Forbes Field

Pirates Wins

Game 1: 6–4, Forbes Field
Game 4: 3–2, Yankee Stadium
Game 5: 5–2, Yankee Stadium
Game 7: 10–9, Forbes Field

16. KIRK GIBSON: THE UNBELIEVABLE HOME RUN

It might be the most implausible home run ever hit in a World Series game.

On October 15, 1988, the Los Angeles Dodgers' Kirk Gibson, playing on legs so bad that he had difficulty walking to the plate, hit a bottom-of-the-ninth, pinch-hit two-run home run that won Game 1 of the 1988 World Series. It was the first time that a World Series game had ever been won on a come-from-behind home run in the last inning. Many Dodger fans regard it as the greatest home run in the history of that storied franchise.

The Dodgers trailed the series favorite Oakland Athletics 4–3 that night as the bottom of the ninth began at Dodger Stadium. Dennis Eckersley, with 45 saves that year as the premier reliever in the major leagues, came in to pitch for the Athletics. Eckersley easily retired the first two Dodger batters before walking pinch hitter Mike Davis. In a surprise move, Dodger manager Tommy Lasorda then called on Gibson to pinch-hit for relief pitcher Alejandro Pena. Injured during the National League Championship Series, Gibson was hobbling badly. Practice swings in the Dodger clubhouse drew agonizing groans with each swing.

Gibson fouled off tough pitches by Eckersley and took two others barely off the outside corner as the count eventually reached 3–2. With the count full, Eckersley's next pitch was a "backdoor slider." Gibson reached across the plate and hit it into the lower right-field stands. The Dodgers won 5–4. Replays of the gimpy Gibson going around the bases—right arm pumping like an exaggerated double-clutch of a floor shift on an 18-wheeler—are shown repeatedly on sports program segments. Announcer Jack Buck's call—"I don't believe what I just saw"—captured the moment precisely and became one of the sport's historical icons.

Gibson later credited a report from Dodger scout Mel Didier for identifying the backdoor slider as the likely pitch that Eckersley would throw on a 3–2 count to a left-handed hitter.

The Athletics never seemed to recover from that first-game loss, as the Dodgers took the series four games to one.

17. BABE RUTH: "THE CALLED SHOT"

Did he or didn't he? Did Babe Ruth really point to the stands and then hit the very next pitch over the fence in that exact spot? That play in the 1932 World Series remains one of the most debated in baseball history.

The Yankees and the Cubs were battling both on and off the field when the series moved to Wrigley Field for Game 3 on October 1. On the field, the Yankees led the series two games to none, having won the first two games at Yankee Stadium. Off the field, emotions ran high as the bench-jockeying insults traded by the teams became increasingly heated.

In statements to the press, some Yankee players, Ruth among them, had called the Cubs cheapskates. The main source of contention was the decision by the Cubs players to award Mark Koenig, a former Yankee player now with the Cubs, only a half share of World Series money. The Cubs resented the cheapskates label, pointing out that Koenig had played only 33 games for the team and was unable to play in the series because of injury. A second circumstance also fueled the fire: only two years previously, Yankee manager Joe McCarthy had managed the Cubs. Indeed, he had managed the team to the World Series in 1929 before being fired after finishing second the following year. From the start, the trash talk between the teams was intense. The Cubs called Ruth fat and washed up and shouted slurs questioning his ethnicity.

Into this charged atmosphere, Ruth—who had hit a three-run home run in the first inning—stepped to the plate in the fifth with the score tied 4–4. There is general agreement regarding the first pitches of his at bat. Cubs pitcher Charley Root threw a first-pitch fastball for a strike, which Ruth acknowledged with a raised hand. Most observers agreed that Ruth indicated "strike 1" to the Cubs dugout or perhaps to Root or the crowd in general. With the count two balls and one strike, Ruth took another strike from Root, and raised two fingers, indicating strike 2. Before the next pitch, Ruth apparently said something to Root. Ruth's version is that he told Root what he was going to do with the ball. Ruth then made some kind of gesture with his right hand. Exactly what it was and what it intended remain controversial to this day.

The version that has become legend is that Ruth pointed to the center-field wall and then hit Root's next pitch over the fence at that exact spot. That story might be true: Lou Gehrig, who watched the action from his vantage point in the on-deck circle, said immediately after the game that Ruth had "called his shot." Or it might not: Pitcher Charley Root disagreed, saying that if Ruth had pointed like that, Root would have knocked him down with the next pitch.

Fuzzy images found years later from the reels of two small handheld movie cameras are not definitive. They appear to show Ruth making some kind of motion with his right hand, but the film is too grainy and the shots taken too far away to be conclusive.

Ruth himself was equivocal. On occasion over the years, he affirmed the version of legend. In other circumstances, the story differed. In one account, he said that he had indeed made a sweeping gesture, not specifically directed at center field, to indicate that he was going to hit it somewhere over the fence. In another, he stated that he pointed to Root, saying that he was going to "hit the ball down his throat." At least once when questioned, he replied something to the effect that "whatever happened, it made for a great story."

That, at least, is something that all can agree on. Nearly eight decades later, whatever happened remains a great story.

Led by Ruth and Gehrig (who each hit two home runs), the Yankees went on to win the game 7–5 and sweep the series.

18. BUCKY DENT: THE UNPRINTABLE MIDDLE NAME

In one entire section of the country, Yankees shortstop Bucky Dent's name is seldom mentioned without adding an expletive (and deleted) middle name.

What malicious combination of factors made the name "Bucky Dent" alone insufficient to appropriately convey Boston fans' sense of hurt, outrage, and disgust?

Here's what happened: (1) Dent's heroics came in a one-game playoff to decide the American League East Division Championship; (2) the game between the bitter rivals Yankees and Red Sox was played at Boston's home field, Fenway Park; (3) during the year, the Yankees had overcome a seemingly insurmountable 14-game Red Sox lead to force the playoff game; (4) Dent's three-run home run led the Yankees to a 5–4 victory.

Dent was the least likely hero. In 1978, he batted only .243 (his lifetime average was .247) and hit five home runs. Worse, during the final 20 games of the season, he batted .140. It was only a shortage of other infielders that put him in the lineup that day. Dent's seventh-inning hit off Boston pitcher Mike Torrez carried about 315 feet, just far enough for it to land in the screen on top of Fenway's "Green Monster" left-field wall.

The drama of the October 2, 1978, contest made the game and Dent's role in its outcome one of the most memorable in baseball history. For Red Sox fans, whose team at the time had not won a World Series since 1918, the loss seemed particularly cruel, coming as it did at the hands of a nonslugger such as Dent.

Hence, in the Boston area, Bucky (*bleeping*) Dent is what his name will always be.

19. AL GIONFRIDDO: THE CATCH THAT FRUSTRATED DIMAGGIO

A catch made by Brooklyn Dodger center fielder Al Gionfriddo in the 1947 World Series is remembered for two reasons. The first and foremost is that the catch—made on a drive hit to deep left center field by the Yankees' Joe DiMaggio—was phenomenal. The second is that the grab caused DiMaggio to shake his head and kick the dirt near second base in frustration. It was one of the few times in his storied career that the imperturbable DiMaggio showed his emotions.

Gionfriddo, a 5'6" utility player, was put into the game for defensive purposes in the bottom of the sixth inning with the Dodgers leading 8–5. With two on and two out, he was playing deep in the cavernous center field at the original Yankee Stadium when DiMaggio hit a long line drive. The ball was struck so sharply that Gionfriddo, off with the crack of the bat, never had time to fully turn around. Instead, moving slightly to his side and angling backward, he went to the fence in left center field. There, near a small gate to the bullpen marked at 415 feet, just as it seemed the ball might carry over the short wall, he reached out at the last instant and caught it.

Films of the action make it appear doubtful that the ball would have cleared the fence, but even if it had stayed in the park, two runs would have scored, and DiMaggio would have been at second or third with the tying run. The Dodgers held the lead and won the game 8–6 (although they lost the seventh and deciding game).

Observers have commented that while the catch itself was outstanding, equally as remarkable was how far Gionfriddo had to backpedal before making it. Announcer Red Barber's "back, back, back" call quickly became famous and remains widely imitated.

Gionfriddo did not make any more putouts in game 6 and did not play in game 7. By the next year, he was out of the major leagues. Thus, the ironies: the game was his last in the big leagues, and the catch that made him famous was the last putout he would ever make as a major league ballplayer.

NOTES

1. Some scholars include a disputed play during a game in 1878 as the first unassisted triple play and thus list a total of 16.

2. The Toronto Blue Jays' Joe Carter's notable series-ending home run in 1993 came in the sixth game.

Chapter Four

The Most Famous Misplays

Baseball involves a series of individual confrontations—pitcher against batter, catcher against runner, fielder against batted ball—all performed within a team context. Even in an era of power pitchers and long ball hitters, sometimes it is the outcome of a single defensive play in the contest between fielder and ball that is so remarkable or decisive that it becomes ingrained as a part of baseball's institutional memory.

When the fielder prevails in an extraordinary way, such as Mays with his catch in the 1954 World Series or Jeter with his full-speed backhand toss, both the play and the player are recalled as part of the game's lore.

Sometimes, though, the ball wins.

20. MICKEY OWEN: THE DROPPED THIRD STRIKE

The Brooklyn Dodgers were one pitch—one strike—away from tying the 1941 World Series with the crosstown New York Yankees at two games apiece. The Dodgers got the strike, a swinging strikeout, and lost the game!

The fourth game of the series was played October 5 at Ebbets Field, home of the Brooklyn Dodgers. The Yankees led two games to one; a Dodger win would even the series.

The Dodgers appeared to have victory in hand. After trailing early 3–0, they had rallied to take a 4–3 lead into the ninth inning. Relief pitcher Hugh Casey was especially sharp, entering the game in the fifth inning to shut down the Yankees, leaving the bases loaded, and then pitching shutout ball through the sixth, seventh, and eighth. The ninth inning began well for Casey and the Dodgers. Casey retired the first two Yankee hitters on easy ground balls. With two out, outfielder Tommy Henrich came to the plate for the Yankees. Casey and Henrich battled to a 3–2 count: one more strike would tie the series.

The Dodgers got the strike: Henrich swung and missed the low, sharp-breaking curve thrown by Casey.

They did not get the win: the ball caromed off the side of catcher Mickey Owen's mitt and rolled away toward the Dodgers' dugout.

Henrich hurried to first base, reaching safely on Owen's passed ball. Owen's misplay opened the floodgates: Joe DiMaggio singled; Charlie Keller doubled, driving in two runs; Bill Dickey walked; and Joe Gordon hit another two-run double. When the inning was over, the Yankees had scored four runs—all coming after two outs with the bases empty—and led 7–4. They won the game by that score, closing out the Dodgers in order in the bottom of the ninth and went on to take the series four games to one.

21. FRED SNODGRASS: "THE $30,000 MUFF"

The 1912 World Series between the New York Giants and the Boston Red Sox was one of the most closely competed of all time. In only one game was the winning margin more than three runs. Four games were decided by one run, one by two runs, and another ended in a tie, called because of darkness. In two games, the losing team had the tying and winning runs on base when the game ended. Two more, including the decisive final game, went into extra innings.

Two notable firsts highlighted the series: It was the first to be decided in the last inning of the final game and the first where a team within one inning of losing came back to win. It was Giant center fielder Fred Snodgrass's role in the latter circumstance that brought him lasting notoriety.

The series was tied three games apiece, and the game, played at Boston's new Fenway Park, was knotted 1–1 going into extra innings. In the top of the 10th, the Giants managed a run off Boston reliever Smokey Joe Wood, taking a 2–1 lead and putting them only three outs away from winning the series.

The bottom of the inning began when Boston pinch hitter Clyde Engle (batting for pitcher Wood) led off with a high, lazy fly to center field. Snodgrass took a step back, setting up to make a routine catch—and dropped the ball! Meanwhile, Engle hustled into second base putting the tying run in scoring position.

The next batter, Harry Hooper, followed with a wicked line drive to center. This time, Snodgrass made an excellent running catch of the hard-hit ball, but Engle advanced to third base after the catch. Giant pitcher Christy Mathewson then walked the next batter, Steve Yerkes, putting the winning run on base and bringing Tris Speaker to the plate.

Snodgrass's muff is the most remembered misplay of the series, but what happened next was equally decisive. Speaker popped up Mathewson's pitch, lofting the ball foul between home plate and first base. Neither Mathewson nor first baseman Fred Merkle nor catcher Chief Meyers made a play on the ball, which fell harmlessly among them. Given new life, Speaker singled, tying the game and sending Yerkes to third with the potential winning run. Mathewson then issued an intentional walk, loading the bases and setting up a force play at every base. However, Boston's next batter, Larry Gardner, hit the ball in the air to right field, scoring Yerkes with the winning run on a sacrifice fly.

Snodgrass's error, called "Snodgrass's muff," or "the $30,000 muff" (the difference between the teams' winning and losing share), became part of the baseball history.

22. FRED MERKLE'S BONEHEAD PLAY

The Chicago Cubs and the New York Giants were in the closing days of a tight pennant race when the teams met at the Polo Grounds, the Giants' home park, on September 28, 1908.

With the score tied at 1–1 in the bottom of the ninth, the Giants put runners on first and third with two outs. Al Bridwell, the next Giant batter, singled to center, sending home the runner at third, Moose McCormick. The Giants' runner on first, Fred Merkle, seeing McCormick score what appeared to be the winning run, trotted toward second base but did not touch it, turning instead to run to the Giants' clubhouse in center field.

As fans poured onto the field, Cubs second baseman Johnny Evers, noting that Merkle never touched the bag, retrieved the ball (some argued that it was not the game ball) and stepped on second base, claiming a force out. Amid chaos, umpire Hank O'Day agreed, ruling that because Merkle never reached the base, he was the third out of the inning, and thus McCormick's run did not count.

The teams finished the season tied with 98–55 records. When the National League then ordered the contest replayed, the Cubs won the game and, with it, the National League pennant.

Fred Merkle, a 19-year-old rookie at the time, played an additional, productive 16 years in the major leagues. While his teammates never blamed him for his mental lapse, "Merkle's Boner," as the play became known, followed him for the rest of his career.

23. BILL BUCKNER'S ERROR

In the 10th inning of game 6 of the 1986 World Series, a ground ball was hit toward Boston first baseman Bill Buckner. The slow roller struck by the New York Mets' Mookie Wilson slipped under Buckner's glove. The winning run scored as the ball trickled into right field. The Mets' victory that night of October 25 tied the series at three games apiece. Two nights later the Mets won again, taking the seventh and deciding game.

For the Red Sox, who were within one pitch of winning their first World Series since 1918, it must surely have seemed that the "Curse of the Bambino"[1] was alive and present in the ballpark.

The game had gone into extra innings tied 3–3. Boston scored twice in the top of the 10th to lead 5–3. When Boston reliever Calvin Schiraldi retired the first two batters in the bottom of the inning, it appeared that the Sox were well on their way to victory. But down to their last out, Mets catcher Gary Carter singled. Outfielder Kevin Mitchell followed Carter with another base hit. Schiraldi then got quickly ahead of the Mets' next batter, third baseman Ray Knight. With the count no balls and two strikes, the Sox were one strike from the World Series title.

Knight spoiled the Sox's moment with an 0–2 base hit that scored Carter and moved Mitchell to third. With the score now 5–4, the Sox brought in Bob Stanley to pitch to Mookie Wilson. Stanley and Wilson battled through a tense, anguishing 10-pitch duel that riveted the 55,078 fans at Shea Stadium and the millions in the television audience.

With the count two balls and one strike, Wilson fouled off three consecutive pitches. Then pandemonium broke loose as Stanley's seventh pitch went wild, eluding Boston catcher Rich Gedman and allowing Mitchell to race home with the tying run and Knight to move to second as the ball rolled toward the backstop.

The count then moved to 3–2 with Wilson still at the plate when Stanley delivered his 10th pitch of the confrontation. Wilson hit it slowly toward Buckner, who was playing behind the first base bag. Somehow, the ball stayed under his glove and dribbled out into the right field grass. Knight scored from second and the Mets won.

As with Fred Snodgrass's miscue, it is that particular play that is most often remembered and not the circumstances surrounding it in the game. While the image that remains in the minds of viewers is that of the ball trickling past Buckner, often overlooked is that Boston left 14 base runners stranded that night and blew a 5–3 lead with two outs in the 10th inning. Buckner's presence in the game at that stage was in itself an issue. Painfully hobbled, Buckner was playing on two bad ankles. Boston's manager was later faulted for having left him in the game while trying to protect a lead that would have won the series. Furthermore, even with that game lost, it is useful to remember that the Sox led 3–0 into the sixth inning of the seventh game and blew that lead also.

Buckner—a former National League batting champion regarded by his teammates as a consummate professional—never made excuses. Boston would have to wait another 18 years before winning a World Series and finally removing the "Curse of the Bambino."

NOTE

1. The Sox had not won a series since an owner desperate for money traded Babe Ruth to the Yankees.

Chapter Five

Streaks and Sustained Excellence

At any one time, there are about 750 players in the major leagues. They come from many parts of the world. They have been scouted, weeded out, shaped, and trained until, eventually, barring injuries or bad breaks, a special few with extraordinary talent make the cut and find places on major league rosters.

Against that best-of-the-best competition perhaps the surest measure of excellence is to perform at a level superior to that of even those exceptional contemporaries: to excel day in and day out over a series of games, or a season, or a lifetime.

24. DIMAGGIO'S HITTING STREAK

In 1941, Joe DiMaggio captivated the nation by getting at least one hit in 56 consecutive ball games. News broadcasts and newspaper headlines highlighted the story as, day by day, the streak continued. For fans nationwide, the answer to the burning question "Did Joe get a hit yesterday?" was the first thing they looked for when they opened their sports pages in the morning.

The streak began on May 15. From that day until July 17, DiMaggio had at least one hit in every game. During that time, he batted .409 with 91 hits in 223 at bats. The streak ended only when Cleveland third baseman Ken Keltner made two dazzling plays on balls hit hard by DiMaggio.

On occasions during the streak, luck played a part. DiMaggio twice benefited on close calls by official scorers and got one hit when a catchable fly ball fell untouched and another hit on a ground ball dribbler that an infielder, playing deep, could not get to in time to throw him out. Still, it is a little-known fact that after the streak ended at 56 games, DiMaggio then hit safely in the next 17 games that followed. [1]

The entire 1941 season was a magical one for DiMaggio: he hit .357 with 125 RBI, 30 home runs, and was voted the league's most valuable player. Incredibly, he struck out only 13 times the entire year.

25. TED WILLIAMS: CONSECUTIVE GAMES AND TIMES ON BASE

Although Joe DiMaggio's 56-game hitting streak is the much better-known record, in 1949 Ted Williams reached base via hits, walks, or errors in an astounding 84 consecutive games—more than half the games in the season. Eight years later, in 1957 Williams accomplished a feat that would be difficult even if the competition involved Class Z city league slow-pitch softball: With 2 singles, 4 home runs, 9 walks, and 1 hit by pitch, he reached base on 16 consecutive plate appearances.

26. JOHNNY VANDER MEER: TWO CONSECUTIVE NO-HITTERS

Johnny Vander Meer of the Cincinnati Reds is the only pitcher in major league history to pitch two consecutive no-hit games. When Vander Meer took the mound on two June nights in 1938, no one had ever pitched two no-hitters in a season, much less in back-to-back games.

The magic began on June 11, when Vander Meer no-hit the Boston Braves 3–0. Four nights later on June 15, 40,000 fans crammed Ebbets Field in Brooklyn not only to witness the first night game ever played in that storied ballpark but also to watch Vander Meer try for two no-hitters in a row. Using a fastball and a sharp-breaking curve, the left-hander moved easily through the opening and middle innings before escaping trouble after walking two batters in the seventh.

Carrying the no-hitter into the bottom of the ninth with a 6–0 lead, Vander Meer retired the first man up and then walked three consecutive batters loading the bases. After a visit by the Reds' manager, Vander Meer got the next batter to hit a ground ball. The Cincinnati infielder elected to throw to the plate, forcing out the runner coming from third base. With two outs and the bases still loaded, Vander Meer faced Brooklyn's player/manager Leo Durocher. After hitting a long foul ball, Durocher—on Vander Meer's second pitch—lofted a soft fly ball that was caught in short center field, preserving the no-hitter and Vander Meer's place in baseball history.

In the first no-hitter against Boston, Vander Meer walked three and struck out four. No runner advanced beyond first base. The second no-hitter was a rockier road: Vander Meer walked eight and struck out seven, leaving two runners on in the seventh inning and the bases loaded in the ninth.

It is perhaps conceivable that someone, someday, might again pitch two consecutive no-hitters, thus tying Johnny Vander Meer's record. But beating his record with three consecutive no-hitters seems nearly impossible.

Executing two consecutive no-hitters is indeed an astonishing feat, but some experts believe that the exploits of "Iron Man" Joe McGinnity of the New York Giants equal Vander Meer's achievement. Incredible as it may seem, three times in the same month, McGinnity pitched complete-game doubleheader victories.

McGinnity's streak began on August 1, 1903, when he pitched and won both ends of a twin bill against the Boston Braves. A week later on August 8, he repeated with doubleheader victories against Brooklyn. Then, on August 31, McGinnity pitched and won a third doubleheader, this time against the Philadelphia Phillies.

27. OREL HERSHISER: 59 CONSECUTIVE SCORELESS INNINGS PITCHED

There has been no record of sustained pitching excellence to match that accomplished by Los Angeles Dodger pitcher Orel Hershiser from September 5 to September 28, 1988.

After giving up two runs in the fifth inning on September 5 against the Montreal Expos, Hershiser allowed no more runs in that game or, as it turned out, for the rest of the regular season! Starting with the first inning of the following game, Hershiser pitched six consecutive shutouts, closing the regular season on September 28 with a 10-inning shutout victory.

Interestingly, even that remarkable official record does not tell the whole story. After closing the regular season with a record-setting 59 consecutive scoreless innings, Hershiser added 8 more starting the first game of the National League Championship Series. Had the playoff numbers counted as regular season stats, he would have been credited with 67 consecutive scoreless innings.

Incredibly, there is more: Hershiser pitched the 12th inning in relief to save game 4 of the National League Championship Series and then won game 7 with a complete-game shutout.

More still: He pitched another complete-game shutout in game 2 of the World Series, becoming the first pitcher to throw same-year shutouts in both the National League Championship Series and the World Series.

Overall, between September 5 and the last game of the World Series, Hershiser pitched eight complete-game shutouts. Hershiser's official consecutive scoreless inning streak ended on April 6, 1989, in the first inning of the first regular season game of the following season, when he gave up a single run to the Cincinnati Reds.

28. ERIC GAGNE: 84 CONSECUTIVE SAVES

From August 26, 2002, until July 4, 2004, Eric Gagne, closer for the Los Angeles Dodgers, converted 84 consecutive save opportunities. In the midst of the skein, Gagne converted all 55 of his save chances during the 2003 season. That year, more than half of all the batters he retired came by strikeout. In 82 1/3 innings pitched in 2003, he struck out 137 batters and walked only 20, a performance that earned him the Cy Young Award, a rare accomplishment for a relief pitcher. After that stellar year, Gagne's remarkable string continued for almost half the following season.

29. CHARLES RADBOURN: 60 VICTORIES IN A SEASON (OR MAYBE ONLY 59)

Pitching for the Providence Grays in 1884, Charles "Old Hoss" Radbourn won 60 games—or 59—either way compiling a record that will likely never be broken.

In July, after the Grays' other pitcher was kicked off the team, Radbourn offered to pitch every game in return for a raise and contract revisions. For the rest of the season, he did indeed pitch the majority of the Grays' games, and on the few days when he did not pitch, he often played a position in the field.

Considering the record that Radbourn compiled that year, it seems strange to relate that his year did not begin particularly well. When the season opened, Radbourn shared pitching duties, and although on one occasion he won both games in a doubleheader and then pitched a 10-inning victory the following day, his overall record was spotty. In early June, he was disciplined for a contract violation (probably for breaking a no-drinking pledge). Nonetheless, Radbourn returned on a hot streak, for a time pitching every day for his sore-armed colleague before his own arm temporarily gave out. His arm trouble ended a series of six straight victories, and he was hit hard while losing two of the next three games.

In mid-July, frustrated by a balk call at a crucial point in a game, Radbourn was again suspended by the team's management, who believed that he had intentionally pitched poorly after being called for the balk, giving up three more runs in a losing game.

Then, when the Grays' other pitcher was released from the team following a midgame altercation, Radbourn's year turned around in remarkable fashion. Taking over in the midst of a close pennant race, Radbourn compiled a 31–2 record into late September when the race was well in hand. During August and early September, the Grays won 20 straight games; Radbourn pitched 18 of them. When in late September management gave him a day off, Radbourn had pitched every inning of the Grays' previous 22 games and, counting 3 games in the outfield, had played in every game since July.

Radbourn's regular season record officially wound up as 60 wins, 12 losses, and 2 ties. He then followed up by pitching all three games as the Grays swept New York in an interleague championship series.

Although in Radbourn's era other pitchers occasionally approached his totals for games and innings pitched, none ever pitched so well over such an extended period. Radbourn paid a price for his great year, however. The season apparently took something out of his arm, and although he played seven more years in the major leagues, his success never again approached that of 1884.

The question regarding number of wins comes from a game against Philadelphia played on July 28. Rules in effect at the time correctly gave Radbourn the win in a game where he pitched four innings of relief. Current-day rules would have credited him with a save. Some sources apply the modern standard and revise Radbourn's record by deducting that game from his win column. *Baseball Encyclopedia* and *Sporting News Baseball Record Book* credit Radbourn with 60 wins. MLB.com and some others show his win total as 59. Entire books—such as *Fifty-Nine in '84*, by Edward Achorn—have been written on the subject.

Interestingly, a few early sources—and Radbourn's tombstone—show as many as *62* wins.

30. CARL HUBBELL: 24 CONSECUTIVE PITCHING VICTORIES

Considering the magnitude of the achievement, it is one of the least known of all the major "streaks" in the long history of baseball.

Beginning in the 1936 season and extending into the first weeks of the 1937 campaign, New York Giants pitcher Carl Hubbell won 24 consecutive games. Hubbell began his streak by winning his last 16 decisions in 1936 and then followed with 8 more consecutive victories in 1937. Taken together, the

24 pitching victories in a row is the longest streak ever recorded in either league. Hubbell's final 16 wins in 1936 propelled him to a 26–6 record that year (and selection as the most valuable player in the National League). In 1937, the first 8 triumphs started him on the road to a 22–8 record.

A left-handed pitcher who spent his entire career with the New York Giants, Hubbell was known for a slow delivery and a remarkable sharp-breaking screwball that dived down and away from right-handed batters and low and into left-handed hitters. During the course of his 16-year major league career, Hubbell threw the pitch—a delivery that places unusual torque on a pitcher's arm and elbow—so often that his left arm became permanently twisted, leaving his palm facing outward.

31. HOME RUNS IN EIGHT CONSECUTIVE GAMES

Three players share an extraordinary record: each hit a home run in eight consecutive games. Dale Long, Pittsburgh Pirates first baseman, established the mark in 1956, hitting home runs in an eight-game stretch that spanned May 19 to May 28. Thirty-one years later, on July 18, 1987, Yankees first baseman Don Mattingly equaled Long's standard. In July 1993, Ken Griffey Jr., center fielder for the Seattle Mariners, earned a share of the record with Long and Mattingly.

Mattingly actually hit 10 home runs during his eight-game stretch. Long and Griffey hit single home runs in each game. All three were left-handed hitters.

Mattingly is also known for a second, separate hitting record. In 1987, he hit for extra bases in 10 consecutive games. In 1979, Del Unser of the Philadelphia Phillies hit pinch-hit home runs on three consecutive at bats.

Extra-Innings Coverage about Home Runs

American fans are sometimes surprised to learn that the all-time home run champion in professional baseball is not Babe Ruth, Hank Aaron, or Barry Bonds but Sadaharu Oh of the Yomiuri Giants in the Japanese Central League. In 22 seasons (1959–1980), Oh hit 868 home runs. A left-hand-hitting first baseman, Oh led the Central League in home runs 15 times and in RBI 13 times while winning five batting titles, two triple crowns, and nine Most Valuable Player Awards.

Oh's career was noted for its consistency. Although his overall home run total was more than 100 higher than the 762 hit by Barry Bonds, Oh's single-season high was 55 (also the Japanese single-season record).

After retiring as an active player, Oh began a career as a manager in Japan's Central and Pacific leagues. On three occasions (1984, 2001, 2002) when foreign players in Japan approached Oh's single-season record, Oh's teams were criticized for allegedly not pitching to the players who threatened his record when the teams met in late-season games.

In 1974, Oh and Hank Aaron, his close friend and contemporary in major league baseball, staged a home run–hitting contest preceding an exhibition game in Japan. Aaron won 10–9. In 1988, the two of them collaborated to create the World Children's Baseball Fair, aimed at increasing interest in baseball among young people.

In 2006, Oh managed Japan's national team that won the World Baseball Classic.

32. NEW YORK YANKEES: FIVE CONSECUTIVE WORLD SERIES CHAMPIONSHIPS

From 1949 to 1953, the New York Yankees won an unprecedented five consecutive World Series titles.

The Yankee teams combined excellent pitching (Allie Reynolds, Vic Raschi, Eddie Lopat, Whitey Ford) with a lineup that was deep and solid throughout, led by Phil Rizzuto, Yogi Berra, and Joe DiMaggio. Mickey Mantle broke in as a rookie in 1951. Manager Casey Stengel astutely "platooned" several position players, such as Hank Bauer and Gene Woodling, depending on whether the Yankees were facing left- or right-handed pitching.

The Yankees' streak is all the more remarkable in that three of the series victories were achieved against the Brooklyn Dodgers, a truly exceptional ball club.

Yankees' World Series Triumphs

1949: Brooklyn Dodgers, 4–1
1950: Philadelphia Phillies, 4–0
1951: New York Giants, 4–2
1952: Brooklyn Dodgers, 4–3
1953: Brooklyn Dodgers, 4–2

In 1954, the Yankees won 103 games but were denied the chance to compete for a sixth consecutive World Series title by the Cleveland Indians, who took the American League pennant while winning a record-setting 111 games.

Less remembered is that after missing the series in 1954, the Yankees appeared in eight of the next nine, winning four. In fact, beginning in 1947 and going through 1963, the Yankees appeared in 14 out of 17 World Series, missing only 1948, 1954, and 1959. The Yankees' record of sustained excellence during those nearly two decades is surely one of the most remarkable in all of professional sports.

33. LONGEST WINNING STREAK

By its nature, baseball at the major league level is a sport that discourages long winning streaks. For the most part, there is general competitive balance: even last-place teams typically win 60 to 70 games per year. There are 25 players on a major league team, which plays day in and day out from April through September; it is not unusual for a club to go through short cycles where things seem to either click or not go as well as they should. The teams travel; there are injuries; there is fatigue; players get hot or go cold. During the course of a long season, many games are decided by close plays or bounces of the ball. For all those reasons, prolonged streaks where a team wins and then wins again and again through road trips, adversity, close calls, and the rhythms of highs and lows are difficult and uncommon.

Depending on how you count the beans, the major league record for the longest winning streak is either 21 games by the 1935 Chicago Cubs or 26 games by the 1916 New York Giants. The reason for the confusion is that after the Giants won 14 games in a row, they played a tie game before winning 12 more. Thus, there were 26 official games without a loss. The Cubs won 21 consecutively. You decide.

The American League record is 20, held by the 2002 Oakland Athletics.

34. AT THE TOP OF THEIR GAMES . . . FOR YEARS AND YEARS

Pitching: Nolan Ryan—Strikeouts and No-Hitters

Nolan Ryan played a record 27 years in the major leagues (1966–1993). During that time, he struck out an astonishing 5,714 batters and pitched seven no-hit games. In 1973, Ryan set the single-season record for strikeouts, with 383. He is currently the only pitcher to accomplish a nine-strike, three-strikeout inning in both leagues. Ryan's seven no-hitters were spread over 18 years, during which he pitched for three teams: California Angels (1973 [twice], 1974, 1975); Houston Astros (1981), and Texas Rangers (1990, 1991).

While lauding these achievements, critics point out that Ryan also walked 2,795 batters (50 percent more than any other pitcher in major league history), that on two occasions he walked more than 200 batters in a season, and that his overall won-loss record was a modest 324–292 (.526), a winning percentage only slightly better (.023) than the teams he played for. It is worth noting, however, that Ryan holds the American League record for victories by a pitcher on a last-place team, winning 22 games for the 1974 cellar-dwelling California Angels.

All else aside: 5,714 strikeouts and seven no-hitters . . . it is quite possible that neither achievement will be surpassed.

Hitting: Ty Cobb—Consecutive .300 Seasons

Twenty-three years in a row. The number seems astounding. From 1906 through 1928, Detroit Tiger hall of famer Ty Cobb hit more than .300 every season. During that time, he hit higher than .350 sixteen times and twice batted .400. From 1907 through 1919, Cobb won 12 of 13 batting crowns, including a never-equaled 9 in a row from 1907 to 1915.

Base Running and Runs Scored: Rickey Henderson

On August 29, 2003, Rickey Henderson, playing for the Los Angeles Dodgers (his ninth big league club), stole second base. In a career that spanned 25 years, the steal was his final stolen base in the big leagues: It was number 1,406—almost 500 more than runner-up Lou Brock.

Two years prior, on October 4, 2001, Henderson had achieved another milestone, breaking Ty Cobb's 73-year-old record for runs scored in a career. The run that Henderson scored that day was his 2,246th. He ended his career with 2,295.

Fielding: Greg Maddux—18 Gold Gloves

From 1990 to 2008, Greg Maddux won 18 Gold Gloves, perhaps fielding the pitcher's position better than anyone else who has played the game. During that remarkable stretch, he won Gold Gloves with the Chicago Cubs (3), the Atlanta Braves (10), the Cubs again (3), the San Diego Padres (1), and the Los Angeles Dodgers (1). Aided by his fielding prowess and remarkable control, Maddux won at least 15 games for 17 consecutive seasons, also a record.

Consecutive Games Played: 2,632 — Cal Ripken Jr.

For decades in baseball, it was "conventional wisdom" that the record set by the Yankees' Lou Gehrig for consecutive games played would quite likely never be surpassed: 2,130 consecutive games seemed unattainable, almost too many to fathom.[2]

But, on September 6, 1995, the unattainable was exceeded. On that night, Cal Ripken Jr., playing for the Baltimore Orioles, beat Gehrig's record—and then went on to add three additional years' worth of games to it!

Ripken's streak began on May 20, 1982. For the next 18 years, day in and day out, he played every game. When Ripken finally chose to end the streak on September 20, 1988, he had played a total of 2,632 consecutive games.

Making Ripken's streak even more remarkable is that for many of those 18 years, he played shortstop, a physically demanding position where bumps, bruises, contact plays, and the spikes of sliding runners are part of the cost of doing business. The position requires a strong arm, another potential injury hazard, as well as range on fielding plays. The final years of Ripken's streak were at third base; there, as well as at shortstop, his performance was of all-star caliber.

A lesser-known fact about Ripken but one that again illustrates his incredible resilience is that in 1983 he became the first player ever to play every inning of every game for his team. Beginning on opening day on April 4 through the 162-game regular season, 4 league championship playoff games, and 5 World Series games—171 games total—Ripken played every pitch of every inning.

Ten Consecutive 200-Hit Seasons: Ichiro Suzuki

Ichiro Suzuki, Seattle Mariners outfielder, is the only player to have made 200 hits in each of his first 10 big league seasons (2001–2010). Only one other player (Wee Willie Keeler of the Baltimore Orioles) had eight consecutive 200-hit seasons at any point in his career. During the course of his career, Pete Rose amassed ten 200-hit seasons, but they were not consecutive.

In 2004, Ichiro set the major league single-season record with 262 hits. His string of consecutive 200-hit seasons ended in 2011.

A Decade of Multiple Firsts: Albert Pujols

Before moving to the Los Angeles Angels in 2012, Albert Pujols spent his first 11 years in the major leagues as a member of the St. Louis Cardinals. Pujols's achievements as a Cardinal during the first decade of his career fill several "sustained excellence" categories—or, perhaps, a separate category needs to be invented just for him. He is the only player in major league history to start his career with 10 consecutive seasons with a batting average higher than .300, 30 or more home runs, and more than 100 RBI. Let's be sure we understand: He did all those things every year.

Along the way, he was the fastest to reach 300 or more home runs, the second (along with Ralph Kiner) to hit 300 home runs in his first eight seasons, and only the third (along with Al Simmons and Ted Williams) to start a career with eight 100-plus RBI seasons.

Plagued by an early-season slump and a midseason injury, Pujols's consecutive string of seasons with a .300 batting average, 30 or more home runs, and 100 or more RBI ended in 2011. Although he played in only 147 games, a late spurt brought him remarkably close to adding an 11th consecutive season to his phenomenal record. Pujols ended the season with a batting average of .299 and 99 runs driven in, while hitting 37 home runs.

Not surprisingly, Pujols is a multiple most valuable player and all-star selectee, as well as a National League batting champion. ESPN chose him as its player of the decade (2001–2009).

NOTES

1. An even lesser-known facet of DiMaggio's career is that in 1933, as a minor leaguer playing with the San Francisco Seals of the Pacific Coast League, he had a 61-game hitting streak.

2. Some have called it the most famous headache in all of big league history. On June 1, 1925, Yankees' first baseman Wally Pipp was kept out of the lineup because of a headache. Pipp was replaced by a youngster named Lou Gehrig, who did not come out of the Yankees' starting lineup for the next 14 years. From the day that Gehrig stepped onto the field to take Pipp's place, he played the next 2,130 consecutive games. The next time someone other than Lou Gehrig started at first base for the Yankees was May 2, 1939.

Chapter Six

Streaks and Sustained (Lack of) Excellence

Except for rainouts, national catastrophes, or other acts of God, in every one of the more than 2,400 ball games played each year in the major leagues, there is a winning team and a losing team. When teams win repeatedly, history marks them as special. But history doesn't play favorites: from the beginning, there have been equal numbers of instances where clubs have consistently failed, losing game after game after game.

Similarly, in almost every one of those hundreds of games, there are players who have had good days and others who have had bad days (or bad luck). When a player's bad days string together one after another over a prolonged period, that player's name is also remembered in the record books. Good or bad, the print size is the same for all.

35. ZERO FOR 2011

In 2011, Eugenio Velez, a utility player for the Los Angeles Dodgers, set the record for a position player by going 46 consecutive at bats without a hit. Velez concluded the 2010 campaign with a 0-for-9 performance with the San Francisco Giants. Traded after the season to the Dodgers, he was called up to the majors in July 2011 and went 0 for 37 for the rest of the season. For a position player, Velez's 0-for-37 performance was the most at bats in a season without a hit in major league history. His consecutive 0-for-46 total established the record for the most consecutive at bats without a hit spanning more than one season.

36. LONGEST LOSING STREAK

In the modern era, the record for sustained futility is held by the 1961 Philadelphia Phillies. From July 26 to August 20, they lost every time they played: 23 consecutive games.

The American League record is 21 consecutive losses, posted by the 1988 Baltimore Orioles. The Orioles' streak was made more painful by the fact that it came at the start of a new season. The Orioles were beaten 12–0 on opening day and then followed with 20 more losses.

37. ANTHONY YOUNG: 27 CONSECUTIVE LOSSES

During 1992 and 1993, New York Mets pitcher Anthony Young lost 27 straight decisions.

Young, a right-handed pitcher, posted two wins early in the 1992 season, then did not win again until midseason of the following year, 15 months later. The streak—from May 6, 1992, until July 24, 1993—involved 27 pitching decisions in 74 appearances. During that time, Young went 0–14 as a starter and 0–13 in relief.

On many occasions, Young did not pitch badly. His overall earned run average was a respectable 3.89. Moved to the bullpen midyear in 1992 to cover for an injured teammate, he converted 12 straight save opportunities and at one point threw 23 2/3 scoreless innings in relief. Prosperity did not last, however, and for the remainder of that season and the beginning of the next, he shuttled back and forth between the starting rotation and the bullpen.

Finally, on July 28, 1993, after giving up an unearned run to the Florida Marlins in the top of the ninth that put him behind 4–3 and threatened him with yet another loss, the Mets rallied for two runs in the bottom of the inning. The 5–4 victory gave Young the win and ended the streak.

The record for the most consecutive losses in a single season is 19. In 1916, Jack Nabors, pitching for the Philadelphia Athletics—then in the second year of their record seven consecutive last-place finishes—lost 19 straight while compiling a season record of 1 win and 20 losses.

The most losses without ever winning a game in the big leagues is 16. During the years 1979–1982, Terry Felton compiled an 0–16 mark while pitching for the Minnesota Twins.

38. THE WORST TEAM

To the 1899 Cleveland Spiders of the National League goes the dubious honor of being the worst team in major league history. During the 1899 season, the Spiders won only 20 of 154 games.

The horrendous season was not entirely the fault of the players on the field. The Spiders' owner, Frank Robison, owned a second National League club, the St. Louis Browns. Robison stripped the Spiders' roster early and often to provide additional talent to his team in St. Louis.

Understandably, as the season wore on, attendance at the Spiders' home games plummeted; often, fewer than 200 fans came to see them play. Disgusted, Robison then ordered the team to play the final two months of the season on the road, earning the club a second nickname: the "exiles" or the "wanderers."

During a season in which no pitcher won more than four games, the Spiders' 24 consecutive losses set the all-time major league standard in that category, although in the modern era, the 1961 Phillies and the 1988 Orioles came close to equaling it.

Chapter Seven

Highs and Lows

Sometimes things happen in major league games that must appear as fantasies. Surely, one would think, they could exist only in dreams like those of the kid in the backyard who hits a rock with a stick and pictures himself launching a homer out of Yankee Stadium: things like hitting the first ball thrown to you in the big leagues for a grand-slam home run . . . hitting two grand slams in one inning . . . pitching a no-hitter in your first start.

But none of those are fantasy. They, as well as a record book full of equally implausible events, actually happened.

Of course, it is the nature of baseball that for every high, like a first-pitch grand slam, there is at the other extreme a corresponding low. Things sometimes happen that even the cruelest person wouldn't wish on his worst enemy on a bad day. Lows of that kind are best remembered with compassion or humor (although embarrassment was the emotion most likely felt by the player involved).

39. FIRST-PITCH GRAND SLAM

What is the most ideal start you could possibly imagine for a major league career? How about hitting the first pitch ever thrown to you as a big league hitter for a grand-slam home run? Astounding as it may seem, it has happened twice.

Kevin Kouzmanoff did it first when he came to the plate as the Cleveland Indians' designated hitter on September 2, 2006. Kouzmanoff became the first—and, at that point, the only—batter ever to hit a grand slam on the first pitch he saw in a big league game.

On June 12, 2010, Daniel Nava, an outfielder of the Boston Red Sox, equaled Kouzmanoff's feat. With the bases loaded in the second inning of an interleague contest with the Philadelphia Phillies, Nava hit a first-pitch fast ball over the right-field fence at Fenway Park. Just called up from the minor leagues, Nava had never before played in a major league game or swung at a major league pitch.

40. FIRST-GAME NO-HITTER

For a pitcher, probably the only accomplishment that could match Kevin Kouzmanoff's and Daniel Nava's first-pitch grand slams would be to throw a no-hitter in one's first start in the big leagues. In all of major league history, that has only been done once.

On May 6, 1953, Bobo Holloman of the St. Louis Browns no-hit the Philadelphia A's 6–0 in his first major league start. Holloman had made four unspectacular relief appearances before taking the ball as a starter in a game frequently interrupted by rain delays. Holloman worked through the soggy weather, striking out three and walking five. While any no-hitter is an exceptional event, by most accounts the game was not particularly well pitched. The A's hit several balls hard, but solid fielding by the Browns, including a spectacular play by shortstop Billy Hunter in the ninth inning, saved the no-hitter for Holloman.

Unfortunately for Holloman, his early success was short-lived. Later that season, after first being sent to the bullpen, Holloman was returned to the minors sporting a 3–7 record and a 5.27 earned run average. He never again pitched in the big leagues.

41. HOME RUNS ON FIRST TWO AT BATS

In the annals of remarkable big league beginnings, there may be one more feat that compares with first-pitch grand-slam achievements. On September 14, 1951, Bob Nieman of the St. Louis Browns became the only player ever to hit two home runs on his first two at bats in a single game in the major leagues. Later, Bert Campaneris of the Kansas City Athletics (July 23, 1964), Mark Quinn of the Kansas City Royals (September 14, 1999), and J. P. Arencibia of the Toronto Blue Jays (August 7, 2010) would hit two home runs in their first major league games. Nieman's, however, came on his first two times at the plate.

Speaking of exceptional debuts in the big leagues—in the modern era, 12 players have gotten four hits in their first major league game. Familiar names among them include Casey Stengel, Willie McCovey, and Kirby Puckett. On April 25, 1933, Russ Van Atta, a pitcher for the New York Yankees, got off to a truly extraordinary start: Van Atta not only got four hits in his first major league game but also threw a shutout against the Washington Senators. In 2001, Jason Jennings of the Colorado Rockies paralleled Van Atta's achievement by hitting a home run and pitching a shutout in his first major league appearance.

42. TWO GRAND SLAMS IN ONE INNING

It seems almost too incredible to believe—hitting two grand-slam home runs in the same inning. Maybe, just barely, it might be possible in Little League play but in major league competition? No way.

In the thousands of games played up until April 23, 1999, it had never happened. That day it did. In the third inning of a game between the St. Louis Cardinals and the Los Angeles Dodgers, Fernando Tatis of the Cardinals hit two grand-slam home runs. The slams gave him the record for RBI in an inning—eight.

Irony 1 was that before the two that he hit in the same inning, Tatis had never before hit a grand-slam home run. Irony 2 was that both slams came off Dodger pitcher Chan Ho Park—which made him the first pitcher to give up two grand slams to the same batter in the same inning.

And speaking of grand slams, on October 10, 2011, Nelson Cruz of the Texas Rangers hit the first walk-off grand slam in postseason play. Batting against Detroit pitcher Ryan Perry in the American League Championship Series, Cruz hit an 11th-inning grand slam that won the game for Texas 7–3.

43. THREE HITS IN ONE INNING

It takes a rare circumstance—an enormous inning with lots of batters coming to the plate—to give a player the opportunity to bat three times in the same inning. After that, of course, there is the small matter of converting every one of those chances while hitting against major league pitching.

Fifty years and nine days separated the accomplishments of the only two players who have ever gotten three hits in an inning. Their names are Gene Stephens and Johnny Damon. Both were members of the Boston Red Sox when fortune gave them the opportunity for a place in the record books.

For outfielder Gene Stephens, at first there was nothing unusual about the game with Detroit on June 18, 1953; it was a tight contest that Boston led 5–3 through six innings. Then the Sox came to bat in the seventh: 23 batters and 17 runs later, Stephens had been at the plate three times. He made a hit every time: a double and two singles off three different Detroit pitchers. It was five decades before anyone did anything like it again.

When it happened, the circumstances were also unusual, although the pattern of the game was much different from the one in which Stephens had set the record. Where Stephens's heroics took place fairly late, for Boston center fielder Johnny Damon, the fireworks came early in Boston's game with Florida on June 27, 2003. Damon, Boston's leadoff hitter, started the game with a hit. Tens runs later, Damon had been to the plate two more times, and Florida still hadn't retired a single batter. (Ten runs before an out was made is also a major league record.) Damon's three hits in the first inning—a single, a double, and a triple—helped the Sox roll to a 25–8 victory.

44. TWELVE RBI IN A GAME

For most batters, 12 runs batted in is a productive two- or three-week stretch (or longer). For two players, though, it was all in a day's work: St. Louis Cardinal ballplayers Jim Bottomley and Mark Whiten share the record.

On September 16, 1924, Bottomley, the Cardinals' left-hand hitting first baseman, drove in a dozen runs as the Cards beat the Brooklyn Dodgers. Bottomley's six hits that day included two home runs, a double, and three singles.

On September 7, 1993, Whiten, a switch-hitting outfielder, equaled Bottomley's mark. Whiten's route to the record was much different from Bottomley's. Whiten did it all on home runs. Four of them, in fact. His home runs came in the first inning with the bases loaded, in the sixth with two runners on, in the seventh with two more on, and in the ninth with one on. Whiten hit home runs from each side of the plate as the Cardinals hammered the Cincinnati Reds 15–2. The Cards and the Reds played a doubleheader that day; Whiten's 13 RBI in a doubleheader also set a record.

A bit more about RBI: In 2010 Alex Rodriguez of the New York Yankees tied Lou Gehrig and Jimmie Foxx by driving in 100 or more runs for the 13th consecutive season. With a career total of fourteen 100 RBI seasons, Rodriguez holds the major league record.

45. TWELVE HITS IN A ROW

Walt Dropo, Detroit Tigers first baseman, has the record for consecutive base hits. In games played on July 14 and 15, 1952, Dropo came to the plate 12 times and hit safely every time without a walk, sacrifice, or hit by pitch intervening. Twelve times up, 12 hits: that is 28 fewer at bats than it normally takes a .300 hitter to collect a dozen hits.

Some historians believe that Johnny Kling, a catcher with the Chicago team in the National League, made 12 consecutive hits during the 1902 season. Kling's accomplishment went unrecognized for more than a century.

46. SEVEN FOR SEVEN

Even for a .300 hitter, seven hits normally take 23 at bats. Figuring four at bats per game, that's about six games. Rennie Stennett of the Pittsburgh Pirates did it in one game . . . and he did it in seven consecutive times at the plate.

Stennett set the modern-day record for hits in a nine-inning game on September 16, 1975. Stennett, the Pirates' second baseman and leadoff hitter, opened the game against the Cubs with a double, then followed with six more hits in succession his next times up. Stennett wound up with three doubles and four singles off five different pitchers. It was not a good day for Cubs pitching. In the game at Wrigley Field that afternoon, the Pirates pounded the Cubs 22–0.

Others have gotten seven or more hits during extra-inning games. Stennett, however, remains the only player to accomplish the feat in nine innings.

47. THREE SWINGS, SEVEN OUTS, AND OTHER BAD TIMES

Sometimes when you are having a really bad day, it is useful to put things in perspective. In the annals of baseball history, perhaps no one has ever had as bad a day at the plate as Burleigh Grimes of the Brooklyn Dodgers.

On September 25, 1925, Grimes, later a Hall of Fame pitcher, came to bat three times. He took three swings. He hit into two double plays and a triple play: three swings, seven outs. On July 21, 1945, George Kell of the Detroit Tigers also had a historically bad day. In a 24-inning game against the Philadelphia A's, Kell, a lifetime .306 hitter, went 0 for 10.

In terms of season-long frustration, the award may go to Boston Red Sox outfielder Jim Rice, who during the 1984 season hit into 36 double plays. And during the course of an otherwise illustrious career, the Baltimore Orioles' Brooks Robinson hit into a record four triple plays.

Chapter Eight

Special Games

There is a quality about certain games that sets them apart from all others. In some cases, it is that something about them was truly spectacular—like 12 perfect innings of baseball that will live in memory for as long as baseball is played.

In other instances, the games themselves may not have been particularly good or well played; nonetheless, some unique feature associated with them was so extraordinary that years later they remain the subjects of conversation, interest, and wonder.

48. THE SHORT AND THE LONG

Fifty-one minutes. Less time than most State of the Union speeches. Less time than it takes to watch a rerun of *Law and Order*.

Fifty-one minutes was how long it took two major league teams to play a complete, nine-inning game. On September 28, 1919, hardly before fans had settled in their seats, the game between the New York Giants and Philadelphia Phillies was over. The Giants won 6–1.

At the other extreme, the longest nine-inning game on record happened at Fenway Park on April 18, 2006, when it took the Yankees 4 hours and 45 minutes to beat the Red Sox 14–11. On May 31, 1964, after 23 innings and a mind-boggling, seat-numbing 7 hours and 23 minutes,[1] the San Francisco Giants beat the New York Mets 8–6. That remains the longest single game in major league history.

By the way, fans got their money's worth that day: the 23-inning game was the second game of a doubleheader. The total time elapsed, counting both games of the twin bill, was 9 hours and 52 minutes (also a record).

Before we leave the subject, consider for a moment another really long day at the ballpark: a triple header. The last one in the major leagues was played at Forbes Field in Pittsburgh on October 2, 1920. The Pirates played three against the Cincinnati Reds that day. The third game was mercifully halted by darkness in the sixth inning.

49. THE MOST INNINGS

On May 1, 1920, the Boston Braves and the Brooklyn Dodgers battled for 26 innings. The game ended in a 1–1 tie. It remains the longest contest in major league history. Remarkably, both pitchers—Joe Oeschager of the Braves and Leon Cadore of the Dodgers—pitched the entire game.

In the major leagues, two 25-inning games have been played to conclusions. On May 8, 1984, the Chicago White Sox beat the Milwaukee Brewers 7–6. On September 11, 1974, the St. Louis Cardinals defeated the New York Mets 4–3.

The longest game in the history of professional baseball actually stretched over two playing dates. Play began at Pawtucket, Rhode Island, on April 18, 1981. At 4:07 the next morning, the game—between the Pawtucket Red Sox and the Rochester Red Wings of the International League—was suspended after 32 innings with the score tied 2–2. When the game was resumed on June 23, Pawtucket pushed across a run in 18 minutes to win in the 33rd inning.

50. SEVENTEEN RUNS IN ONE INNING

On June 18, 1953, the Red Sox were leading the Detroit Tigers by a modest 5–3 score at the end of six innings. Then came an inning that lives on in Red Sox—and baseball—history. In the seventh inning at Fenway Park, the Sox sent 23 batters to the plate. The inning took 47 minutes to play. When it was finally over, the Red Sox had scored 17 runs. The Sox went on to win the game 23–3.

Not surprisingly, perhaps, this was the same inning of the same game in which Boston outfielder Gene Stephens made three hits.

The scorecard must have been a sight to behold.

51. MOST RUNS SCORED

It was not your classic pitchers' duel. On August 25, 1922, Chicago Cubs pitchers gave up 23 runs to the Philadelphia Phillies. Normally, 23 runs should be good enough to win a ball game (or four or five ball games). The thing is, though, Phillies pitchers gave up 26 runs to the Cubs. Phillies batters had the unique experience of scoring 23 times in a nine-inning game and losing by 3 runs. The 49 runs scored in the Cubs 26–23 victory remain the most ever to cross the plate in a big league ball game.

The modern record for most runs scored by one team in a major league game is 30. The Texas Rangers hung the big "three oh" on the Baltimore Orioles on August 22, 2007. Texas won that game 30–3. Down 27 runs, it is uncertain whether Baltimore fans, if any remained in the stands, put on rally caps in the bottom of the ninth.

By the way, the record at the opposite end of the spectrum—the most innings without scoring in one day—is 27. On July 2, 1933, the St. Louis Cardinals set a still-standing record for futility: 27 innings without scoring a run. The Cards lost an 18-inning first game of a doubleheader 1–0 and then were shut out again by the same score in the nightcap.

52. TWELVE PERFECT INNINGS

It was one of the most extraordinary games in all of major league history. On May 26, 1959, Pittsburgh Pirates left-hander Harvey Haddix pitched 12 perfect innings of baseball, retiring the first 36 Milwaukee Braves batters he faced. No one else before or since has ever pitched a perfect game beyond 9 innings. Haddix's achievement is in itself almost unbelievable. What made the game even more remarkable is that Haddix lost it!

Although Pittsburgh had 12 hits, the Pirates could not score against Braves pitcher Lew Burdette. Meanwhile, Haddix's gem continued batter after batter, inning after inning. Finally, in the bottom of the 13th, Felix Mantilla, the 37th Braves batter to face Haddix, reached first base when the Pirates' third baseman booted a routine ground ball for an error. Haddix's perfect game was gone, but at this point the no-hitter was still intact. The second batter in the inning sacrificed Mantilla to second base. Haddix then intentionally walked Hank Aaron. Two on now, but the no-hitter was still working. It all ended when Joe Adcock, the fourth Braves batter in the bottom of the 13th, drove a ball out of the park. The perfect game: gone. The shutout: gone. The pitching victory: gone.

Later, the hit would be ruled a double because Adcock passed Aaron on the bases. Thus, the game officially went on the books as a 1–0 Milwaukee win.

Because of the repeated three-up, three-down sequence inning after inning, the 13-inning contest took only 2 hours and 54 minutes to play. The 19,194 fans at Milwaukee County Stadium who saw that game that night witnessed one of the most brilliant pitching performances of all time. Haddix struck out eight batters, but despite his masterpiece—12 innings of what many believe might have been the greatest game ever pitched—Haddix was the losing pitcher.

Memories of Haddix's masterpiece were rekindled in July 2009, when Chicago White Sox pitcher Mark Buehrle retired 45 consecutive batters over a three-game span. On July 18, Buehrle retired the last batter he faced in a game with Baltimore. Then, on July 23 he pitched the 18th perfect game in major league history, against the Tampa Bay Rays. On his next start after the perfect game, on July 29, Buehrle retired the first 17 Minnesota Twins batters he faced before walking Alexi Casillas in the sixth inning. All together, 1 + 27 + 17 = 45 consecutive batters—surely one of the great stretches of pitching excellence in baseball history.

53. DOUBLE NO-HITTER

May 2, 1917: A game like the one that took place that day has happened only once in major league history. When the Cincinnati Reds and the Chicago Cubs battled that afternoon, neither team made a hit through nine innings. Cincinnati pitcher Fred Toney and Chicago pitcher Hippo Vaughn each pitched no-hit ball for the entire regulation game.

The drama ended in the 10th inning, when Vaughn gave up a run on two hits. With Toney preserving his 10-inning no-hitter, the Reds won 1–0.

54. THE MOST UNUSUAL NO-HITTER—OR WAS IT A 26-OUT PERFECT GAME?

It was a no-hitter for sure. But was it a perfect game? Or maybe a 26-out perfect game?

One of the most unusual games of all time took place on June 23, 1917. The starting pitcher for the Boston Red Sox against the Washington Senators that day was a young left-hander named Babe Ruth.

Ruth walked the Senators leadoff hitter, Ray Morgan, to start the game. Ruth was incensed by the ball 4 call and argued heatedly with a home plate umpire named—appropriately, perhaps—Brick Owen. Ruth apparently crossed the line with his comments, and Owen threw him out of the game.

With Ruth gone, the Sox brought in Ernie Shore to take Babe's place on the mound. Base runner Morgan was immediately thrown out trying to steal second. Ernie Shore than retired the next 26 Washington batters. No other Senators reached base that day. Only 27 Washington batters came to the plate during the game. Shore was on the mound for all 27 outs, pitched to 26 Senators, and retired them all.

55. LARSEN'S PERFECT GAME

For as long as major league baseball has been played, only 22 perfect games have been pitched. Only one has come in the World Series.

On October 8, 1956, Don Larsen, a journeyman right-hander pitching for the New York Yankees, retired 27 consecutive Brooklyn Dodgers. Using a no-windup delivery that he began employing late in the season, Larsen threw only 97 pitches that day as the Yankees won the fifth game of the series 2–0.

Larsen's control was masterful: only one batter, Pee Wee Reese in the first inning, went to a ball 3 count. Larsen survived three close calls as the game progressed. In the second inning, Jackie Robinson hit a line shot that ricocheted off Yankee third baseman Andy Carey's glove straight to shortstop Gil McDougal who threw out Robinson on a close play at first. In the fifth inning, the Dodgers' Gil Hodges hit a sinking liner to center field that Mickey Mantle ran down and caught at knee level. Sandy Amaros, the next Dodger batter, followed with a ball hit deep down the right-field line that cleared the fence but was barely foul.

With two out in the ninth inning, the Dodgers called on Dale Mitchell to pinch-hit against Larsen. Larsen struck out Mitchell on a 1–2 count to secure the perfect game and a place in baseball history.

The picture of Yankee catcher Yogi Berra leaping on Larsen after the final out is one of the most famous of all sports photos. (Appendix D provides a list of perfect games.)

56. THE PINE TAR GAME

On July 24, 1983, at Yankee Stadium, the Kansas City Royals trailed the Yankees 4–3 in the top of the ninth inning. Royals' third baseman George Brett came to the plate with two outs and a runner on base. Brett, facing Yankee closer "Goose" Gossage, homered to give the Royals a 5–4 lead. At that point, things quickly became unstuck (no pun intended).

The Yankees had noticed in games earlier in the year that Brett's bat was smeared with an unusual amount of pine tar. After Brett's home run, Yankee manager Billy Martin protested, arguing that the bat was illegal and asking rookie umpire Tim McClelland to look at it.

Following an extended discussion involving the entire crew, the umpires determined that the pine tar on Brett's bat exceeded the allowable limit. (The governing rule states that a substance cannot cover the barrel of the bat more than 18 inches up from the tip of the handle.)

The officials' decision erased the home run. Brett was ruled out for using illegal equipment. Brett's at bat constituted the third out of the inning, thus ending the contest and giving New York a 4–3 victory. Replays aired innumerable times show Brett enraged, bolting out of the dugout and charging toward umpire McClelland, barely restrained by Kansas City manager Dick Howser and Royal players.

In the days that followed, American League president Lee MacPhail upheld Kansas City's protest. MacPhail allowed the home run and directed that the game be restarted from that point (although Brett, Howser, and Royal player Gaylord Perry were ordered ejected from the game).

The two clubs had an open date on August 15 and met then to resume the game with Kansas City now leading 5–4 with two outs in the top of the ninth inning. The game ended that same way after the Yankees went down in order in the bottom of the inning. Fewer than 1,200 fans showed up to watch the few minutes of play.

In 1987, the famous pine tar bat was given to the Hall of Fame.

57. THE BLOODY SOCK

Like the pine tar bat, this item is one of the most unusual in the Hall of Fame. Among the museum's thousands of exhibits, there is only one bloody sock. As it turns out, it is not the one from the contest that made the "bloody sock game" label famous.

That game, now firmly ingrained in baseball lore, occurred at Yankee Stadium on October 19, 2004. The Boston Red Sox went into the game that night trailing the Yankees three games to two in the American League Championship Series. The Sox had lost the first three games before rallying to win the next two. Another victory would tie the series. Still, the final games were in New York, and the Yankees needed only one more win to advance to the World Series.

On the mound for Boston was Curt Schilling, whose physical condition was in question. Schilling had injured his right ankle during the season and damaged it again in game 1 of the series only seven days earlier. A poised veteran, Schilling was 21–6 during the regular season and had an exceptional record in playoff competition. His presence on the mound in the key game was of special importance to the Red Sox club.

Schilling's injury was officially a torn tendon sheath. To enable him to pitch, team doctors devised a procedure, unprecedented by most accounts, that involved suturing the damaged tendon to hold it in place. Three stitches connected the skin with the ligament and tissue near the bone, creating a protective barrier to keep the tendon from interfering with Schilling's pitching motion and delivery.

His sock soaked with blood, Schilling pitched masterfully through seven innings, leaving with a 4–1 lead. The Sox won the game 4–2 and went on to win game 7 of the playoffs and then the World Series. After the game, Schilling discarded the sock in the clubhouse.

Five days later, on October 24, Schilling pitched and won the second game of the World Series, again stitched together by what was already known as the Schilling tendon procedure. As before, the sock was bloody. This one, though, wound up in the Hall of Fame.

NOTE

1. Had the *Concorde SST* still been flying, an international traveler could have flown from New York City to London and back in the time it took to play the game (and still have a half hour for duty-free shopping).

Chapter Nine

Moments to Remember

Certain moments, some lasting only an instant, others encompassing an entire game, have carved themselves into baseball's collective memory. Some evoke warm feelings about the game or the player involved. Others are most remembered for the shocks they caused: Bolt-out-of-the-blue surprise interventions that changed the flow of the game and, some would argue, influenced the outcomes of pennant races and World Series games.

58. THE GARBLED PHONE CALLS GAME: "CAN YOU HEAR ME NOW?"

The outcome of a World Series game influenced by phone calls? You're kidding me again, right? Not really. Here's how it happened.

The scene: Rangers Ballpark in Arlington. The date: October 24, 2011. The St. Louis Cardinals and the Texas Rangers were tied 2–2 in the fifth game of a World Series even at two games apiece. In the bottom of the eighth, St. Louis manager Tony LaRussa called on right-hander Octavio Dotel to replace Chris Carpenter, who had pitched through the first seven innings. Dotel started the inning by giving up a double to Texas batter Michael Young before striking out Adrian Beltre and issuing an intentional walk to Nelson Cruz.

At about this point, the confusion began. LaRussa had earlier called the Cardinals' bullpen coach, Derek Lilliquist, intending that both left-hander Mark Rzepczynski and right-hander Jason Motte begin warming up. Somehow in the noise and excitement, Lilliquist heard only Rzepczynski's name. LaRussa speculated later that Lilliquist may have hung up after hearing the first name.

Playing the percentages, LaRussa brought in Rzepczynski to face left-handed batter David Murphy. During the season, left-handers had hit only .161 off Rzepczynski, while right-handers had batted .275. Murphy grounded a ball right back at the pitcher, which deflected off Rzepczynski's bare hand. Murphy beat the throw to first for an infield hit. Instead of a double play that would have ended the inning, the Rangers now had the bases loaded, still with only one out.

In the meantime, LaRussa learned that Motte—the Cardinals' closer—was not warming up and again called the bullpen to have him start throwing. Incredibly, this second message was also garbled. In the clamor and noise of the sellout crowd of 51,459, Lilliquist did not hear Motte's name. Instead, he thought he heard LaRussa say "Lynn" for right-handed pitcher Lance Lynn. Lynn, another reliever, was supposed be resting in game 5 after having pitched in game 3.

LaRussa, again playing the percentages, had intended to bring in right-hander Motte to oppose Texas's right-handed hitting catcher, Mike Napoli. During the season, right-handed batters had hit only .162 off Motte. However, with Motte still not warm, LaRussa stayed with the southpaw Rzepczynski to pitch to Napoli. Napoli promptly belted one of Rzepczynski's sliders into the gap in deep right-center field. When the dust settled, Napoli was on second with a double, and two runs had scored for Texas—the eventual margin of victory in a 4–2 game.

Still waiting for Motte to get warm, LaRussa brought in Lynn to issue an intentional walk. Finally, with Motte now ready, LaRussa called on his closer to get the Cardinals out of the inning.

LaRussa later assumed responsibility for the mix-ups, although some of his managerial colleagues noted in his defense that the bullpen is not visible from the visitors' dugout at the Rangers' ballpark. As with so much about the game of baseball, there is no assurance that Motte, had he been warmed up and available, would have gotten Napoli out. Percentage-wise, though, his presence would have unquestionably improved the Cardinals' prospects. Thus, in an era of cell phones, text messaging, and Twitter, baseball fans found it ironic that two misunderstood phone calls sent on a direct landline might have influenced the outcome of a World Series game.

The Cardinals recovered nicely from the telephone trauma of game 5. The sixth game, played two nights later in St. Louis, turned out to be one of the most exciting World Series games ever played. The Cardinals—twice within one strike of losing the game and, with it, the series—found a way to win. Down by two runs in both the ninth inning and the tenth—each time with two outs and two strikes on the batter—the Cardinals tied the game before winning it 10–9 with a walk-off home run in the 11th inning. The hero of game 6 was David Freese, a St. Louis–area native. In the bottom of the ninth, Freese hit a two-out, two-strike triple that tied the game. After Lance Bergman drove in the tying run in the 10th with another two-out, two-strike hit, Freese hit an 11th-inning walk-off blast to dead center field that sent the series to the seventh and deciding game.

The seventh game, played the following night in St. Louis, saw the Cardinals again fall behind early as the Rangers scored twice in the top of the first inning. The Cardinals came back with two runs to tie the game in the bottom of the inning and then dominated the rest of the game, winning 6–2.

For the Cardinals, the victory climaxed a spectacular closing run—down by 10 1/2 games on August 24, down 7 with 20 games left in the season, down 3 with only 5 days left in the wild card race, and assured a playoff berth on the last day of the season. Three days after the embarrassment of the telephone game, they were world champions.

59. THE FAN IN AISLE 4, ROW 8, SEAT 113

Wrigley Field, October 14, 2003: The Chicago Cubs were only five outs away from their first World Series appearance since 1945 and perhaps their first World Series championship since 1908. The Cubs led the National League Championship Series three games to two and were ahead of the Florida Marlins 3–0 in the top of the eighth inning. Only five more outs . . .

With a runner on second base and one out, Florida Marlins batter Luis Castillo lifted a high, shallow fly ball down the left-field line. Cubs left fielder Moises Alou hurried to attempt a play as the ball traveled down the line to a section of the park where the seats directly butt up against the field, with almost no space in foul territory.

While Alou moved to the ball as it dropped toward the stands at only an arms-length distance in foul territory, several fans reached for it. Fate placed one of them almost directly in its path. Steve Bartman—sitting in aisle 4, row 8, seat 113 (just inside the stands closest to the playing field)—was one of many who stood up and attempted to catch it. Art Looney, sitting to Bartman's right, also tried to snare the ball, only to have it fall just outside his grasp. Bartman, though, was right under it. As the ball came down, Bartman reached for it, as did Alou, who, positioned against the wall, leaned into the stands, jumped, and stretched for the ball with his glove arm fully extended. Bartman—positioned a bit higher than what Alou could reach—touched the ball. Although he did not catch it, Bartman deflected the ball away from Alou's outstretched glove.

Alou was not a particularly good fielder, but most simulations that remove the fan involvement appear to indicate that he could have caught the ball. Bartman's action, the attempt of a dedicated fan to take home a valued souvenir, started a cascade of events that spelled disaster for the Cubs. The Marlins went on to score eight runs in the inning. They won the game 8–3 and then took game 7 the next night to advance to the World Series.

As the eighth inning progressed that night, Cubs security personnel, fearing for Bartman's safety, escorted him from the field. In the days immediately following, he was subjected to threats of violence. And in recent years, the "Bartman seat" or the "Bartman play" have become part of baseball's vocabulary, often associated with instances of fan interference.

For the Cubs, a tantalizing five outs away, the wait would continue.

60. JETER HITS A HOME RUN — OR MAYBE NOT

This is the second notable game whose outcome was influenced by a fan's involvement in a key play.

While the incident happened seven years before the night that made the name Steve Bartman a household word, there are similarities between the games. Like the Bartman game, the episode also occurred in a league championship series. In both cases, historic venues framed the scene: Wrigley Field with Bartman, Yankee Stadium in game 1 of the American League Championship Series. In each case, the fireworks occurred in the eighth inning: it was in the eighth when Bartman famously reached for the ball in Chicago, and it was in the same inning in New York when a 12-year-old named Jeffrey Maier gained instant notoriety.

The 1996 American League Championship Series pitted the Yankees against the Baltimore Orioles. In the close, hard-fought contest, the Orioles sought to take the important first game and capture the lead in the series on the Yankees' home field. In the bottom of the eighth, Yankee shortstop Derek Jeter stepped to the plate with the Orioles leading 4–3. Jeter then hit a long, high fly deep to the right-field wall. Orioles right fielder Tony Tarasco moved to the fence and with his back against the wall settled in to wait for the ball. As Tarasco reached for it, Jeffrey Maier leaned over the top of the fence. Maier attempted to catch the ball but instead deflected it backward into the stands.

Tarasco and Baltimore protested vehemently that Maier had interfered, arguing that the fan reached into the field of play and intercepted a ball that Tarasco might otherwise have caught. Umpire Rich Garcia disagreed, ruling Jeter's hit a home run. The Yankees went on to win the game 5–4 and take the series four games to one.

Television replays showed that Garcia's call was probably incorrect: young Jeffrey Maier did appear to reach out into the field of play. In 2008, major league baseball introduced an instant replay capability to help arbitrate questions of fan interference and close fair/foul calls on home runs.

61. STIRNWEISS'S BATTING TITLE

September 30, 1945: The last day of the 1945 season, the New York Yankees are playing the Boston Red Sox. Yankee second baseman George "Snuffy" Stirnweiss went three for five that day. The three hits raised Stirnweiss's batting average to .3085443, just enough to give him the American League batting title.

Stirnweiss's performance on closing day edged him past the Chicago White Sox's Tony Cuccinello, who finished with an average of .3084577. Stirnweiss won the batting crown by .000866 of a point.

Stirnweiss not only won the batting title by the merest sliver but did so on the last day in a year in which he did not lead the league in batting on a single other day during the entire season. Because it was the last day, Cuccinello could not catch up, and Stirnweiss took the title.

Despite losing the closest batting title race in major league history, Cuccinello was released by the White Sox after the season and never played another big league ball game.

62. TED WILLIAMS: .406 ON THE LAST DAY

Ted Williams's batting average stood at .39955 as the Boston Red Sox prepared to meet the Philadelphia A's in a doubleheader on the last day of the 1941 season. The average would have been rounded up to .400. By taking the day off, Williams would have been assured of a .400 average and a place among baseball's immortals.

Nineteen forty-one had been a wondrous year for Williams. Counting the .39955 going into the final games, his average had dropped under .400 only twice during the season, having also briefly slipped under on July 25.

Boston manager Joe Cronin asked the 23-year-old Williams if he wanted to sit out the two games. Williams declined, indicating that doing so would cheapen the accomplishment. Now, having refused to sit out, he put the .400 average at risk as he stepped into the batter's box at Shibe Park in Philadelphia. In an astounding display of batting excellence under enormous pressure, Williams got a hit his first time up . . . and then in his next three also. After starting the game 4 for 4, he was retired the fifth time up. At the end of the first game, his average stood at .4048.

Offered the chance to sit out the second game, Williams again declined. He made two more hits, going 6 for 8 in the doubleheader.

Williams finished the season with a .406 average. No one has hit .400 since.

63. SEPTEMBER 28, 2011: HOURS AND HOURS OF EXCITEMENT

On one incredible Wednesday, baseball provided not just a single moment but an entire day to remember.

For many who follow the game, September 28, 2011, ranked as one of the most dramatic days in baseball history. On the last day of the regular season, wild card races in both leagues were in dead-even ties. In the National League, the Atlanta Braves and St. Louis Cardinals took the field with identical 89–72 records. In the American League, the Tampa Bay Rays and the Boston Red Sox were also knotted, each with 90 wins.

Late into the night, the suspense continued to build as the games themselves conspired to add to the drama. Two of the four went deep into extra innings. One winning team came within one pitch of losing. One losing team came within one out of winning. Down 7–0 in the eighth inning, one made a remarkable comeback to win. In a game of inches, a normally reliable fielder did not come up with a catch, and the game slipped away. One of baseball's best relief pitchers, needing only one more out, gave up three straight hits, ending both the game and the team's season.

The schedule that day had Atlanta hosting Philadelphia and St. Louis traveling to Houston, while the Rays played the Yankees at home and Boston closed at Baltimore. One after another, memorable, near-miraculous games began to unfold. During the course of several nail-biting hours, no lead was safe, and the most extraordinary happenings became commonplace.

In the National League, the Atlanta Braves faced an especially tough challenge. The Braves, already slumping, played their final series against Philadelphia. With 102 victories, the Phillies had the best record in baseball.

In early September, the Braves had built an eight-and-a-half game lead in the wild card race. After going 9–18 and losing their last five, their season came down to one game.

It began well. The Braves went ahead 3–1 in the third inning and clung to a 3–2 lead going into the ninth. Needing only three outs, the Braves called in rookie closer Craig Kimbrel, who during the course of a remarkable season had saved 46 games. Sandwiched around two outs, Kimbrel walked three and gave up a hit and the tying run. With the bases loaded, Braves pitcher Kris Medlen entered the game and retired the side.

The teams went scoreless through the 10th, 11th, and 12th innings before, with two outs in the 13th, the Phillies' Hunter Pence hit a broken-bat single that drove in the go-ahead run. Trailing 4–3 in the bottom of the 13th, the Braves managed a base runner, but Freddie Freeman hit into a game-ending double play.

Meanwhile, the St. Louis Cardinals, the Braves' competitors for the National League's wild card slot, were at Houston playing the Astros. For St. Louis, the closing days of the season had taken on a near-mystical quality. With the Braves faltering, the Cards—down 10 games in the race on August 24—went 22–9, finally catching the Braves on the 161st game of the year.

Of the deciding games that night, the St. Louis–Houston contest was the only one of the four that did not go down to the wire. The Cardinals won 8–0. The only excitement involved pitcher Chris Carpenter's mastery as he held the Astros to two hits. St. Louis's win, coupled with Atlanta's loss, gave the Cardinals the National League playoff berth.

In the American League wild card race, Boston, like Atlanta, stumbled late in the season, while Tampa Bay, like St. Louis, closed with a rush. On September 3, Boston led Tampa Bay by nine games. From that point through the end of the season, the Sox lost 18 of 24. At no time during the month did they win back-to-back games.

Even so, Boston's prospects looked favorable. Although the Sox were on the road for the final game, their opponents were the Baltimore Orioles. With a record of 68–93, the Orioles were in last place in the American League East Division. During the season, though, the Orioles had played well against the Red Sox, winning five of the seven most recent games between the teams.

It was an uncomfortable evening to watch major league baseball in Baltimore. The weather had no respect for playoff implications. In the middle of the seventh inning, heavy showers forced a rain delay of 1 hour and 26 minutes.

Despite its recent travails and a soggy field, Boston carried a one-run lead into the bottom of the ninth. The Sox had ample opportunities throughout the game to expand that margin but failed to do so. In the top of the eighth, Marco Scutaro was thrown out at home plate. In the top of the ninth, with the bases loaded and one out, Ryan Lavanway grounded into an inning-ending double play.

Still, as Baltimore came to bat in the bottom of the ninth, Boston retained a one-run lead. Boston also had Jonathan Papelbon, one the game's premier closers. Red Sox manager Terry Francona called on Papelbon to get the final three outs and extend Boston's season.

Papelbon promptly struck out the first two batters. Then, just three strikes away from ensuring at least a one-game playoff, Papelbon gave up a double to Chris Davis. Nolan Reimold followed with a double, driving in pinch runner Kyle Hudson. With two outs and the game now tied, the Orioles' Roberto Andino, a .245 hitter, stepped to the plate. Still needing only one out to continue the game and the season, Papelbon fired a fastball toward the plate. Andino drove the ball to the outfield where Boston left fielder Carl Crawford could not make the play. The two runs with two outs in the bottom of the ninth gave Baltimore a 4–3 win. With Boston's loss and Tampa Bay's win over the Yankees, the Red Sox became the first team to miss the postseason after leading by as many as nine games in September.

If Boston's loss made history, Tampa Bay's victory surely ranked as one of the most improbable of all time. Only days before, just getting to the deciding game seemed beyond possibility. Apparently out of the race in early September, the Rays caught fire and in face-to-face encounters beat the Red Sox six out of seven times. On September 26, they pulled into a tie with Boston. The tie continued until the final day.

Everything came down to September 28, the last day of the season. What happened next seemed taken from the pages of a novel. At the end of the second inning, the Rays were behind 5–0. They trailed 7–0 going into the eighth.

In the bottom half of the eighth inning, the Rays loaded the bases, and the miracle began to unfold. Sam Fuld drew a bases-loaded walk: 7–1. Sean Rodriguez got hit by a pitch: 7–2. B. J. Upton hit a sacrifice fly: 7–3. Evan Longoria hit a three-run home run: 7–6. That's where it stood after eight innings.

In the ninth, the first two Rays struck out. Down to their final out, the Rays sent Dan Johnson to the plate to pinch hit. Johnson, little used during the season, was batting .108. Johnson immediately fell behind in the count, picking up two quick strikes. With many fans already having left the park, the Rays were down to their last strike . . . and Johnson hit a home run: 7–7.

The teams remained scoreless through the top half of the 12th inning. In the bottom half of the inning, Evan Longoria hit a walk-off home run: 8–7 Tampa Bay. The Rays were in the playoffs.

Wednesday, September 28, 2011: an incredible day for baseball.

64. MOMENTS THAT TRANSCEND THE GAME

Over the course of the game's history, a few extraordinary events—unique in their capacity to inspire, captivate, or amuse—have become inseparable parts of baseball's story.

July 4, 1939: Lou Gehrig Appreciation Day at Yankee Stadium

In one of the most poignant scenes in baseball history, Lou Gehrig, fatally stricken with amyotrophic lateral sclerosis, the ailment that would forever be linked to his name as "Lou Gehrig's disease," said good-bye to a sellout crowd at Yankee Stadium. Forced by the effects of the disease to end his consecutive-games-played string at 2,130 and retire earlier in the year, Gehrig's remarks included one of the most famous comments ever delivered by an American sports personality: "Today, I consider myself to be the luckiest man on the face of the earth." Gehrig's uniform number was retired that day, the first ever by a major league team. Gehrig died two years later at age 38.

June 13, 1948: Babe Ruth's Farewell at Yankee Stadium

It was not just the occasion—Ruth's final public appearance at the "House That Ruth Built"—but also a picture taken of the event that has become ingrained in the game's history. Taken from behind, the photo shows Ruth frail, stooped, and leaning on a bat—the famous number 3 on the back of his uniform—addressing the massive throng of fans and players. Shot by Nat Fein, press photographer for the *New York Herald Tribune*, the photo, "The Babe Bows Out," won a Pulitzer Prize. Ruth's comments describing his affection for the game were delivered in a raspy voice, his throat ravaged by the cancer that would take his life two months later. After his death, his body lay in state at Yankee Stadium, visited by tens of thousands of fans.

July 13, 1999: Ted Williams Returns to Fenway Park

Williams, 80 years old and in failing health, was the centerpiece of one of the most marvelous moments in baseball history. At Fenway Park, as pregame festivities for that year's All-Star Game were under way, Williams was driven in a golf cart from center field to the pitcher's mound to throw the ceremonial first pitch. As soon as Williams entered the field, the sellout crowd, lifted as if one from its chairs, launched into a long, loud, emotional standing ovation. As the cart moved toward the mound, Williams doffed his cap to the Red Sox fans, something he had never done during his long and often contentious relationship with them.

When the cart reached the center of the field, Williams was engulfed—not only surrounded by fellow Hall of Fame immortals but swamped by the young, present-day all-stars who hurried from both dugouts to gather around him, unabashedly enthralled and in awe. For several minutes in the midst of the still-standing ovation, Williams sat in the cart laughing and talking, immersed in the adulation of his young admirers.

The game was considerably delayed. No one who loves the sport of baseball would have had it any other way.

October 21, 1975: Carlton Fisk's Home Run Changes the Way Games Are Covered

If the picture of Babe Ruth's farewell at Yankee Stadium is one of the most memorable still photos in baseball history, the iconic television shot is that of Carlton Fisk in game 6 of the 1975 World Series. In the bottom of the 12th inning at Fenway Park, Fisk hit a one-ball, no-strike pitch high down the left field line. What happened next was television magic.

As the ball flew toward the foul pole, the camera stayed with Fisk as he side-hopped down the first base line, waving both hands over his head, motioning to the right, seeming to will the ball to stay in fair territory. It did, just barely. Fisk's home run gave the win to Boston. In one of the best-ever World Series, the Cincinnati Reds would win the deciding game 7 the next night. Years later, though, it is the recollection of Fisk's hop down the line, followed by a joyful bound, that forever memorializes the moment.

That the camera followed Fisk and not the flight of the ball, as was standard practice at the time, was apparently accidental. However, so remarkably did the depiction capture the drama of an incredible instant that it quickly and permanently altered the protocol for covering the sport—and along the way provided an enduring memory for fans of the game.

August 19, 1951: The Shortest Batter in Major League History

It turned out to be a memorable game but for reasons far different from those surrounding the appearances of Gehrig, Ruth, and Williams. Indeed, there was nothing solemn or poignant about what took place in St. Louis at the beginning of the second game of a doubleheader between the woeful Browns and the Detroit Tigers. On that date, as a publicity stunt, consummate showman Bill Veeck, owner of the (as usual) cellar-dwelling Browns, sent 3'7" Eddie Gaedel to the plate to lead off the game. With a minuscule strike zone, Gaedel walked on four pitches thrown by Tiger pitcher Bob Cain. Laughing visibly, Cain soft-tossed the last two pitches to the plate. Gaedel, wearing number 1/8, went to first base, where he was immediately replaced by a pinch runner.

Veeck was also known for other stunts aimed at increasing attendance. A second famous instance also took place in St. Louis, where he instituted a "Grandstand Manager's Day" allowing fans to decide (by vote) moves that the team should employ in various situations during the game. Interestingly, the Browns won the game 5–3, breaking a losing streak. A few years later, as owner of the Chicago White Sox, Veeck installed an "exploding scoreboard," the first of its kind, using fireworks, electronics, and sound effects.

October 5, 2011: The "Rally Squirrel"

In the fifth inning of game 4 of the National League Division Series, the most famous gray squirrel in baseball history ran across home plate at Busch Stadium in St. Louis.

Phillies pitcher Roy Oswalt was delivering a pitch to Cardinals batter Skip Schumaker when the squirrel chose the moment to make its historic scamper. When umpire Angel Hernandez called the pitch a ball, Oswalt and Phillies manager Charlie Manuel argued that the squirrel had distracted Oswalt and that Hernandez should have ruled "no pitch."[1] As it turned out, Schumaker eventually flied out. What mattered to St. Louis fans, though, was that the Cardinals won the game. The legend of the Rally Squirrel was born.

The squirrel was instantly adopted as an unofficial mascot by the Cardinals ball club and, indeed, by the entire city of St. Louis. Rally Squirrel T-shirts, towels, a Twitter account, and a theme song quickly followed. The squirrel's notoriety would be enhanced considerably over the following days when the Cardinals went on to win the division series, the National League championship, and the World Series title.

At game 5 in Philadelphia two nights later, Phillies fans threw a stuffed squirrel into the Cardinals bullpen. St. Louis pitcher Octavio Dotel picked it up and kept it as a good-luck charm. After St. Louis won the National League championship, the stuffed squirrel was honored with a champagne bath during the postgame celebration.

A squirrel had also appeared on the Busch Stadium field the day before the celebrated incident, although it is uncertain if it was the same creature that made history the following night. Eventually, four squirrels were captured inside the stadium. Along with its companions, the squirrel believed to be the Rally Squirrel was released at a Wildlife Rescue Facility near St. Louis.

NOTE

1. In terms of physical distractions, though, the squirrel's antics were mild in comparison with those that afflicted Yankee pitcher Joba Chamberlain at Jacobs Field in Cleveland on October 5, 2007. With the Yankees leading 1–0 during the eighth inning of game 2 of the American League Division Series, thousands of small insects swarmed the area around the pitcher's mound. Close-up television shots showed hundreds of the midges crawling on Chamberlain's face, neck, and arms. Repeated douses of insect repellent did no good. Chamberlain threw two wild pitches, giving up the tying run without surrendering a hit. The Yankees lost the game and, eventually, the series.

Chapter Ten

Hall of Fame

The Hall of Fame—officially, the National Baseball Hall of Fame and Museum—is on Main Street in Cooperstown, New York. Since opening on June 13, 1939, more than 14 million visitors, on average about 350,000 each year, have toured the facility. On display at any one time are a portion of the museum's 35,000 artifacts, 2.6 million library items, and 130,000 baseball cards. The hall's main features include the gallery, where plaques of all Hall of Fame members are displayed, as well as the museum, museum store, museum bookstore, and library. The library includes a file on every player to appear in a major league game; it is the world's largest repository of baseball information. The museum collection contains bats, balls, gloves, caps, helmets, uniforms, shoes, and other items reflecting the hall's charter to honor excellence, preserve history, and connect generations to the game.

The Cooperstown site was chosen after a disputed 1907 study concluded that Abner Doubleday, later to achieve notoriety in the Civil War, had laid out a rudimentary diamond-shaped field and developed initial rules for the game while in town in 1839. Later historians discounted the story that Doubleday "invented" baseball; most now view the sport as having evolved from several bat-and-ball games that were being played throughout the country in the early 1800s. At most, Doubleday's game might have reflected the arrival of a version of the sport in the small town in upstate New York.

Nonetheless, the Doubleday tale, while no longer given great credence as fact, remains part of baseball's enduring—and endearing—mythology. The Cooperstown site adds to the charm of an institution that many baseball fans regard as a national treasure.

Generally speaking, players are inducted into the Hall of Fame through election by either the Baseball Writers' Association of America or the Veterans Committee. Players with 10 years of major league experience become eligible for consideration 5 years after retirement. After an initial screening process removes players clearly less qualified, baseball writers may vote for up to 10 players from a pool of eligibles that usually numbers from 25 to 40 candidates. Any player whose name appears on 75% of the ballots is elected. Players named on less than 5% of the ballots are dropped from further consideration. If a player fails to be elected within 20 years after retirement, he may be considered by a Veterans Committee. Other committees evaluate managers and umpires, executives and builders, and players whose active careers ended earlier than 1942.

When plans for the hall were being formulated, a panel of baseball writers met to choose the first Hall of Fame class. That initial election, held in January 1936, honored five players with election as the first members of the Hall of Fame—Babe Ruth, Ty Cobb, Honus Wagner, Walter Johnson, and Christy Mathewson. It is the story of those baseball immortals that we turn to in this chapter. (Hall of Fame membership is shown at Appendix E.)

65. BABE RUTH

No one occupies a place in the history of American sports quite like Babe Ruth.

- In 1969, he was named "Greatest Player Ever" in voting associated with the 100th anniversary of professional baseball.
- In 1998, *The Sporting News* ranked Ruth first among "Baseball's 100 Greatest Players."
- In 1999, baseball fans named him to the Major League Baseball All-Century Team.
- In 1999, the Associated Press named him Athlete of the Century.
- The Hall of Fame devotes an entire room to him—the only player so honored.

The first true superstar in American sports, Ruth dominated the game like no other player before or since. In 1919, his first full year as an outfielder, he hit 29 home runs, shattering by 15 a record that had stood since 1903. In 1920, his 54 home runs exceeded the total of every other team in the American League. He was the first player ever to hit 30, 40, 50, and 60 home runs.

Ruth's records are remarkable and enduring. During the period 1918–1934, Ruth led the American League

- 12 times in home runs,
- 13 times in on-base percentage plus slugging percentage,

- 13 times in slugging percentage,
- 8 times in runs scored, and
- 6 times in RBI.

Except for RBI, each of these statistics established an all-time record.

Because of attention given to his accomplishments as a power hitter, often overlooked is the fact that Ruth was a remarkably gifted athlete. His lifetime batting average was .342, placing him in the all-time top 10. Before the Yankees converted him to a full-time outfielder, Ruth was the best left-handed pitcher in baseball. In 1916, he set a still-existing record for the longest complete-game victory in World Series history, when he beat Brooklyn 2–1 in 14 innings. For 43 years after he last pitched in 1918, he held the World Series record for consecutive scoreless innings, with 29 2/3.

Ruth's prodigious achievements on the diamond were matched by his exuberant personality off the field. Everything about Ruth was extraordinary: his efforts on behalf of children's charities; his size, strength, and appetite; and his extracurricular carousing.

More than any other player in any other sport, Ruth's name is inextricably linked with the game he played. Decades after Babe Ruth last stepped on to a diamond, he remains larger than life.

66. WALTER JOHNSON

Walter Johnson won 417 games while pitching his entire career for a ball club that was often only average and many times far below average. The Washington Senators seldom fielded a seriously contending team, yet Johnson's personal winning percentage was .599—a figure that has led some analysts to believe that had he played for a more competitive club, his winning total might have exceeded the 511 achieved by Cy Young. There is, of course, no way of knowing, but it is useful to point out that during his career, the Senators were shut out in 65 of his starts and got only one run in 38 others. In 1909, they were shut out 10 times in games pitched by Johnson. The 1909 team scored only 380 runs the entire season, setting a record that stands to this day. In 1913, Johnson won 36 of the team's 90 victories, personally accounting for 40 percent of the Senators' wins.

Johnson—a powerful, raw-boned right-hander with a side-arm delivery—was known for his blazing fastball. The debate remains whether he was one of the "fastest" of all time. He threw a record 110 career complete-game shutouts, including an incredible 11 in one season. He holds the record for number of 1–0 victories, with 38.

Nicknamed the "Big Train," Johnson was a complete player: in 1913, he fielded 1.000 (with 103 chances); in 1925, he hit .433, a record for a pitcher.

67. TY COBB

Ty Cobb's lifetime batting average covering 24 seasons in the major leagues is .367. It is the highest ever recorded. Using a unique grip with his hands slightly separated on the bat, the left-handed Cobb's career average was an astounding 100 points higher than the league average.

Cobb's achievements are breathtaking: During the course of his career, he was credited with setting as many as 90 records. Among those still standing are career batting average, most batting titles, and most consecutive .300 seasons. Cobb won the American League batting crown 12 times, including a never-equaled 9 in a row. He batted .300 for 23 consecutive years. Often overlooked, because he was not a power hitter, is that he led the league in slugging percentage eight times.

In 1909, Cobb won the Triple Crown, batting .377, driving in 107 runs, and hitting 9 home runs. All the home runs were inside the park, for which Cobb became the only player in modern times to lead the league in home runs without hitting a ball over the fence.

For decades, Cobb held numerous other major records. Until 1985, when Pete Rose surpassed him, Cobb had the most hits (4,191). Rose finished with 65 more career hits but had 2,624 more at bats.

Likewise, for years, Cobb's numbers for runs scored (2,245) and stolen bases (892) were major league highs. Ricky Henderson eventually broke both, winding up his long career with 2,295 runs and 1,406 stolen bases. Earlier, Cobb's single-season stolen-base record of 96 had been eclipsed by Maury Wills. Still not surpassed is another of Cobb's accomplishments: three times in his career he stole second, third, and home in consecutive attempts.

Cobb remains the only player to have two 35-game hitting streaks. He also had six streaks of 20 or more games. On May 5, 1925, Cobb went six for six in a single game, hitting three home runs, a double, and two singles. His 16 total bases set the American League record.

Despite his remarkable achievements on the diamond, there is a dark side to the legacy left by the "Georgia Peach." Ty Cobb was possibly the most intensely and universally disliked ballplayer in the history of major league baseball. Cobb fought—with insults and fists—almost everyone: fans, umpires, opponents, and teammates. Baseball historians describe his conduct and personality in menacing terms: "noisy, combative"; he intimidated opponents with "spikes, fists, bat, biting tongue"; "violent and outrageous"; Cobb viewed the game as "something like war." His numerous fights on and off the field are well documented. On one occasion, he went into the stands to assault a partially handicapped heckler. On another, he fought an umpire under the stands. On another, he beat up a butcher's assistant in an argument over a disputed price. When Cobb's son got less-than-satisfactory grades at a university, Cobb drove to the school and struck him with a whip. He was accused on at least two occasions of slapping black women. Even at a time when racist attitudes were far more rigid, Cobb's were noted for being extreme and profane. Through his years in the big leagues, Cobb ate and roomed alone. When he died, only three people from major league baseball attended his funeral.

There were many facets to Cobb's personality. He was an astute buyer and seller of stocks and bonds. He invested early in, and became a major shareholder of, Coca-Cola as well as General Electric, eventually accumulating an estate of several million dollars. When two of his three children died and a second marriage failed, Cobb became more generous with his wealth, endowing the Cobb Memorial Hospital, the Ty Cobb Healthcare System, and the Cobb Educational Fund. The latter charity assisted needy children in attaining quality schooling. It, like the healthcare system, was open to all races. When baseball broke the color line, Cobb supported the decision to integrate the game.

Cobb's colleagues in the profession disliked him with an abiding intensity, yet they recognized his transcendent skills. When the balloting took place to choose the first inductees to the Hall of Fame, Cobb received the most votes—more than even Babe Ruth. Baseball historian Benjamin Rader best described Cobb's complicated legacy: "Rarely has a more successful, more violent, or more maladjusted personality passed through the annals of American sport."

68. HONUS WAGNER

At the time when the two of them played, Honus Wagner shared with Ty Cobb the reputation of being one of the greatest hitters in the game. Like Cobb, Wagner had blazing speed, but the two of them had little else in common either on or off the field. Cobb was loud, profane, hated; Wagner was quiet, amiable, liked by nearly everyone. Cobb was a lean left-handed outfielder; Wagner was a "stout, barrel-chested, bowlegged" right-handed shortstop. Cobb spent his entire career in the American League, primarily as a member of the Detroit Tigers; Wagner was a National Leaguer with the Pittsburgh Pirates.

Wagner led the National League in batting eight times, in slugging percentage six times (surpassing the league average by an astounding 200 points), and in stolen bases five times. The "Flying Dutchman" was equally famous for his remarkable fielding. Many accounts describe Wagner using his huge hands "like a scoop shovel" to swallow up ground balls. Perhaps because of his fielding, some contemporaries of Cobb and Wagner regarded Wagner as being the better all-around ballplayer. Almost all who played or managed against him placed him at shortstop on their all-time team lists. Many baseball historians still rank him as the greatest shortstop in the game's history. In the first election for Hall of Fame membership, Wagner tied for second in the balloting with Babe Ruth.

Long after his retirement, honors for Wagner continued. In 1969, on the 100th anniversary of professional baseball, Wagner was voted the all-time shortstop. In 1999, more than 82 years after he last played, he was still the highest-ranking shortstop on *The Sporting News's* list of the 100 greatest players.

69. CHRISTY MATHEWSON

Christy Mathewson was appreciated for his legendary skills as a pitcher (373 career wins) and for his conduct on and off the field. In an age where the game and those who played it were known for their rough edges, "no one was more successful in enhancing the reputation of professional baseball" than Mathewson.

In modern terms, Mathewson would be called "poster boy" for the sport. Tall (6'2"), blond-haired, and blue-eyed, he was held up as an ideal example for the game. Unlike most players at the time, Mathewson had a college education (Bucknell). He cautioned against smoking and drinking, and fulfilling a promise to his mother, he refused to play on Sundays.

For a decade at the peak of his career, no pitcher was more consistent than "Matty," or "Big Six" as he was called. Using a fastball that some said was the equivalent of Walter Johnson's, a big-breaking roundhouse curve, and a pitch that he called a "fadeaway" (likely what would now be called a screwball), the right-hander won at least 22 games each season for 12 consecutive seasons (1903–1914). Four times during that span, he won 30 or more games.

In 1913, when he won 25 games, and in 1914, when he won 24, Mathewson actually gave up fewer walks than he had victories: he walked 21 batters in 1913 and 23 in 1914. In 1913, he walked only 0.62 batters per nine innings, a record still.

During World War I, Mathewson enlisted in the army. Sent to France as a captain in a chemical warfare company, he was accidentally subjected to poison gas during a training exercise. As a result of the accident, Mathewson developed tuberculosis, which led to his early death seven years later.

Mathewson's selection as one of the first five inductees to the Hall of Fame was well deserved. In 1999, *The Sporting News*'s list of the 100 greatest ballplayers ranked him as the highest National League pitcher. ESPN chose his pitching performance in the 1905 World Series as the greatest playoff performance of all time: three shutouts over a six-day span as his New York Giants bested the Philadelphia A's four games to one.

Chapter Eleven

The All-Star Game

In 1933, to help celebrate Chicago's Century of Progress Exposition, *Chicago Tribune* sports editor Arch Ward proposed a game pitting all-star teams from the American and National leagues. Although club owners were at first reluctant, the game was a resounding success. Played to a full house at Comiskey Park (home of the White Sox), excitement surrounding the contest was enhanced considerably when, with one out in the third inning, Babe Ruth hit the first home run in all-star competition. The caliber of players in that first game is evidenced by the fact that of the 18 players in the starting lineups, only one—Wally Berger of the Boston Braves—was not later selected to the Hall of Fame. Originally conceived as a one-time event, the game was so well received that the "Mid-Season Classic" became a fixture on the major league schedule.

The site of the All-Star Game alternates among cities in each league. Beginning in 2003, the champion of the league that wins the game has received home field advantage in the World Series. Rules for selecting all-star players have changed a bit over the years. In 2007, rules were revised to provide for 32 players on each roster. Starting lineups are selected by fans. Eight pitchers are chosen by players, coaches, and managers. Managers then lift the roster to 31 players and ensure that every team is represented by at least one player. After the first 31 are chosen, fans vote for one additional player from a list of five provided by the managers and the commissioner's office. Managers come from the two league champions that competed in the prior year's World Series.

This chapter recounts some of the most memorable moments in all-star competition.

70. THE WINDBLOWN BALK

Fans can look at it in any one of three ways: It was the most famous balk, the most exaggerated episode, or the most potent wind gust in All-Star Game history. The game's most notorious meteorological event took place on July 11, 1961, at Candlestick Park in San Francisco, a stadium famous for its high and unpredictable winds.

With runners on first and second, National League pitcher Stu Miller, representing the San Francisco Giants, came into the game in the ninth inning. Working to protect a 3–1 lead, Miller set himself on the mound and began his windup. Suddenly, a violent gust of wind erupted and, in the exaggerated version, blew him off the mound. In reality, the burst of wind disrupted his windup, causing him to shift or sway on the pitching rubber. Umpires immediately called a balk, advancing the runners to second and third. Exaggerated or not, so heavy were the gusts that day that one batter later, catcher Smokey Burgess dropped a foul pop-up in the wind. The American League eventually tied the score on an infield error, sending the game into extra innings.

With Miller still pitching, the American League scored again on another error to take a 4–3 lead in the top of the 10th inning. The National League then came back in the bottom of the inning to score twice on hits by Willie Mays and Roberto Clemente and win the game 5–4, making Miller, despite the most famous balk in All-Star Game history, the winning pitcher.

71. CARL HUBBELL: 5 KS IN A ROW

It is the most famous pitching performance in All-Star Game history. The scene was the second All-Star Game, played July 10, 1934, at the Polo Grounds in New York City.

Carl Hubbell, New York Giants left-hander, was on the mound for the National League. With two runners on and no outs in the top of the first inning, Hubbell faced a daunting task. The next five hitters were among the most feared and famous sluggers in baseball—Babe Ruth, Lou Gehrig, Jimmie Foxx, Al Simmons, and Joe Cronin. All would eventually be selected for the Hall of Fame.

Hubbell struck them out. All five of them.

Using a devastating screwball, Hubbell whiffed Ruth, Gehrig, and Foxx to end the first inning and then fanned Simmons and Cronin to start the second. In the process, Hubbell fanned—in order—players who at the time ranked first, second, third, and fourth on the American League's career home run list.

Although in 1986 Fernando Valenzuela of the Los Angeles Dodgers also struck out five consecutive all-star batters, decades later Hubbell's feat is still recognized as one of the great pitching performances not just in All-Star Game annals but in baseball history.

72. THE EEPHUS PITCH

The Eephus[1] (sometimes Ephus), or "blooper pitch," played a major role in one of the most memorable moments in All-Star Game history.

Right-handed pitcher Rip Sewell of the Pittsburgh Pirates is credited with inventing the Eephus after a hunting accident permanently damaged the foot he stepped off on, causing him to modify his pitching motion and delivery. The pitch that resulted had a high, arcing trajectory like that of a slow-pitch softball. Big league hitters found it difficult to hit solidly. The Eephus topped out at about 25 feet at its highest point, and that strange-sight picture, coupled with the pitch's slow speed (only 50–60 miles per hour), caused problems for batters accustomed to swinging at 90-mph fastballs. Although Sewell was a veteran pitcher—he eventually pitched in more than 300 major league games—no one had ever hit a home run off an Eephus delivery.

The 1946 All-Star Game, played July 9 at Fenway Park in Boston, was in the bottom of the eighth inning when Ted Williams stepped in to face Sewell. Accounts vary whether Sewell told Williams in advance that he was going to throw the Eephus or whether Williams challenged Sewell to throw it. Regardless, Sewell delivered an Eephus for a strike. (By yet another account, Williams challenged Sewell to throw it again.) When Sewell lofted the second Eephus toward the plate, Williams waited, cocked once, stepped forward, and hit the pitch over the wall and into the bull pen in right-center field. It was Williams's second home run of the game in what turned out to be a 12–0 American League victory.

Photos appear to show that as he moved forward to get to the pitch, Williams may have stepped out of the batter's box. Nonetheless, the drive went for a home run. Sewell—and the pitch—would be remembered not for the countless occasions when the Eephus was thrown successfully, but for the one time when it was hit out of the park.

73. THE COLLISION

For those who saw the game in person or on television or in one of the countless replays shown over the years, the scene remains etched in memory: Pete Rose barreling full out around third; third base coach Leo Durocher running with Rose about halfway down the line, arms windmilling, trying to hurry him on; catcher Ray Fosse moving slightly up the third base line to take the incoming throw from the outfield . . . and then there is the collision. Rose races full speed down the line; Fosse shifts a bit to the left to receive the throw from center fielder Amos Otis. As Fosse reaches the ball, Rose slams violently into him, knocking him backward, sprawling on the ground, clutching his shoulder. The ball comes loose, and with Rose's run, the National League wins 5–4 in 12 innings.

The game, played July 14, 1970, helped celebrate Cincinnati's new Riverfront Stadium. With two out and the score tied 4–4 in the bottom of the 12th, Rose singled and moved to second on a follow-on single by Bill Grabarkewitz. With Rose now in scoring position, Jim Hickman drove a hit to center. American League center fielder Amos Otis fielded the ball cleanly and came up throwing. Otis made a good throw that was slightly up the line on the third base side of home plate. The rest is history.

Rose, of course, went on to greater notoriety. For Fosse, an up and coming young star, already an all-star in his second major league season, the collision altered the course of his career. Although he played nine more big league seasons, the injury (untreated at first and then eventually diagnosed as a fractured bone) caused persistent pain and made it difficult for him to raise his arm above the shoulder. A power hitter until the collision, he was never again a consistent long-ball threat.

NOTE

1. The name apparently has no meaning. It is thought to have been coined by a teammate of Sewell who said, "Eephus means nothin' and so does the pitch."

Chapter Twelve

The Most Famous Teams

Over the past 100-plus seasons, more than three dozen franchises past and present have fielded major league teams. Many of those teams have been very good. Some have been great. Still others, far fewer in number, are in a category by themselves—so exceptional that they have received identifying labels that have persisted through the years.

While arguments about the "greatest teams" are as old as the sport itself, what is less debatable about these few is that they are—or are among—the most famous teams of all time. All of them played with such unique brilliance or accomplished feats so astounding that they have come down to us as "named" teams: "Murderers' Row" . . . "The Big Red Machine" . . . "The Miracle Braves" . . . "The Hitless Wonders."

74. MURDERERS' ROW

In 1969, the Baseball Writers' Association voted the 1927 New York Yankees as the greatest team of all time. Statistically, it is hard to argue the point.

The 1927 club set team records in every category except stolen bases. In first place every day of the season, it eventually won the pennant by 19 games and then swept Pittsburgh in the World Series.

The team led the league in home runs, runs scored, slugging percentage, and batting average (a remarkable .307) and outscored opponents by a record 376 runs. The pitching staff's league-leading 3.20 earned run average was better than the second-best team's by three-quarters of a run per game and almost a full run per game (0.92) lower than the league average.

The tandem of Babe Ruth and Lou Gehrig finished first and second in home runs, slugging, runs scored, and walks. They also finished first and second—this time with Gehrig ahead of Ruth—in RBI, total bases, and extra-base hits. Ruth alone hit more home runs than every opposing team in the American League.

The club featured extraordinary depth throughout the powerful lineup. Center fielder Earle Combs and Gehrig finished first and second in hits and triples. Combs finished third behind Ruth and Gehrig in runs and third behind Gehrig and Ruth in total bases. Second baseman Tony Lazzeri finished third behind Ruth and Gehrig in home runs.

Five members of the starting lineup hit .300: Combs (.356 with 231 hits), Ruth (.356 with 60 home runs and 164 RBI), Gehrig (.373 with 47 home runs and 175 RBI), left fielder Bob Meusel (.337 with 103 RBI), and Lazzeri (.309 with 18 home runs and 107 RBI). Ruth scored 158 runs, walked 137 times, and slugged .722. Gehrig was voted the league's most valuable player, having had not only 47 home runs and 175 RBI but also 52 doubles and 18 triples among his 218 hits. Six players from the 1927 Yankees would eventually be elected to the Hall of Fame, plus manager Miller Huggins and general manager Ed Barrow.

The team was labeled the Murderers' Row—particularly the first six batters: Combs, shortstop Mark Koenig, Ruth, Gehrig, Meusel, and Lazzeri. Seldom has a nickname seemed more appropriate.

75. THE BIG RED MACHINE

Some analysts make the case that the Big Red Machine—a name given to the 1970–1976 Cincinnati Reds ball club—was, if not the best, then certainly among the best teams of all time. During those several years of sustained excellence, the team won five division titles, four National League pennants, and two World Series championships. With the World Series victories of 1975 and 1976, the Reds became the first National League team in 75 years to win back-to-back series championships. The team's overall winning percentage for the seven-year period was a robust .607.

Those who argue on behalf of the Big Red Machine note that the eight position players in the lineup were collectively among the best ever as an overall unit. Superstars among the group included infielder/outfielder Pete Rose (all-time hit leader), catcher Johnny Bench, first baseman Tony Perez, and second baseman Joe Morgan. During 1970–1979, team members earned six Most Valuable Player Awards, led the league in home runs four times, won three batting titles and 25 Gold Gloves, and were selected to the All-Star Team a combined 63 times. Bench, Perez, and Morgan were later inducted into baseball's Hall of Fame.

The Reds' starting pitching was not exceptional, but for much of the period, the team was bolstered by a solid corps of relief pitchers. The Big Red Machine was managed by Sparky Anderson.

76. THE MIRACLE BRAVES

In mid-July 1914, the Boston Braves were 15 1/2 games down, dead last in the National League. By the end of September, they were National League champions, having won the league title by an impressive 10 1/2 games. In early October, they swept the overwhelmingly favored Philadelphia A's to win the World Series.

At their last-place low point, the Braves' 33–43 record seemingly put them far out of pennant contention. The miracle turnaround began on July 19 with a doubleheader victory that pulled the team out of the cellar. A six-game winning streak moved them into fourth place. Soon after, the Braves reeled off nine victories in a row and were in second place by August 10. As the team continued to roll, it touched first place for a time by the end of August, fell back briefly, and then on September 8 moved in front to stay.

The team's incredible climb was made possible by winning 61 of its last 77 games, including 34 of its last 44. From last place in July to World Series champions, the 1914 Braves accomplished the greatest comeback in major league history.

The Braves' turnaround was made possible by the outstanding pitching of Lefty Tyler (16 wins), Bill James (26 wins), and Dick Rudolph (26 wins). James posted an amazing 19–1 record during the second half of the season. In the field, the team was sparked by shortstop "Rabbit" Maranville, second baseman Johnny Evers (the league most valuable player), and catcher Hank Gowdy, who hit .545 in the team's World Series victory over Philadelphia.

The "Miracle Braves" were skippered by George Stallings in what must surely rank as one the most outstanding managing jobs in baseball history.

77. THE HITLESS WONDERS

In 1906, the Chicago White Sox won both the American League and World Series championships. They did so with a team batting average of .230 and while hitting only seven home runs the entire season.

Despite the low batting average and the lack of power, the team finished third in the league in scoring, as Chicago batters led the league in drawing bases on balls. The Sox pitching staff allowed the fewest runs in the league (2.99 per game), and the masterful pitching—the team finished with 32 shut-outs—kept the club in almost every game. The pitching staff was anchored by Frank Owen (22 wins), Nick Altrock (20 wins), Doc White (18 wins, with the league's lowest earned run average at 1.52), and Ed Walsh (17 wins with 10 shutouts).

As late as August 1, the White Sox were in fourth place, trailing the league-leading Philadelphia A's by seven and a half games. Nineteen consec-utive wins later—an American League record that stood until 2002—they were in first place by five and a half games. Still, the season was not over, and the New York Highlanders responded with a 15-game winning streak of their own to take the lead by a game on September 12. The rest of the season was a roller-coaster ride with the Sox and the Highlanders exchanging the lead. Eventually, the White Sox closed with another rush, including five wins in a row in a 9–1 run, to take the pennant.

The team finished the year last in home runs and slugging percentage. No regular player hit higher than .279, and none drove in more than 80 runs.

The Sox were decided underdogs to the Cubs in the crosstown World Series that followed. The 1906 Cubs finished the year with a 50–8 run on the way to 116 victories (a record that still stands). In bitterly cold Chicago weather, the teams split the first four games. The Sox hit only .097 but somehow managed to win two while getting only nine hits during the entire first four games.

In the final two games, something miraculous happened to the Hitless Wonders: they exploded for 12 hits in game 5 and 14 in game 6. They won both, taking the series four games to two. The team hit only .198 over the six games but held the Cubs to a .196 batting average.

The Sox's superb pitching, combined with making the most of a minus-cule number of hits, propelled the 1906 Hitless Wonders to the top of the baseball world.

Chapter Thirteen

Franchises and Leagues

Since 1901, teams from 42 franchises representing 27 American and Canadian cities have competed on the major league stage. A handful of those cities have fielded teams in both leagues. In others, teams have left, then returned, and a few have left again. Except for a brief period (1914–1915), major league baseball over the past century has consisted of the American and National leagues.

It has not always been that way. Sometimes forgotten is that baseball's past has at times included other major leagues. Four leagues in fact have been designated as major league equivalents for specific periods during their years of operation.

Far too often overlooked is a separate cluster of teams and organizations that enriched the sport beyond measure: the Negro Leagues. Until Jackie Robinson broke the color barrier, the Negro Leagues were home to some of the country's greatest ballplayers and provided almost the only showcase for their remarkable talents.

78. MAJOR LEAGUE FRANCHISES

The information that follows traces franchise moves and additions over the years.

American League

Original Franchises

Baltimore Orioles

1903: move to New York City, becoming the Highlanders
1913: renamed the Yankees
Boston Red Sox
Chicago White Sox
Cleveland Indians
Detroit Tigers
Milwaukee Brewers
1902: move to St. Louis, becoming the Browns
1954: move to Baltimore, becoming the Orioles
Philadelphia Athletics
1955: move to Kansas City
1968: move to Oakland
Washington Senators
1961: move to Minnesota, becoming the Twins

New Franchises

1961: Los Angeles Angels
1961: Washington Senators
1972: move to Texas, becoming the Rangers
1969: Kansas City Royals
1969: Seattle Pilots
1970: move to Milwaukee, becoming the Brewers
1998: transfer to the National League
1977: Seattle Mariners
1977: Toronto Blue Jays
1998: Tampa Bay Rays
2013: Houston Astros transfer from National League

Moves and Additions by Year

1902: Milwaukee Brewers to St. Louis (Browns)
1903: Baltimore Orioles to New York City (Highlanders)
1954: St. Louis Browns to Baltimore (Orioles)
1955: Philadelphia Athletics to Kansas City
1961: Washington Senators to Minnesota (Twins)
1961: (New franchise) Washington Senators
1961: (New franchise) Los Angeles Angels
1968: Kansas City to Oakland
1969: (New franchise) Kansas City Royals
1969: (New franchise) Seattle Pilots
1970: Seattle Pilots to Milwaukee (Brewers)
1972: Washington Senators to Texas (Rangers)

1977: (New franchise) Seattle Mariners
1977: (New franchise) Toronto Blue Jays
1998: (New franchise) Tampa Bay Rays
2013: Houston Astros transfer from National League

Transfers

1998: Milwaukee Brewers to National League
2013: Houston Astros to American League

National League

Original Franchises

Boston Braves
1953: move to Milwaukee
1966: move to Atlanta
Brooklyn Dodgers
1958: move to Los Angeles
Chicago Cubs
Cincinnati Reds
New York Giants
1958: move to San Francisco
Philadelphia Phillies
Pittsburgh Pirates
St. Louis Cardinals

New Franchises

1962: Houston Cole .45s
1965: renamed the Astros
2013: Transfer to American League
1962: New York Mets
1969: Montreal Expos
2004: move to Washington, DC, becoming the Nationals
1969: San Diego Padres
1993: Colorado Rockies
1993: Florida Marlins
2012: name changed to Miami Marlins
1998: Arizona Diamondbacks
1998: Milwaukee Brewers transfer from American League

Moves and Additions by Year

> 1953: Boston Braves to Milwaukee
> 1958: Brooklyn Dodgers to Los Angeles
> 1958: New York Giants to San Francisco
> 1962: (New franchise) Houston Colt .45s
> 1962: (New franchise) New York Mets
> 1966: Milwaukee Braves to Atlanta
> 1969: (New franchise) Montreal Expos
> 1993: (New franchise) Colorado Rockies
> 1993: (New franchise) Florida Marlins
> 1998: (New franchise) Arizona Diamondbacks
> 1998: Milwaukee Brewers transfer from American to National League
> 2004: Montreal Expos move to Washington, DC (Nationals)
> 2013: Houston Astros transfer from National to American League

Interleague Play

Regular season competition that matched teams from the American and National leagues began on June 12, 1997, with a game between the Texas Rangers and the San Francisco Giants. Through the 2001 season, teams from each division played against clubs from the corresponding division in the other league: American League West vs. National League West, American League Central vs. National League Central, American League East vs. National League East. Beginning with the 2002 season, the format was changed. Teams now play interleague games against clubs from various divisions in the other league. As in World Series competition, the designated hitter rule is used in home games in American League ballparks.

79. OTHER MAJOR LEAGUES

The Federal League

Perhaps because the American and National leagues have been the "only games in town" during the lifetimes of today's fans, we sometimes forget that at times in baseball's past, other major leagues have existed as well.

The Federal League (1914–1915) was the last major attempt to establish a third league.[1] For the two years of its existence, the league's eight teams were in direct competition with the two other leagues and were regarded by American and National league club owners as a serious threat. The new league extended generous salary offers and, by one count, lured away 81 American and National league ballplayers (about one-third of the total number then playing in the major leagues). Included in the players that "jumped" to the new league were six future Hall of Famers. The older leagues responded by blacklisting the players who "deserted," obtaining court injunctions and significantly raising player salaries. One interesting side effect of the threat posed by the Federal League was that the average salary for players on American and National league clubs doubled during the two years of the Federal League's existence.

Particularly worrisome to American and National league owners were the four Federal League teams "planted" in big league cities (Chicago, St. Louis, Pittsburgh, and Brooklyn). When the 1915 season ended, the weakening financial condition of the Federal League, coupled with its threat to place a franchise in New York City, induced American and National league club owners to buy out several owners of Federal League teams. Additionally, three major owners and financial backers of the Federal League were allowed to buy stock in National League teams at cut-rate prices, while two were allowed to purchase a franchise in difficulty in each established league. The owner of the St. Louis Terriers bought the St. Louis Browns of the American League, while the owner of the Chicago Whales purchased the Chicago Cubs in the National League. Both merged players from their Federal League teams with those from the newly acquired franchises. When the Federal League folded, owners of teams not in direct competition with major league cities received little compensation other than for the sale of players to American and National league clubs.

There remain two lasting legacies from the Federal League. While the league was in operation, club owners brought an antitrust suit against the American and National leagues. The lawsuit was assigned to the court of federal judge Kenesaw Mountain Landis, who would later become the first commissioner of baseball. Hoping for a negotiated settlement, Landis allowed the suit to linger. "Both sides must understand," Landis said, "that any blow at . . . baseball would be regarded by this court as a blow to a national institution." In the meantime, while the suit languished, the Federal League's financial problems continued to deepen, eventually resulting in the buyout by the established leagues.

In 1922, six years after the Federal League went out of business, a suit brought by the St. Louis franchise eventually reached the Supreme Court. In baseball's most famous legal decision (*Federal Baseball Club v. National League*), the court ruled that major league baseball was primarily entertainment, not conventional interstate commerce as intended by the Sherman Antitrust Act, and thus was exempt from the statute. The exemption remains mostly intact today.

The second so-called silent monument to the Federal League is a stadium originally known as Weeghman Park. Charles Weeghman built the field in 1914 to be the home of his Federal League franchise, the Chicago Whales.

When the league collapsed, Weeghman purchased a National League club. In 1916, Weeghman Park became home to the Chicago Cubs. Today, Weeghman Park is Wrigley Field.

Federal League Teams

  Baltimore Terrapins
  Brooklyn Tip-Tops
  Buffalo Blues
  Chicago Whales[2]
  Indianapolis Hoosiers (1914)[3] / Newark Peppers (1915)
  Kansas City Packers
  Pittsburgh Rebels
  St. Louis Terriers

Other Major League Equivalents

In 1961, the commissioner of baseball appointed a Special Baseball Records Committee to examine extinct leagues from baseball's past and determine which of them qualified for major league status. The committee concluded that four leagues, all long out of existence, were at times major league equivalents during their years of operations.

In addition to the Federal League (1914–1915), the committee identified the following three leagues.

American Association

Years of operation qualifying as a major league: 1882–1891.
  League champions:
  Cincinnati (1882)
  Philadelphia (1883)
  New York (1884)
  St. Louis (1885)
  St. Louis (1886)
  St. Louis (1887)
  St. Louis (1888)
  Brooklyn (1889)
  Louisville (1890)
  Boston (1891)

Union Association

Year of operation qualifying as a major league: 1884.
  League champion:

St. Louis (1884)

Players' League

Year of operation qualifying as a major league: 1890.
   League champion:
   Boston (1890)

80. NEGRO LEAGUES

Baseball has a long and rich tradition in the African American community. Ironically, the first known baseball game between black teams was played September 28, 1860, at the Elysian Fields in Hoboken, New Jersey—the same general site used by Alexander Cartwright and his New York Knickerbocker ball club. By 1885, the first black professional team, the Cuban Giants, was formed and drew audiences from the New York / New Jersey area.

Two professional leagues quickly followed: the Southern League of Base Ballists and the National Colored Baseball League. Both soon folded. Indeed, the history of Negro League baseball is marked by continually shifting franchises, financial difficulties, and territorial disputes.

In the modern era, the most significant Negro Leagues were as follows:

- Negro National League (1920–1931)[4]
- Eastern Colored League (1923–1928)[5]
- American Negro League (1929)
- East-West League (1929–partial season)
- Negro Southern League (1932)[6]
- Negro National League (1933–1948)[7]
- Negro American League (1937 to late 1950s)[8]

After 1947, interest in Negro League baseball faded as the "color barrier" was broken and major league clubs began signing black players to big league contracts. The Negro National League folded in 1948. The Negro American League was soon reduced to minor league status and ceased operations in 1958.

Barnstorming was a major feature of Negro League baseball. Although banned from major league participation, Negro League players and teams barnstormed across the country, playing with considerable success against teams composed of major leaguers.

Notable Negro League teams over the years included the Homestead Grays, the Kansas City Monarchs, and the Pittsburgh Crawfords. In 1932, the Crawfords must surely have fielded one the greatest batteries in all of baseball history. On opening day, the pitcher was Satchel Paige; the catcher was Josh Gibson.

In 1971, a special committee identified Negro League players for Hall of Fame induction. Selectees included Paige and Gibson as well as Cool Papa Bell, Oscar Charleston, Martin Dihigo, Monte Irvin, Judy Johnson, Buck Leonard, and John Henry Lloyd.

NOTES

1. With Branch Rickey and William Shea as the driving forces, the Continental League was proposed in 1959 and projected to begin play in 1961. The threat of the proposed league led to the expansion of the two other leagues, which was perhaps the motive all along. Unlike the Federal League, the Continental League never actually fielded teams or began operations.

2. League champion, 1915.

3. League champion, 1914.

4. The first league to bear this name.

5. From 1924 to 1927, the champions from the Eastern Colored League and the Negro National League met in a postseason World Series competition.

6. A minor league operation from 1920 into the 1940s, when the first Negro National League folded, the Southern League absorbed some of the teams and for one year operated as a major league.

7. The second league so named.

8. From 1942 to 1948, the National and American league champions met in a World Series. After 1950, the league operated in a haphazard fashion, with many teams on the barnstorming circuit.

Chapter Fourteen

Elysian Fields

From midway in the nineteenth century, when Alexander Cartwright first marked out diamonds in a meadow in Manhattan and on a corner of the Elysian Fields in Hoboken, ballparks have been a feature of the American landscape. In the early days, some fields were of remarkable shapes and sizes. Like dinosaurs, those oddities have become extinct, their place in baseball's evolution taken by parks with more traditional dimensions and accommodations fine-tuned for fans, players, and media. In some cities, domed stadiums and parks with retractable roofs have transported baseball to less conducive climates, and at those locations, "playing indoors" has given the game immunity from the vagaries of weather.

Still, there is no mistaking the charm of many of the early parks; the two oldest that remain are regarded with near reverence by fans of the game. (Appendix F provides names, seating capacities, and dimensions of current major league ballparks.)

81. BALLPARKS

The Oldest

By far, the two oldest stadiums still being used by major league teams are Fenway Park in Boston and Wrigley Field in Chicago.

When Fenway Park opened in 1912, the dimensions were extreme. While left field was a comfortable 321 feet, it was a whopping 488 feet to center and a distant 414 down the right field line. Over the years, the park has been reshaped to its present configuration: 315 to the "Green Monster" in left, 420 to center, and 302 to right field. Though still one of the smaller parks in the major leagues, the addition of seats in recent years has increased Fenway's capacity to 39,928.

When the park was first built, a 25-foot wall in left field was put up to keep people in the apartments across the street from watching the game for free. In 1934, the original wall was torn down and rebuilt to its current height of 37 feet. When green paint was applied in 1947, the result—the Green Monster—eventually became one of baseball's most revered and recognizable landmarks.

The ballpark that opened in 1914 at the corner of Clark and Addison streets in Chicago was first known as Weeghman Park. It was the home of the Chicago Whales of the short-lived Federal League. When the park was built, the Whales' owner, Charles Weeghman, introduced features such as the placement of concession stands in the back of seating areas to not obscure fans' views of the game. In 1916, after the Federal League went out of business, the Cubs moved into the park. Two years later, William Wrigley Jr. bought the team, and in 1926 the ballpark officially became Wrigley Field.

Among several other early changes, Wrigley added a second deck to the original structure in 1927. Then in 1937 came the two features most associated with Wrigley Field: the ivy-covered walls and the three-story-high scoreboard in center field—both courtesy of Bill Veeck Jr., then a young assistant to Wrigley.

The scoreboard measures 27 by 75 feet. It is operated by three people inside the structure who manually place five-pound steel numbers on the board that tell the story, not only of the Cubs game, but also of action throughout the major leagues.

For much of its existence, there was also another feature associated with Wrigley Field: it had no lights. Wrigley was the last park in the majors to play only day games on its home field. Finally, on August 9, 1988, the first night game was played at Wrigley, although the team continues to play more day games at home than any other club.

The stated capacity of the present day park is 41,118. Additional numbers watch from atop nearby buildings.

The Oddest

Several of the early ballparks were unusual for their extreme dimensions. Consider, for example, Huntington Avenue Grounds in Boston, built in 1901 and used by the Boston Pilgrims (later the Red Sox): the center-field wall was an incredible 635 feet from home plate. Center field was so unreachable that for a time a utility shed positioned near the wall actually stood in the field of play. The left-field line was only slightly less distant at 440 feet. Right field, strangely enough, was pop-up distance: 280 feet.

In 1903, Hilltop Park in New York City, home of the Highlanders (later the Yankees), also featured a gargantuan distance to center field: 542 feet. Even the original Yankee Stadium, built in 1923, had a center-field fence 490 feet from home plate. As late as 1967, the center-field distance stood at 463 feet before a further, final reconfiguration placed the wall at 385 feet.

Extreme center-field distances were found in many early parks. Center field at the original 1912 Fenway Park was 488 feet; at Shibe Park in Philadelphia, built in 1909 and home to the Philadelphia A's, the distance to center was 515 feet.

Griffith Stadium in Washington, DC, earned the reputation of being one of the most difficult parks to hit home runs in. The original dimensions of the 1911 park were 407 (left), 421 (center), and 320 (right). In later years, the distance to the left-field wall was reduced slightly, but at 388 feet it was nearly as distant as many center-field walls in modern ballparks.

Baker Bowl in Philadelphia, built in 1895, was used by the Philadelphia Phillies until 1938. The park was wildly out of proportion. Left- and center-field distances were a fairly reasonable 341 and 408 feet, respectively. In right field, however, there stood a 40-foot-high wall that was only 279 1/2 feet from home plate. The Phillies often featured left-handed batters who hit easy line drives off that "short porch" and who often led the league in doubles as a result.

Although used well into baseball's more modern times, the Polo Grounds in New York City—home to the New York Giants through 1957 when the club moved to San Francisco—was a park with some of the most radical dimensions in baseball history. During the final years of play at the Polo Grounds, the park's dimensions were 288 to left field, 475 to center, and 258 feet down the right-field line. That layout contributed to some notable plays, perhaps the most famous being Willie Mays's catch of Vic Wertz's enormous blast to center field in the 1954 World Series. While Wertz belted the ball more than 450 feet and got nothing from it (except a long out), in the same game Dusty Rhodes, a Giants pinch hitter, hit a 259-foot pop fly down the right-field line that barely cleared the fence and won the game in extra innings. In terms of fan convenience, the Polo Grounds was the site of a notable first: in 1929, a public address system was used for the first time at a major league game.

The extreme opposite of the parks with gigantic dimensions was Lake Front Park in Chicago, used for a time by the Chicago White Stockings during the dawn of major league baseball. Lake Front Park had the shortest outfield dimensions in major league history: 180, 300, and 196 feet to left, center, and right fields, respectively. In all but one year (1884), balls hit over the left-field fence were considered ground rule doubles. However, for that one year, balls that cleared the wall were ruled as home runs. The White Stockings' home run totals for 1884 were the highest recorded to that point;

in fact, four Chicago hitters all surpassed the existing record. Their figures stood among the four highest home run totals of all time until Babe Ruth shattered all records in 1919.

Some of the early parks had unusual features other than just their strange shapes. Baker Bowl, for example, already renowned for its shell-shocked right-field wall, had a "hump" in center field. The raised area was formed by elevated ground that allowed for a subway tunnel that ran underneath that part of the ballpark. Not surprisingly, the ballpark was sometimes called "The Hump." It also had a less charitable nickname: Because the ballpark was in a seedy part of town and was in a badly rundown condition—during the Great Depression years, few repairs were made—Baker Bowl was sometimes called "The Dump by the Hump."

Crosley Field in Cincinnati, used by the Reds until 1970, had a feature called "The Terrace" in left field. Although the outfield ramped upward from foul line to foul line, the slope was most pronounced in left field, where fielders had a 15-degree climb for the last 15 feet in front of the wall.

A recently built ballpark, Minute Maid Park in Houston, incorporates a Crosley Field–like terrace in center field. Called "Tal's Hill," the slope begins 90 feet in front of the fence and slants upward at a 30-degree incline.

Some fans might label as oddities the swimming pool behind the outfield wall at Chase Field (formerly Bank One Ballpark) in Phoenix and the tank full of manta rays at Tropicana Field where the Tampa Bay Rays play.

The Domes

The era of "indoor baseball" began in 1965 with the opening of the Houston Astrodome. Called the "Eighth Wonder of the World," the Astrodome introduced the baseball world to synthetic turf (after natural grass failed to grow inside the dome), luxury suites, and air-conditioned ball games. Originally configured to hold 42,217 for baseball, the seating capacity was increased to 54,816 in 1990.

The Astrodome was home to the Houston baseball club until 2000, when the Astros moved to what is now called Minute Maid Park, a stadium with a 9,000-ton retractable roof advertised to open or close within 12 minutes. Minute Maid Park seats 40,950.

Like the Houston Astros, the Seattle Mariners moved from an original dome facility to a newer park with a retractable roof. From 1977 until 1999, the Mariners played in the Kingdome, an arena with a seating capacity of 59,166. After an extended period of structural problems, in midseason 1999 the team moved to Safeco Field, a new facility seating 47,447.

The Montreal Expos played in Olympic Stadium from 1977 until the franchise moved to Washington, DC, for the 2005 season (and became the Nationals). Designed with a retractable feature, the roof was plagued from the outset with mechanical difficulties. When the roof stopped working completely, the Expos closed it permanently and played inside the dome. In its final days of operation, Olympic Stadium seated 43,739 for baseball.

In 1982, the Minnesota Twins began playing ball in the Hubert H. Humphrey Metrodome in Minneapolis. Originally configured to hold 54,711 for baseball, in 1994 the interior was redesigned to more comfortably accommodate 48,678 fans. Although adequate for baseball, the Metrodome was never ideal. Its most notable feature (other than its high noise level) was the "Big Blue Baggy," or the "Hefty Bag," a drape feature constituting the right-field wall. The "bag" was a plastic sheet that covered folded up football seats to form a 23-foot fence. In 1987, the Metrodome became the first indoor stadium to host a World Series. The Twins moved to a new outdoor park (Target Field) on opening day 2010.

When the Sky Dome (now renamed Rogers Centre) opened in Toronto in 1989, it was regarded as baseball's most advanced facility. With a seating capacity of 50,516 and a technologically state-of-the-art retractable roof, the stadium features a hotel, restaurant, and shops.

Tropicana Field was built in 1990 to accommodate sporting events in the Tampa Bay / St. Petersburg area. The Tampa Bay Rays have used the stadium, which seats 43,772 for baseball, since 1998. The rafters, catwalks, and interesting ground rules make the stadium one of the more unusual places for a major league ballgame.

In Phoenix, Chase Field (formerly Bank One Ballpark) was opened in 1998 as home to the Arizona Diamondbacks. The convertible roof can be set to adjust the amount of sunlight reaching the turf and the interior of the stadium, allowing the park to cool quickly and efficiently in the Arizona heat. Chase Field seats 49,033.

On opening day 2001, the Milwaukee Brewers began playing in Miller Park, a $400-million stadium with a retractable roof. Stadium designers took note of Wisconsin's chilly April and September weather: when the roof is closed, the air inside the park can be heated 30 degrees higher than the outside temperature. Miller Park seats 41,900.

In April 2012, the Miami Marlins moved into a retractable roof facility to handle the heat, humidity, and frequent showers in South Florida.

Chapter Fifteen

The Equipment

If at some point a time traveler should drop in on an early game of baseball, he or she might, depending on the date of arrival, see a piece of history that looks like this: a nine-man team wearing blue wool pants, white shirts, and "boater" hats . . . trying to hit a ball perhaps weighing only three ounces, possibly made of small clumps of lead wrapped in twine and covered with sheepskin . . . with a bat made of hickory or bamboo, heavier than today's version, with no knob at the end, and maybe even flat on one side. And gloves, you ask? . . . Well, there weren't any.

How did baseball get from there to here? This chapter traces the development of the game's major pieces of equipment.

82. THE BASEBALL

In the early dawn of baseball history, balls were mostly homemade, sometimes built of small clumps of lead wrapped in twine and covered with animal hide (often sheepskin or chamois). When rubber eventually replaced the lead core, the early baseballs that resulted sometimes weighed only three ounces or so. The interesting influence of the lightweight ball was that the shortstop became more of an outfielder, positioned to help relay the light ball back to the infield. In 1854, rule changes put the weight of the ball between 5 1/2 and 6 1/2 ounces with an inscribed diameter between 2 1/2 and 3 1/2 inches. Since 1872, the weight of the baseball has been not less than 5 ounces or more than 5 1/4 ounces, and the ball has been a constant 9 to 9 1/4 inches in circumference.

The controversy about the liveliness of the ball—"dead ball" versus "rab-bit ball"—is almost as old as the game itself. Around 1904, big league pitchers began more routinely soiling game balls with dirt or tobacco juice to make them harder to see. In 1910, the major leagues replaced the rubber core with a cork-centered ball. Though sometimes cited as being the beginning of a livelier ball era, statistics from the time reveal only a short-term, slight increase in hitting and run production.

Babe Ruth's power explosion, which shattered all existing home run records, added intensity to the "live ball" controversy. Some have said that 1919—when Ruth destroyed long-standing records by hitting 29 home runs—was evidence that the ball had been doctored. Baseball historians re-plied that, if so, Ruth was the only player to benefit from it.

Other proponents of the livelier ball theory have conjectured that the yarn on the inside of modern baseballs may be wound tighter or that the stitches may be smoother (causing breaking pitches to flatten out and reducing wind resistance on batted balls). The yarn theorists point to a change to the ball in 1920. In that year, both leagues began using yarn from Australia. Australian yarn was stronger than American yarn and could be wound tighter, giving the ball more bounce. Baseball historians note that if the ball became livelier that year, the liveliness did not extend to the National League (where Cy Williams of the Phillies led the league in home runs, with only 15). In any event, the only recent known official change to the baseball occurred in 1975, when cowhide replaced horsehide as the cover.

Each baseball has 108 stitches hand sewn in Haiti. Because the stitches are hand sewn, they are not always exactly the same. For that reason, some balls have a different "feel," and the stitching may influence the selection/effectiveness of a pitch—for example, many pitchers prefer a ball with a high seam when throwing a curve ball—or cause the pitcher to request another ball.

The key test of a ball's liveliness is called the "coefficient of restitution." The coefficient of restitution is measured by firing a baseball from an air cannon at a velocity of 85 feet per second at a slab of wood 8 feet away. Major league baseball requires "a rebound rate of 54.6 percent of the original velocity, with a permitted deviation of no more than plus or minus 3.2 per-cent." It is the contention of the baseball hierarchy that the coefficient of restitution has not changed or been changed.

By the way, the substance that umpires use to "rub up" baseballs before a game—officially Baseball Rubbing Mud—comes from a secret site on the New Jersey side of the Delaware River. After the smooth, creamy mud is cleaned and screened, a secret ingredient is added to it. Baseball Rubbing Mud removes the sheen and slipperiness from the ball and makes it easier for the pitcher to grip.

83. THE BASEBALL BAT

Over the course of baseball history, baseball bats have been made from several types of wood, including at times hickory (eventually discarded because of its heavy weight) and bamboo. In modern bats, ash is used most frequently, although the popularity of maple is increasing despite its greater tendency to shatter.

Bats are manufactured by companies such as Louisville Slugger, Rawlings, Mizuno, Wilson, and Brett Brothers, by "turning" the wood on a lathe and then branding the bat with the company's name, the bat's serial number, and the player's signature. The brand is applied on the "hard side" of the bat, so the batter can see it and control the batting surface. Most bats are shaped into a rounded head, although significant numbers of players prefer a "cup-balanced" head, featuring a recess scooped out of the top of the bat, making the club lighter and shifting the center of gravity down the shaft closer to the bat handle. As a final step, bats are stained in one of seven standard colors.

Major league specifications require that bats be no more than 42 inches long and no more than 2.75 inches in diameter at their thickest point. Over the years, baseball bats have featured knobs of different sizes and appearances at the ends of bat handles. Babe Ruth may have been among the first to order a bat with a knob similar to those used in the present day.

Over the years, weights of bats have undergone a significant transformation. Earlier bats were much heavier; until fairly recent times, it was not totally unheard of for a major league batter to swing a 36-ounce bat. Beginning in the early 1990s, the trend has been toward lighter bats. Possibly as an influence of the lightweight aluminum bats now used almost exclusively in high school and college baseball, the average weight of the bat used by major league ballplayers has dropped to 31 ounces, down from 33 ounces as late as 1991.

In baseball history, some interesting tales concern the bats used by Babe Ruth, some of which were reputed to be remarkably weighty. By current standards, Ruth's bats were indeed heavy. According to the Baseball Hall of Fame and Museum, Ruth used bats 35 to 36 inches in length that weighed between 37 and 47 ounces.

Historically, the earliest rules from Alexander Cartwright's time placed no restrictions on bat size or shape. About 1858, bats were limited to 2 1/2 inches in diameter. Before that time and reflecting the game's ties with cricket, bats with a 4-inch flattened side were sometimes used. Bats with one side flattened were again briefly legalized in 1885. Seldom employed, use of the cricket-like club was permanently rescinded in 1893. Present-day rules on bat length and size are long-standing: the 42-inch limit on length has existed since 1868; the 2 3/4-inch maximum diameter has been on the books since 1893.

84. GLOVES AND MITTS

For a considerable time in the early days of the game, fielders played bare-handed. It is thought that in 1875, much to the initial derision of fans and fellow players, first baseman Charles Waite began wearing a glove.[1] The glove was small, not much bigger than a modern batter's glove with the fingers cut off. Waite's glove, like those that first followed it, was not intended so much to aid in receiving a ball as to reduce the sting from catching one. For a time, gloves were flesh colored, so fielders would not be embarrassed by wearing protective gear. Perhaps reflecting the evolution of the glove to a piece of equipment more focused on fielding, in 1887 Charles Cushman, manager of Toronto in the International League, instructed all of his right-handed players to wear gloves on only their left hands. The last major leaguer to play without a glove was probably Jerry Denny of Louisville, who retired in 1894.

Although gloves were universally worn after Denny, for the next three decades they remained quite small, often weighing less than 10 ounces (even with padding). Still, the effect of gloves on fielding was remarkable. During those three decades, errors were reduced from 6.66 to 2.83 per game.

In 1920, Bill Doak made a significant innovation by introducing a fielder's glove with webbing between the thumb and fingers. In modern times, the web has undergone significant revision. Players can choose between a tight "basket weave" and an "H weave." Those preferring the basket weave think it reduces chances of getting fingers caught in the web while trying to retrieve a ball. Some pitchers believe the closed nature of the basket weave makes it more difficult for opponents to see the grip on the ball as the pitcher prepares for delivery. Advocates of the H weave sometimes cite its usefulness in catching fly balls and pop-ups on days when the sun is troublesome: the weave makes it possible for the fielder to shield his eyes by holding the glove high yet still follow the flight of the ball by looking through the webbing.

The forerunner of the modern catcher's mitt was introduced around 1890 by Harry Decker, and large padded versions for catchers came to the fore by 1891. In the mid-1960s, Randy Hundley of the Chicago Cubs adopted the use of a flexible, hinged catcher's mitt that enabled him to receive the ball without exposing his unprotected throwing hand. Prior to Hundley's innovation, catchers wore a stiff, padded mitt that required them to hold the bare hand next to the mitt and catch the ball with both hands.

Current rules for mitt and glove sizes are shown as follows.

Type of Mitt/ Glove	Rule	Size Specifications
Catcher	1.12	No more than 38 inches in circumference, no more than 15 1/2 inches from top to bottom. The space between the thumb and finger sections cannot be more than 6 inches across the top and 4 inches across the bottom. The webbing cannot be more than 7 by 6 inches.
First baseman	1.13	Not more than 12 inches long top to bottom or 8 inches wide across the palm. The space between the thumb and finger sections cannot be more than 4 inches wide at the top and 3 1/2 wide at the bottom.
Fielder	1.14	Cannot be more than 12 inches long from fingertip to the bottom of the heel of the glove. The glove cannot be more than 7 1/4 inches wide. The web cannot be more than 4 1/2 inches at the top or 3 1/2 at the bottom.

85. UNIFORMS AND ASSOCIATED GEAR

Uniforms have identified specific teams and distinguished them from their opponents since the earliest days of baseball. The first well-known ball club, Alexander Cartwright's New York Knickerbockers, was also the first team known to wear identifying uniforms. The Knickerbockers took the field in the late 1840s wearing blue wool pants, white shirts, and straw "boater" hats. Within a few years, a wide leather belt was added, and a mohair cap replaced the boater. Within a short time, colorful uniforms became commonplace, some of them resembling the apparel of volunteer fire departments or military units.

Certainly by the mid-1870s, however, the trend was toward uniforms styled more nearly in the present-day fashion. Photos from that time show clothing easily distinguishable as baseball uniforms. In 1915, the Detroit Tigers were the last team to have collars on their uniforms. The Tigers later played one additional year, 1917, with collars on their uniform jersey. Foot-to-knee stockings quickly appeared on early uniforms. Teams used different colors, and the stockings became major distinguishing features on many uniforms. In some instances, stockings formed teams' identities as well: Boston Red Sox, Chicago White Sox, St. Louis Browns (originally the Brown Stockings), Cincinnati Reds (originally the Red Stockings).

By the late 1880s, some teams had adopted stripes (the Yankees' adopted their fabled pinstripes in 1915), and by the end of the century, many had begun to use distinct home and road uniforms. Traditionally, white was worn at home and gray on the road, though later altered by some teams to dark, solid colors.

Many accounts have the 1916 Cleveland Indians as the first team to put numbers on jerseys. The Indians positioned those early numbers on left sleeves. In 1929, the Yankees and the Indians added numbers on the backs of uniforms. The Yankees assigned them on the basis of position in the batting order. Hence, Ruth, who hit third, was given number 3; Gehrig, the cleanup hitter, drew number 4; and so forth through the order.

By the early 1930s, the uniforms of all major league teams had numbers on the back. In 1952, the Brooklyn Dodgers placed small numbers on the front as well.

Lettering and logos made early appearances. One of the earliest was the Old English letter "D" worn on Detroit home jerseys. Road uniforms more often spelled out the entire name of the city. By 1901, a small black tiger appeared on Detroit baseball caps, and in 1907 a bear cub logo was introduced on Chicago Cub jerseys.

New styles of close-fitting pants legs, introduced in the 1990s, induced some players to move away from traditional knee-length stockings and begin wearing pants that ran to the tops of the shoes.

Visored caps were introduced by some teams as early as the 1860s perhaps, as some believe, patterned after the soldiers' caps of the recently concluded Civil War or based on jockeys' headgear. Either way, the visor was immediately found useful in "playing the sun" on bright afternoons.

Perhaps the most recent significant addition to baseball equipment and apparel is the batting helmet. Surprisingly, the first recorded use of a helmet occurred as early as 1907 (some sources say 1905), when catcher Roger Bresnahan of the New York Giants created a batting helmet after a beaning incident. The idea never caught on, however, and helmets saw little use, even after the death of a big league ballplayer hit in the head with a pitch. On August 16, 1920, in a game at the Polo Grounds, Cleveland Indians shortstop Ray Chapman was hit by a pitch thrown by the Yankees' Carl Mays.

Although Chapman's death sparked conversations regarding protective gear, the major leagues' primary response to the tragedy was to require umpires to remove soiled, dirty baseballs from games. (Incredibly, on at least one occasion—August 4, 1908—St. Louis and Brooklyn played an entire game using only one baseball.) Prior to that time, it was customary for pitchers to scuff baseballs, darkening them so that they would be more difficult to see. Many observers believed that Chapman did not see the soiled ball thrown by Mays, a pitcher whose "submarine" delivery already made it difficult for batters to "pick up" the ball.

As a result of other injuries over the years, players were using plastic inserts inside their baseball caps by the 1950s. Finally, in 1971, batting helmets were made mandatory throughout the major leagues. Early helmets had no ear flaps. When helmets with flaps were introduced, some players were reluctant to use them because they felt that the flaps were distracting. However, in 1983, the majors made it mandatory for batters to wear helmets with at least one ear flap. Players in the majors at the time were grandfathered and could continue wearing flapless helmets if they wished. The last player to do so was Tim Raines of the Florida Marlins in 2002. Some players continue to wear flapless helmets while fielding their defensive positions. Beginning with the 2008 season, major league first- and third-base coaches were required to wear helmets following the death of a minor league coach hit by a batted ball.

The first protective gear for catchers seems to have been a simple rubber mouth guard similar to the mouth pieces worn by boxers. Masks came fairly quickly, however; the first was thought to have been a modified fencing mask "invented" in 1876 by a man named Fred Thayer and used by the Harvard baseball team. The mask caught on quickly, and by 1878, Thayer's patented version already appeared in Spalding's catalog. By the 1880s, masks were in widespread use at all levels of the sport. An early improvement was made by Roger Bresnahan, who added padding to the cage supports. Other adaptations followed over the years that changed the steel mesh configuration to provide better vision. Carbon steel mesh remains the most often used material.

In the 1970s, catcher Steve Yeager of the Los Angeles Dodgers introduced a mask designed to provide greater protection to the throat. Yeager added a piece to the mask that extended downward from the chin bar. While Yeager's model is still used by some catchers, other recent masks contain a throat protector built in as part of the wire face cage. The most recent notable change features use of a model adapted from a hockey goalie's mask. Currently used by several major league catchers, the polycarbon helmet protects the top, sides, and back of the head. At about 50 ounces, the helmet is slightly heavier than the standard mask-helmet equipment combination.

Among his many other equipment innovations, Roger Bresnahan is generally credited with introducing catcher's shin guards in 1907/1908. Chest protectors for catchers were apparently first used in about 1875. Fred Thayer, inventor of the catcher's mask, is sometimes credited with developing the first inflated chest protector. The first known use of a protective cup was by Claude Berry, a catcher with the Pittsburgh Rebels of the Federal League who used the device in 1915.

When baseball was in its infancy, the athletic shoes of the day were generally high-topped and made of canvas. It is likely that the earliest baseball shoes were similar and without spikes. Soon, however, canvas was replaced by soft, durable leather, and by the late 1860s, spikes similar to those found on present-day golf shoes were introduced.

Further innovation quickly followed, and by the 1870s, traditional metal cleats affixed to three-cornered shoe plates (two sets on each shoe—one under the heel and the other under the toes) made their appearance. An 1874 picture of Boston team members shows the underside of a baseball shoe that looks remarkably like the modern version. The advent of shoe plates and cleats reduced the use of spikes, but it was 1976 before major league baseball explicitly banned them from the game.

In recent years, the frequent presence of artificial turf in major league stadiums led to further modifications of baseball shoes. By the mid-1970s, shoes constructed with hundreds of small rubber bumps (to improve traction on artificial surfaces) were available for use in the new arenas.

The use of batting gloves was pioneered by Montreal Expos outfielder Rusty Staub, who began wearing them in 1969.

NOTE

1. Among other contenders cited as being the first to wear a glove is a player named Al Spalding, who apparently used a padded version.

Chapter Sixteen

Computing the Stats

Few sports are as immersed in statistics as is baseball. Numbers and number comparisons mean much to the game and its history, so those who follow the sport need to understand the significance of the major stats and how they are computed. Computations for statistics most commonly known and used by baseball fans are shown in the next section.

In recent years, more exotic, sabermetric statistics[1] have come into vogue among some baseball analysts and statisticians. A note about the most widely known and discussed sabermetric—wins above replacement—is included at the end of the statistics section.

86. THE MAJOR STATS: WHAT THE NUMBERS MEAN

Batting average: number of hits / number of at bats (walks, hit by pitch, and sacrifices do not count as at bats).

Total bases: number of singles + (2 x number of doubles) + (3 x number of triples) + (4 x number of home runs).

On-base percentage: (hits + walks + hit by pitch) / (at bats + walks + hit by pitch + sacrifices).

Slugging percentage: total bases (home run = 4 bases, triple = 3, double = 2, single = 1) / at bats.

On-base slugging percentage (OPS): on-base percentage + slugging percentage.

OPS is a fairly recent stat that has drawn interest from fans and analysts. OPS is computed by simply adding on-base percentage and slugging percentage. Those who advocate the OPS stat argue that it is accurate for the two main objectives of hitting: avoiding outs by getting on base and advancing runners (including the hitter) around the bases. Critics reply that on-base percentage and slugging percentage partially overlap; that is, they measure parts of the same thing (because a hit adds points to both areas). Others do not object to the stat itself but would like to see it adjusted to account for "hitters' parks" and "pitchers' parks"—thus, the genesis of the adjusted OPS (OPS+) stat.

OPS+: 100 x [(on-base percentage divided by the park-adjusted league on-base percentage) + (slugging percentage divided by park-adjusted league slugging percentage) – 1].

Earned run average (ERA): (earned runs given up x 9) / innings pitched.

Walks, hits per innings pitched: (walks given up + hits allowed) / innings pitched.

Fielding percentage: (assists + put outs) / (assists + put outs + errors).

A note about wins above replacement. Wins above replacement is a saber-metric statistic that attempts to calculate how many more wins a player gives to a team during the course of a season than would a replacement-level ballplayer playing the same position. The stat is computed differently by major statisticians. While there is no accepted standard formula, all are similar in that, for example, position players are assessed using various hitting and fielding statistics, while pitchers are evaluated using measures such as opponents' batting averages, hits and walks allowed, strikeouts, and so forth.

Most computations compare a major league ballplayer against a pseudo replacement whose performance level is assumed to be that of an average call-up from Triple-A ball. The calculation results in a single number that purports to identify the player's value by quantifying the number of wins he provides to the team above what could be expected from the fictitious standard replacement. The computations are complex, and many include special adjustments for positions, leagues, and ballparks.

87. THE STORIES THE NUMBERS TELL: THE MOST/LEAST/BEST/WORST

Hitting

Highest batting average, season: .426.

Nap Lajoie, Philadelphia Athletics, 1901 (Rogers Hornsby, St. Louis Cardinals, hit .424 in 1924).

Highest batting average, career: .367.

Ty Cobb, Detroit Tigers, Philadelphia Athletics, 1905–1928.

Most batting titles: 12.

Ty Cobb. [2]

Most hits, season: 262.

Ichiro Suzuki, Seattle Mariners, 2004.

Most hits, career: 4,256.

Pete Rose, Cincinnati Reds, Philadelphia Phillies, Montreal Expos, 1963–1986.

Most seasons 200 or more hits: 10.

Ichiro Suzuki; Pete Rose (while playing for Cincinnati and Philadelphia).

Most seasons led league in hits: 8.

Ty Cobb, Detroit Tigers.

Most hits in a game: 9.

Johnny Burnett, Cleveland Indians. On July 10, 1932, Burnett went 9 for 11 in an 18-inning game against Philadelphia. (Rennie Stennett, Pittsburgh Pirates, had seven hits in a nine-inning game; see story 46.)

Most total bases, season: 457.

Babe Ruth, New York Yankees, 1921.

Most total bases, career: 6,856.

Hank Aaron, Milwaukee/Atlanta Braves, Milwaukee Brewers (American League), 1954–1976.

Most total bases, game: 19.

Shawn Green, Los Angeles Dodgers, May 23, 2002. Green's 19 total bases came against the Milwaukee Brewers. The 19 bases included four home runs among five extra-base hits.

Most RBI, season: 191.

Hack Wilson, Chicago Cubs, 1930.

Most RBI, career: 2,297.

Hank Aaron, 1954–1976.

Most seasons led league in RBI: 6.

Babe Ruth.

Most consecutive seasons 100 or more RBI: 13.

Lou Gehrig, New York Yankees, 1926–1938;[3] Jimmie Foxx, Philadelphia Athletics, Boston Red Sox, 1929–1941.

Highest on-base percentage, season: .609.

Barry Bonds, San Francisco Giants, 2004.

Most seasons led league in on-base percentage: 12.

Ted Williams, Boston Red Sox.

Most home runs, season: 73.

Barry Bonds, San Francisco Giants, 2001. (See Appendix H for a list of home run champions.)

Most home runs, career: 762.

Barry Bonds, Pittsburgh Pirates, San Francisco Giants, 1986–2007.

Most seasons led league in home runs: 12.

Babe Ruth, Boston Red Sox, New York Yankees.

Most grand-slam home runs: 23.

Lou Gehrig, 1923–1939.

Alex Rodriguez, 1994–2012.

Most times led Triple Crown categories: 19.

Babe Ruth: batting average (1), home runs (12), RBI (6). (Triple Crown winners are shown at Appendix I.)

Most triples, season: 36.

Owen Wilson, Pittsburgh Pirates, 1912.

Most triples, career: 309.

Sam Crawford, Cincinnati Reds, Detroit Tigers, 1899–1917.

Most seasons led league in triples: 5.

Sam Crawford, Cincinnati, Detroit.

Most doubles, season: 67.

Earl Webb, Boston Red Sox, 1931.

Most doubles, career: 792.

Tris Speaker, Boston (American League), Cleveland, Washington, Phila-delphia (American League), 1907–1928.

Most seasons led league in doubles: 8.

Tris Speaker, Boston, Cleveland; Stan Musial, St. Louis Cardinals.

Highest slugging average, season: .863.

Barry Bonds, San Francisco Giants, 2001.

Highest slugging average, career: .690.

Babe Ruth, Boston Red Sox, New York Yankees, Boston Braves.

Most seasons led league in slugging average: 13.

Babe Ruth, Boston Red Sox, New York Yankees.

Highest career batting average as a pinch hitter (100 or more at bats): .333.

Gordy Coleman, Cleveland Indians, Cincinnati Reds, 1959–1967. Cole-man had 40 hits in 120 pinch hit at bats.

Most pinch hits, season: 28.

John Vander Wal, Colorado Rockies, 1995.

Most pinch hits, career: 212.

Lenny Harris, nine teams, 1988–2005.

Most bases on balls received, season: 232.

Barry Bonds, San Francisco Giants, 2004.

Most bases on balls received, career: 2,558.[4]

Barry Bonds, Pittsburgh, San Francisco, 1986–2007.

Most seasons led league in bases on balls received: 12.

Barry Bonds, Pittsburgh, San Francisco.

Most times hit by pitch, season: 50.

Ron Hunt, Montreal Expos, 1971.

Most times hit by pitch, career: 285.

Craig Biggio, Houston Astros, 1988–2007.[5]

Most times struck out, season: 223.

Mark Reynolds, Arizona Diamondbacks, 2009.

Most times struck out, career: 2,597.

Reggie Jackson, Kansas City/Oakland Athletics, Baltimore Orioles, New York Yankees, California Angels, Oakland A's, 1967–1987.

Most difficult batter to strike out: Joe Sewell.

Sewell, who played for the Cleveland Indians and New York Yankees from 1920 to 1933, struck out only 114 times in 7,132 major league at bats, meaning that during the course of his entire 14-year career, he struck out on average only once every 68 plate appearances, or once every 17 or 18 games.

Lowest career batting average (1,000 or more at bats): .175.

Ray Oyler, Detroit Tigers, Seattle Pilots, California Angeles. In recent times, Oyler's .175 is the lowest average. In a six-year career that lasted from 1965 to 1970, Oyler had 1,265 at bats. In Detroit's pennant-winning year in 1968, Oyler, a shortstop, hit only .135 in 111 games. The lowest batting average for a player with more than 2,500 at bats is .170. Bill Bergen, who caught for Cincinnati and Brooklyn from 1901 to 1911, officially went to the plate 3,028 times. Despite his woeful .170 average, Bergen stayed in the big leagues because of his exceptional defensive skills. On August 23, 1909, he threw out six St. Louis Cardinals base runners, a record that still stands.

Pitching

Most wins, season: 41.

Jack Chesbro, New York (American League), 1904.

Most wins, career: 511.

Cy Young, Cleveland (National League), St. Louis (National League), Boston (American League), Cleveland (American League), Boston (National League), 1890–1911.

Most consecutive wins: 24.

Carl Hubbell, New York Giants, 1936–1937.

Most seasons led league in wins: 9.

Warren Spahn, Boston/Milwaukee Braves.

Highest career winning percentage: .690.

Whitey Ford, New York Yankees (236–106).

Most games started, career: 815.

Cy Young, 1890–1911.

Most complete games, season: 48.

Jack Chesbro, New York (American League), 1904.

Most complete games, career: 749.

Cy Young, 1890–1911.

Lowest ERA, season: 0.96.

Dutch Leonard, Boston Red Sox, 1914. In 1994, Greg Maddux of the Atlanta Braves became the first pitcher to achieve an ERA two full runs below the top ERA team in the league. Maddux finished the season with an ERA of 1.56. The Montreal Expos' staff led the National League with an ERA of 3.56.

Most seasons led league in ERA: 9.

Lefty Grove, Philadelphia Athletics, Boston Red Sox. Grove's career spanned the years 1925–1941. His consecutive ERA titles were achieved from 1926 to 1934.

Most shutouts pitched, season: 16.

Grover Cleveland Alexander, Philadelphia Phillies, 1916.

Most shutouts pitched, career: 110.

Walter Johnson, Washington Senators, 1907–1927.

Most seasons led league in shutouts: 7.

Grover Cleveland Alexander, Walter Johnson. Cy Young also led his league seven times; however, five of those years occurred prior to 1901.

Most innings pitched, season: 464.

Ed Walsh, Chicago White Stockings, 1908.

Most innings pitched, career: 7,356.

Cy Young, 1890–1911.

Most seasons led league in innings pitched: 7.

Grover Cleveland Alexander, while pitching for the Philadelphia Phillies and Chicago Cubs.

Most seasons, 300 or more innings pitched: 11.

Christy Mathewson, New York Giants.

Most consecutive seasons, 300 or more innings pitched: 9.

Walter Johnson, 1910–1918.

Most strikeouts, season: 383.

Nolan Ryan, California Angels, 1973.

Most strikeouts, career: 5,714.

Nolan Ryan, New York Mets, California Angels, Houston Astros, Texas Rangers, 1966–1993.

Most strikeouts, game: 21.

Tom Cheney, Washington Senators. Cheney's 21 strikeouts came during a 16-inning game against the Baltimore Orioles on September 12, 1967.

Most strikeouts during a nine-inning game: 20.

Roger Clemens, Boston Red Sox, against the Seattle Mariners, April 29, 1986; Roger Clemens, Boston Red Sox, against the Detroit Tigers, September 18, 1996; Kerry Wood, Chicago Cubs, against the Houston Astros, May 6, 1998.

Most strikeouts in a row: 10.

Tom Seaver, New York Mets, against the San Diego Padres, April 22, 1970.

Most consecutive innings with strikeouts: 40.

Pedro Martinez. In 1999, Martinez, pitching for the Boston Red Sox, struck out at least one batter in 40 consecutive innings. Martinez broke his own record of strikeouts in 33 consecutive innings set earlier in the same season.

Most strikeouts in a World Series game: 17.

Bob Gibson, St. Louis Cardinals, against the Detroit Tigers, October 2, 1968.

Most seasons led league in strikeouts: 12.

Walter Johnson, Washington Senators.

Most seasons 300 or more strikeouts: 6.

Nolan Ryan, Houston Astros, Texas Rangers; Randy Johnson, Seattle Mariners, Arizona Diamondbacks.

Most saves, season: 62.

Francisco Rodriguez, Los Angeles Angels, 2008.

Most saves, career: 608 (through the 2012 season).

Mariano Rivera, New York Yankees, 1995–present.

Most bases on balls allowed, season: 208.

Bob Feller, Cleveland Indians, 1938.

Most bases on balls allowed, career: 2,795.

Nolan Ryan, 1966–1993.

Most bases on balls allowed, game: 16.

Bruno Haas, Philadelphia Athletics, June 23, 1915.

Most consecutive innings pitched without giving up a base on balls: 84.1.

Bill Fischer, Kansas City A's, 1962. Fischer pitched the equivalent of more than nine complete games without surrendering a walk.

Most batters hit by pitch, career: 205.

Walter Johnson, 1907–1927.

Most wild pitches, season: 30.

Red Ames, New York Giants, 1905.

Most wild pitches, career: 156.

Red Ames, New York (National League), Cincinnati, St. Louis (National League), Philadelphia (National League), 1903–1919; Walter Johnson, Washington Senators, 1907–1927.

Most losses, career: 316.

Cy Young, 1890–1911.

Most consecutive losses: 27.

Anthony Young, New York Mets. (See story 37.)

Fielding

First Base

> *Best career fielding average (minimum 1,000 games):* .997.
> Travis Lee, Arizona, Philadelphia (National League), Tampa Bay, New York (American League), Tampa Bay, 1998–2006.
> *Most seasons led league in fielding average:* 9.
> Charley Grimm, Pittsburgh, Chicago (National League).

Second Base

> *Best career fielding average:* .989.[6]
> Ryne Sandberg, Philadelphia (National League), Chicago (National League), 1981–1997; Tom Herr, St. Louis, Philadelphia, New York (National League), Minnesota, San Francisco, 1979–1991; Mickey Morandini, Philadelphia, Chicago (National League), Toronto, 1990–2000.
> *Most seasons led league in fielding average:* 9.
> Eddie Collins, Philadelphia (American League), Chicago (American League).

Third Base

> *Best fielding average, career:* .974.
> Mike Lowell, New York (American League), Florida, Boston, 1988–2011.
> *Most seasons led league in fielding average:* 11.
> Brooks Robinson, Baltimore Orioles.

Shortstop

> *Best fielding average, career:* .985.
> Omar Vizquel, Seattle, Cleveland, San Francisco, Texas, Chicago (American League), Toronto.
> *Most seasons led league in fielding average:* 8.
> Everett Scott, Boston (American League), New York (American League); Lou Boudreau, Cleveland; Luis Aparicio, Chicago (American League), Baltimore; Ozzie Smith, San Diego, St. Louis.

Outfield

> *Best fielding percentage, career:* .995.
> Darryl Hamilton, Milwaukee (American League), Texas, San Francisco, Colorado, New York (National League), 1998–2001.

Most seasons led league in fielding average: 5.
Amos Strunk, Philadelphia (American League), Boston (American League).

Catcher

Best fielding percentage, career: .995.
Dan Wilson, Cincinnati, Seattle.
Most seasons led league in fielding percentage: 8.
Ray Schalk, Chicago (American League).

Notable Fielding Records by Position

First Base

Consecutive errorless games: 238.
Kevin Youkilis, Boston, July 4, 2006–June 6, 2008. Youkilis's record includes 2,002 consecutive errorless chances.

Second Base

Consecutive errorless games: 186.
Placido Polanco, Detroit, July 2, 2006–April 7, 2008. Polanco's record includes 911 consecutive errorless chances.

Third Base

Consecutive errorless games: 99.
John Wehner, Pittsburgh, Florida, April 2, 1993–September 29, 2000; Jeff Cirillo, Colorado, Seattle, June 20, 2001–April 19, 2002.
Consecutive errorless chances: 272.
Vinnie Castilla, Colorado, Washington, July 4, 2004–April 22, 2005.

Shortstop

Consecutive errorless games: 110.
Mike Bordick, Baltimore. April 11, 2002–April 2, 2003. Bordick's record includes 511 consecutive errorless chances.

Outfield

Most chances accepted, season: 544.
Taylor Douthit, St. Louis (National League), 1928.
Most chances accepted, career: 7,290.

Willie Mays, New York/San Francisco Giants, New York Mets, 1951–1973.
Most assists, season: 44.
Chuck Klein, Philadelphia Phillies, 1930.

Catcher

Consecutive errorless games: 252.
Mike Matheny, St. Louis, August 2, 2002–August 2, 2004.
Most chances accepted, season: 1,214.
Johnny Edwards, Houston Astros, 1969.
Most changes accepted, career: 16,233.
Ivan Rodriguez, Texas, Florida, Detroit, New York (American League), Houston, Texas, Washington, 1991–2011.

Pitcher

Most putouts, season: 49.
Nick Altrock, Chicago (American League), 1904; Mike Boddicker, Baltimore, 1994.
Most putouts, career: 530.
Greg Maddux, Chicago Cubs (twice), Atlanta, Los Angeles Dodgers (twice), San Diego, 1986–2008. Maddux also holds the record for most putouts in a game (7) and most times led league in putouts (8).

Overall Fielding

Best fielding average, team: .990.
Colorado Rockies, 2007.

Base Running

Most stolen bases, season: 130.
Rickey Henderson, Oakland, 1982.
Most stolen bases, career: 1,406.
Rickey Henderson, Oakland (four times), New York (American League), Toronto, San Diego (twice), Anaheim, New York (National League), Seattle, Boston, Los Angeles (National League), 1979–2003.
Most seasons led league in stolen bases: 12.
Rickey Henderson.
Most seasons 50 or more steals: 14.
Rickey Henderson.
Most consecutive steals without being caught: 50.
Vince Coleman, St. Louis, 1988–1989.

Most steals of home, career: 54.
Ty Cobb, 1905–1928.
Most times caught stealing, season: 42.
Rickey Henderson, Oakland, 1982.
Most times caught stealing, career: 335.
Rickey Henderson, 1979–2003.
Most runs scored, season: 177.
Babe Ruth, New York Yankees, 1921.
Most runs scored, career: 2,295.
Rickey Henderson, 1979–2003.

Managers

Most games won: 3,582.
Connie Mack, Philadelphia Athletics. Mack managed the team for 50 years, from 1901 to 1950. During that time he lost 3,814 games, also a record. Prior to his 50-year stint with Philadelphia, Mack served three years (1894–1896) as player/manager for the Pittsburgh Pirates. Mack's combined overall record as a manager is 3,731 wins, 3,948 losses.
Most pennants won: 10.
Casey Stengel, New York Yankees; John McGraw, New York Giants (three of McGraw's pennants were won prior to 1900).
Most World Series won: 7.
Casey Stengel, New York Yankees.

Teams

Most wins, season: 116.
Seattle Mariners, 2001; Chicago Cubs, 1906.
Most league championships: 40.
New York Yankees.
Most consecutive league championships: 5.
New York Yankees, 1949–1953, 1960–1964.
Most World Series championships: 27.
New York Yankees.
Most seasons finished in last place: 28.
Philadelphia Phillies.
Most consecutive last place finishes: 7.
Philadelphia Athletics, 1915–1921.
Worst team: Cleveland Spiders, 1899.
See story 38.
Most consecutive sellouts: 455.
Cleveland Indians, 1995–2001. In a formal ceremony, the Indians "re-tired" the number 455.

NOTES

1. Sabermetrics is the specialized analysis of player performance and value derived from statistical data that measure players' in-game and season-long actions. The analyses are used to make determinations about player performance, relative value, and contributions to winning. The sabermetrics term comes from the acronym SABR (Society for American Baseball Research).

2. The 1910 title is disputed. Some recent sources credit Nap Lajoie with winning the title, thus reducing Cobb's total to 11. (A list of batting champions is shown at Appendix G.)

3. From 1931 to 1937, Gehrig had seven consecutive years batting in 150 or more runs.

4. Rickey Henderson, who played for nine teams during a 25-year career, holds the record for the most unintentional walks received, with 2,129. Henderson drew a remarkable 796 walks while leading off an inning.

5. Biggio's is the modern-era record. Hughie Jennings, who played from 1891 to 1918 for Louisville, Baltimore, Brooklyn, Philadelpha, Pittsburgh, and Detroit, was hit 287 times.

6. Placido Polanco, a player active with the Philadelphia Phillies, has a current career fielding average of .990.

Chapter Seventeen

The Awards

Formal recognition for achievements on the field has evolved considerably since the early days of the game. Over the years, awards have been instituted that address all of the sport's major components. "Best of the Best" laurels in areas such as pitching, hitting, fielding, and overall excellence are awarded to honorees in both leagues at the end of each season.

88. HONORS BESTOWED

Most Valuable Player Award

Given annually to one player in each league, the Most Valuable Player Award is voted on by a panel of two writers from each of the league's cities. Voters fill out a 10-place ballot with 10 points awarded for a first-place vote, 9 for second, and so forth. For more than 70 years, the award has been given by the Baseball Writers' Association of America. Known universally as the Most Valuable Player Award, the official title is the Kenesaw Mountain Landis Memorial Baseball Award.

The present award had two brief forerunners. From 1911 to 1914, the Chalmers Award (sponsored by the Chalmers Automobile Company) was for one year presented to the player in major league baseball with the highest batting average at the end of the season. In the following three years, a committee of baseball writers convened to identify the "most important or useful player to the club and the league." Chalmers ceased giving the award after the 1914 season.

From 1922 to 1929, League Awards honored "the baseball player . . . of the greatest all-around service to his club." Selection was made by a committee of eight baseball writers and a committee chairman. Initiated by the American League in 1922, the American League program was ended after the 1928 season when rule restrictions were perceived as leading to flawed outcomes—specifically, voters were required to select one member from each team, and previous winners were ineligible. The National League began a League Award program in 1924. The National League program did not have the same rule restrictions but lasted only a year longer, through 1929. (Most Valuable Player Award winners are shown at Appendix J.)

The Cy Young Award

Implemented in 1956 by commissioner of baseball Ford Frick, the Cy Young Award honors the outstanding pitcher in each league. For the first 11 years, only a single award was given. Awards for both leagues began in 1967.

Award selections are determined by members of the Baseball Writers' Association of America, with one voter from each league city. Beginning in 2010, voters cast ballots ranking their top five choices. A weighted sum of the votes is then used to identify the winner.

The award is named in honor of Hall of Fame pitcher Denton "Cy" Young, the all-time leader in pitching victories, with 511. (Cy Young Award recipients are shown at Appendix K.)

Rookie of the Year Award

The Rookie of the Year Award is given annually to one player from each league. Selections are through a vote of the entire membership of the Baseball Writers' Association of America. Each writer casts a weighted vote for three rookies: first-place votes count for five points, second place for three, and third place for one.

In 1947 and 1948, the award was given to only one player in baseball. Beginning in 1949, the rookie honor has been given to a player in each league. After several modifications over the years, rookie status (and thus eligibility for the award) is currently defined as a player with less than 130 at bats, 50 innings pitched, or 45 days on the active roster of a major league club prior to September 1. Time on the disabled list is not counted.

In 1987, in honor of the 40th anniversary of Jackie Robinson's entry into the major leagues, the award was officially named the Jackie Robinson Award. (See Appendix L for a list of Rookie of the Year Award recipients.)

The Gold Glove Award

Officially the Rawlings Gold Glove Award, statuettes with golden gloves are given annually to players judged to have been the best fielders at their positions. Since 1958, separate awards have been given to players in each league. Gold Glove recipients are selected by votes of managers and coaches. (Appendix M identifies players who have won the most Gold Gloves at each position.)

The Silver Slugger Award

The Silver Slugger Award has been given since 1980 to the best offensive player at each position. Awards are given to players in both leagues as determined by votes of major league coaches and managers.

In the National League, pitchers receive a Silver Slugger Award. In the American League, an award is given to the best designated hitter. (Players who have won the most Silver Slugger Awards are shown at Appendix N.)

Chapter Eighteen

The Black Sox Scandal

The Black Sox scandal shocked the nation. When the story broke in its entirety in the fall of 1920, charges that the 1919 World Series had been fixed dominated the front-page headlines of every major paper, quickly eclipsing coverage of that year's presidential campaign. The scandal remains the most famous blemish on the sport in the long history of major league baseball. Parts of the drama remain controversial to this day.

89. "SAY IT AIN'T SO, JOE"

"Say it ain't so, Joe": Baseball legend has it that those were the words sobbed by a small boy who approached "Shoeless Joe" Jackson as Jackson emerged from a courthouse. Jackson was alleged to have replied, "I'm afraid it is, son."

The nine-game World Series eventually won by the Cincinnati Reds five games to three over the Chicago White Sox opened on October 1, 1919. Even before the first pitch was thrown, rumors circulated among gamblers, players, and newspapermen that the series was fixed. When the regular season ended, the American League champion White Sox had been made solid favorites. Loaded with talent, the team had won the pennant with an impressive 88–52 record (the season following the end of World War I had been shortened to 140 games). Then, in the days before the series opened, heavy betting on the Reds caused the odds to shift dramatically.

Allegedly, the idea to throw the series in return for thousands of dollars in cash came from White Sox first baseman Chick Gandil. Gandil had contacts with underworld figures who in turn had connections with professional gamblers. Gandil brought several of his teammates into the conspiracy. In mid-September, he and others met with gamblers in New York's Ansonia Hotel.

By many accounts, when Sox pitcher Eddie Cicotte hit the Cincinnati leadoff hitter with the second pitch of the opening game, that was the players' signal to the gamblers that the conspirators intended to follow through with the fix. The gamblers, however, did not fully live up to the deal, and only a portion of the agreed-on $100,000 found its way to the players.

The conspiracy might never have come to light if the story had not been doggedly pursued by newspaper reporter Hugh Fullerton of the *Chicago Herald and Examiner.* The day after the series ended, Fullerton published an article predicting that seven players would not return to the Sox the following year. The innuendos caused White Sox owner Charles Comiskey to seek to take the heat off by offering a reward (either $10,000 or $20,000 depending on the version) to anyone who could prove the White Sox had thrown the series. For a time, the situation seemed defused, but at the end of the year, Fullerton ran another series of articles that named the alleged conspirators and the gamblers involved. Fullerton demanded an investigation.

The intensity subsided again for a time, and the 1920 season was mostly complete when the story exploded once more. In response to an allegation of several gambling improprieties—the most recent being a supposedly fixed game on September 4 between the Chicago Cubs and the Philadelphia Phillies—a grand jury in Cook County, Illinois, convened to investigate gambling throughout baseball.

The calling of the grand jury caused the conspiracy to come apart. Embittered because he had not received his promised cut from the series fix, a small-time gambler named Billy Maharg provided details. Maharg told jury members that eight Chicago players had been promised a total of $100,000, although most of the money had never been paid. The day following Maharg's testimony, two alleged conspirators, pitcher Eddie Cicotte and outfielder "Shoeless Joe" Jackson, were called before the grand jury. Both admitted their participation in the fix. They and others signed statements acknowledging their involvement. The grand jury returned indictments, but the trial, held almost a year later, was a sham. During the interval between the indictments and the trial, a new prosecuting attorney took office in Cook County, and three of his predecessor's assistant attorneys hired on with the defense. It was only through the persistence of American League president Ban Johnson, whose primary motive might have been to embarrass Charles Comiskey, that enough evidence and witnesses were made available to sustain the case.

The trial was fraught with difficulty from the outset. No Illinois statute explicitly forbade fixing a sports contest. Accordingly, the judge announced that the players could be convicted of only conspiracy to defraud. In the meantime, the confessions that the players had signed disappeared from grand jury files. (They were found years later in the possession of one of Comiskey's attorneys.) When the signed documents disappeared, the players promptly repudiated their confessions. When the players recanted, only two small-time gamblers were left as substantial witnesses. The jury quickly acquitted the seven defendants.

Celebrations in Chicago were short-lived, however, because Judge Kenesaw Mountain Landis, the newly appointed commissioner of baseball, banished all eight conspirators from baseball for life. Landis's words continue to be frequently cited:

> Regardless of the verdict of juries, no player who throws a ball game, no player who undertakes or promises to throw a ball game, no player who sits in confidence with a bunch of crooked ballplayers and gamblers, where the ways and means of throwing a game are discussed and does not promptly tell his club about it, will ever play professional baseball.

Over the years, there has been considerable speculation regarding the causes of the Black Sox scandal. Baseball pools existed in every major league city, and odds on teams and games were published in newspapers. Players who traveled across the country had the opportunity to meet gamblers at racetracks, saloons, and hotels. It was not uncommon at the time for players to bet on themselves or their teams.

Many have noted that the White Sox team was "susceptible" to bribery. Although the team was one of the best and most profitable in baseball, owner Comiskey paid the lowest or among the lowest salaries to his players. The $10,000 bribe that Eddie Cicotte received for his part in throwing the series was almost double the amount of his regular season salary.

It is the extent of "Shoeless Joe" Jackson's participation in the fix that remains one of the most controversial parts of the scandal. Jackson claimed to have played his best. Some have noted that his .375 batting average in the series was the highest on either team. Perhaps tempering that statistic is the fact that during the five games the White Sox lost, he hit only .268.[1] Jackson's illiteracy has been used as a defense by some. Others say that he and his family were threatened. In later years, some conspirators acknowledged that Jackson had not been present at any meetings with gamblers. One conspirator stated that Jackson's name had been used because the players thought that it would give them more clout with gamblers. Still, there exists the evidence of his oral and signed confessions . . . and so the discussion continues.

NOTE

1. Even that average was padded by a hitting spree in the eighth game, when the Reds were far ahead and the game was out of reach.

Chapter Nineteen

The Steroids Era

One of the charms of baseball is that its many statistics allow rather direct comparisons of players and teams. While changes in conditioning, facilities, equipment, training, and so forth have occurred as the game has evolved over the years, the numbers enable general judgments to be made—overall and within eras—regarding levels of performance and individual achievements.

Therefore, factors that artificially contort statistics and accomplishments are seen by almost all fans as violating the underlying integrity of the game. Since the turn of the century, the baseball establishment has struggled with the use of performance-enhancing drugs by an apparently substantial number of players. The baseball hierarchy was late in acknowledging and addressing a problem that ranks alongside the Black Sox scandal in terms of the stain that it has left on the game.

The villains—other than the players' susceptibility to temptation and willingness to indulge—are anabolic steroids, which elevate the body's testosterone level, increasing muscle mass without changes in diet or activity (although the effect can be enhanced by proper nutrition and strength training). Because of potentially harmful side effects, steroids are illegal in the United States unless prescribed by a physician.

90. THE DOPING DILEMMA

Rumors of drug use had long been whispered inside and outside the baseball establishment when an event—the first of several that would follow—began to move the issue to the public's attention. In 1998, a jar of androstenedione (or "andro") was discovered in Mark McGwire's locker. McGwire, playing for the St. Louis Cardinals, was in the midst of a home run race with Cubs slugger Sammy Sosa. Both were chasing the major league home run record of 61 set in 1961 by Roger Maris. Andro, a testosterone-producing pill, had been banned almost everywhere else in sports—the International Olympic Committee, the National Football League, and the National Basketball Association, among others, prohibited its use; but, at the time, it was not outlawed by Major League Baseball. Both McGwire, with 70 home runs, and Sosa, with 66, would go on to shatter Maris's record.

In 2002, Ken Caminiti, former National League most valuable player, admitted to *Sports Illustrated* magazine that he had used steroids for several years while a major league player. Caminiti estimated that half of all players were steroid users.

At about the same time, Jose Canseco, former American League rookie of the year and most valuable player, made headlines with accusations of rampant drug use by major leaguers—perhaps as initial hype for a forthcoming book. When published in 2005, Canseco's book, *Juiced: Wild Times, Rampant 'Roids, Smash Hits, and How Baseball Got Big*, asserted that 85 percent of all big league players used steroids. Canseco's figure was disputed by many baseball insiders. Nonetheless, Canseco identified players such as McGwire, Rafael Palmeiro, Jason Giambi, Ivan Rodriguez, and Juan Gonzalez as fellow steroid users. Canseco further claimed to have personally injected many of them.

Almost all the players initially denied Canseco's charges. However, Giambi later admitted steroid use to a grand jury. Likewise, after declining under oath to answer questions at a 2005 congressional hearing, McGwire acknowledged in 2010 that he had used steroids. Under oath at the same hearing, Palmeiro forcefully denied steroid use but later drew a suspension after testing positive (although he continues to dispute the results).

Canseco also mentioned Sammy Sosa's allegedly open and visible use of steroids. Later, he would also identify Alex Rodriguez as a user. In 2009, Rodriguez admitted using steroids during the years 2001–2003.

In response to public outcries and increasing congressional pressure,[1] the baseball establishment began tentative steps to address the problem. In 2003, a Survey Testing program began during spring training. Done anonymously, the tests were used to gauge the extent of steroid use among major league players. Released later that year, the results indicated that 5 to 7 percent of 1,438 tests were positive during the 2003 season. The numbers were above the threshold level necessary to begin mandatory testing for performance-enhancing drugs. The results also allowed punishments to be imposed on identified users. However, the initial punishment levels were widely criticized as being too lenient. Significantly strengthened penalties for steroid use and other illegal drugs were announced in late 2005.

Meanwhile, two of the biggest names associated with steroid allegations—Roger Clemens and Barry Bonds—began appearing in the news. Clemens was identified as an anabolic steroid user by his former personal trainer, Brian McNamee, who told investigators that he had begun injecting Clemens with steroids in 1998 and continued to do so for several years thereafter. In 2005, after Clemens denied steroid use under oath during a congressional hearing, federal officials, citing multiple inconsistencies in his testimony, referred his case to the Department of Justice.

Jose Canseco raised Clemens's name earlier, saying that Clemens had expert knowledge regarding steroids. Another major leaguer, Jason Grimsley, also named Clemens as a user of performance-enhancing drugs. When the Mitchell report was released in December 2007, Clemens's name was cited 82 times. Clemens denied the allegations. In 2010, Clemens was indicted on six felony counts involving perjury, false statements, and obstruction of Congress. Clemens pleaded not guilty. In 2011, a first trial was declared a mistrial due to prosecutorial misconduct. In June 2012, jurors in a retrial found insufficient evidence to convict Clemens on any of the charges.

Similarly, questions regarding steroids had long surrounded Bonds, already a player of consummate skill. From the svelte young player of his early major league career, he had bulked up into a massive physical specimen. By some accounts, his hat size increased from 8 to 8 1/2, and his shoe size went from 10 to 13, extraordinary for an individual in his 30s. Bonds allegedly became envious of Mark McGwire's success and the acclaim for his 70 home runs in 1998. McGwire had a reputation in baseball circles as a steroid user. By this account, Bonds turned to steroids in an attempt to match or exceed McGwire's performance.

In 2003, Greg Anderson, Bonds's personal trainer, was indicted by a federal grand jury for supplying anabolic steroids to athletes. In 2006, the book *Game of Shadows* by two San Francisco writers, Mark Fainuru-Wada and Lance Williams, alleged that Bonds had long used a host of steroids. The book famously used leaked excerpts from grand jury testimony. In 2007, Bonds was indicted on four counts of perjury and obstruction of justice (lying to a grand jury). In 2011, he was convicted of obstruction of justice.

When allegations of steroid use began to surface, the name Bay Area Laboratory Co-operative (BALCO) quickly became prominent in sports headlines. Headquartered in Burlingame, California, the company was owned and founded by Victor Conte. Other BALCO officials included Patrick Arnold, a chemist who developed the initially undetectable performance-enhancing steroid tetrahydrogestrinone (called the "clear"), and weight trainer Greg Anderson, who distributed the drugs and became Bonds's personal trainer. Allegedly, after Anderson began working with Bonds, Bonds delivered other baseball contacts to the firm. Eventually, BALCO's customers included several major league ballplayers.

In 2002–2003, U.S. attorneys investigated BALCO for illicitly distributing the "clear" and other steroids. In 2005, Victor Conte pled guilty to conspiracy to distribute steroids and check laundering and served a four-month sentence. Greg Anderson pleaded guilty to similar charges and was jailed for three months. Later, he was found in contempt of court and incarcerated for refusing to testify about Bonds's and others' drug use before a federal grand jury. Patrick Arnold, the chemist, pleaded guilty to supplying BALCO with the "clear" and served three months in prison.

In March 2006, with *Game of Shadows* newly released and public and congressional unease continuing, Baseball commissioner Bud Selig[2] appointed former U.S. senate majority leader George Mitchell to investigate the use of performance-enhancing drugs in major league baseball. Mitchell's report, officially released in December 2007, asserted that performance-enhancing drug use had been pervasive in major league baseball for more than a decade. Eighty-nine current and former major leaguers were mentioned in the report, including Roger Clemens, Andy Pettitte, Miguel Tejada, and Eric Gagne. Mitchell's staff drew heavily on information provided by Kirk Radomski, a former New York Mets batboy and clubhouse employee, and Brian McNamee, personal trainer for Clemens, Pettitte, and Chuck Knoblauch. McNamee was also a former strength coach for the New York Yankees and Toronto Blue Jays. Mitchell's report stated that McNamee acquired performance-enhancing drugs—steroids, amphetamines, and human growth hormones—for many of the players he trained. Among other things, Mitchell recommended an independently administered drug-testing program and more extensive educational efforts.

The more stringent test regime and stronger punishments introduced in 2005 eased the public discontent and reduced the extent of abuse. In the meantime, though, stories of past abuse continued to surface—some linking prominent players such as David Ortiz and Manny Ramirez to performance-enhancing drugs. Ramirez's saga unfolded badly. In 2007, he was suspended for 50 games for using a banned women's fertility drug sometimes used by men to restart natural testosterone after a cycle of steroid use. In 2011, a second drug infraction mandated a 100-game suspension. (The suspension was later reduced to 50 games because Ramirez had sat out much of the season.)

Major League Baseball's drug policy—officially labeled the Joint Drug and Treatment Program—placed the game's testing and punishment standards on a level commensurate with other professional sports. A first positive test for steroid use is punished by a 50-game suspension, a second by a 100-game suspension, and a third results in a lifetime suspension from the game. All suspensions are without pay. In addition to establishing standard punishments for steroid use, the program created a structure of fines and punishments for use of illicit drugs such as cocaine, LSD, and heroin. Unlike the mandatory testing regime associated with steroid use, tests conducted for other drugs require reasonable cause.

Most baseball fans would likely concur with one of the Mitchell report's conclusions: Players' use of performance-enhancing substances is illicit and ethically "wrong." While the baseball hierarchy seems to have addressed steroid abuse to the general satisfaction of the baseball public, albeit belatedly, questions remain about what to make of the suspected steroids users and how to treat the records they shattered while employing performance-enhancing drugs.

A measure of the baseball world's continuing discontent is revealed by the Hall of Fame balloting for Mark McGwire, an acknowledged steroids user. With 583 home runs and the best home run–at bat ratio in baseball history, McGwire would under normal circumstances be a lock for induction into the Hall of Fame. Instead, beginning in 2007 with his first eligibility, in not a single year has his name appeared on as many as a quarter of the voters' ballots. In 2011, his support declined to 19.8 percent.

Like the question of what, if anything, to do with the allegedly tainted records, the Hall of Fame dilemma will continue as other players of prominence move toward eligibility.

NOTES

1. The first of several hearings held over the next three years took place on June 18, 2002—all highly critical of baseball's tepid reaction to the drug issue.
2. Appendix O provides a list of baseball commissioners.

Chapter Twenty

The Impact of World War II

World War II had enormous consequences for major league baseball. Although for morale purposes, President Roosevelt, a fan of the game, rejected proposals for canceling major league play, the quality of play was not the same. With almost all big league players in the military through voluntary enlistment or the draft, major league rosters were typically filled with minor leaguers, older players, youngsters, and others disqualified from military service.

President Roosevelt's response to baseball commissioner Kenesaw Mountain Landis's letter asking if major league play should continue during the war came to be known as the "green light letter." Roosevelt's letter said that "it would be best for the country to keep baseball going," as a valuable recreational outlet for a country coping with an all-out war effort. Roosevelt also expressed the hope that more games would be played at night so that the people working day shifts could have the opportunity to attend games. Roosevelt's words about night baseball also had a profound effect on the game.

The careers of almost all players who were in the major leagues at the time of Pearl Harbor were affected by a war that took most of them away from the game for three years or longer. For many, the period of wartime service came at the height of their careers. For three in particular—Ted Williams, Bob Feller, and Warren Spahn—the impact was enormous. Each saw it as his duty and served proudly and well. Nonetheless, the "what might have been" questions persist. One can only wonder what these players' final statistics would have been had their careers not been interrupted by wartime service.

The war also induced major league executives to develop a women's professional baseball league, an endeavor that initially met with success and lasted for a considerable time into the postwar period.

91. TED WILLIAMS: LEFT FIELDER, BOSTON RED SOX

With one month left in the 1941 season, Ted Williams turned 23 years old. That year he hit .406, the last player to hit .400 in a big league season. The following year, 1942, Williams won the Triple Crown, leading the American League in batting average, home runs, and RBI. Then, because of military service as a Marine Corps fighter pilot—he flew F4U Corsairs—he missed the 1943, 1944, and 1945 seasons.

World War II service was a fate shared by most major leaguers at the time, but, ironically, Williams was again called to active duty when the Korean War began and missed almost all of the 1952 and 1953 seasons as well. Thus, at the peak of his career, military service kept him from five full seasons in the major leagues.

Despite the lengthy absences, Williams compiled remarkable career numbers. Even at age 38 in 1957, he won the American League batting crown with an astounding .388 average. He won it again the next year at age 39, hitting .328.

At the time of his World War II service, based on the three years immediately prior and the three years following as benchmarks, Williams's composite batting average was .359. He averaged 184 hits and 32 home runs per year during those seasons. His Korean War service came at a time when for the three full years preceding[1] and three seasons following, Williams's composite average was .346. He averaged 156 hits and 30 home runs per season during that time.

Taken collectively, Ted Williams's "what might have been's" would have added something like 864 hits and 156 home runs to an already illustrious career.

92. BOB FELLER: PITCHER, CLEVELAND INDIANS

On December 8, 1941, the day after Pearl Harbor, Bob Feller enlisted in the U.S. Navy. He was the first major leaguer to volunteer for military service. Feller missed the next four major league seasons while serving as a gun captain on the battleship *Alabama*.

When the Japanese attacked Pearl Harbor, Feller had just turned 23 years old and had already accumulated 107 major league victories. He was the youngest pitcher in major league history to win 100 games, having done so early in the 1941 season. He had led the American League in wins the preceding three seasons and in strikeouts the preceding four. At age 22, he had already struck out 1,233 batters and was well on his way to breaking the record set by Walter Johnson.

Feller was one of baseball's true "phenoms": He went straight from high school to the major leagues. As a 17-year-old making his first start in the majors (August 23, 1936), he struck out 15 St. Louis Browns. Four starts later, he struck out 17 Philadelphia A's. When the season ended, he went back to Van Meter, Iowa, to finish high school.

On September 9, 1945, after 44 months of combat duty, Feller returned to the major leagues and struck out 12 batters. Feller ended his major league career in 1956 with 266 wins and 2,581 strikeouts.

As with Ted Williams, the "what might have been's" for Feller are enormous. On the basis of the three years prior and three years following his military service—during which he averaged 24 wins and 246 strikeouts per season—he would likely have added around 96 wins and 984 strikeouts during the four years he missed.

It is informative to compare Feller's accomplishments at the time when he entered military service against those of other noted Hall of Fame pitchers—namely, major league victories at age 23 and total major league victories:

Bob Feller	107	266
Walter Johnson	57	417
Cy Young	0	511
G. C. Alexander	0	373

93. WARREN SPAHN: PITCHER, BOSTON/MILWAUKEE BRAVES

Here is the major "what might have been" for Warren Spahn: if not for three seasons missed because of military service during World War II, Spahn would easily have become the winningest pitcher in National League history. The National League record is 373 wins, jointly held by Grover Cleveland Alexander and Christy Mathewson. Spahn ended his career with 363 wins, the winningest left-hander in major league history.

Spahn was called up to the majors briefly during the 1942 season, then enlisted in the U.S. Army, missing the entire 1943, 1944, and 1945 seasons. He fought at the Battle of the Bulge and at the Bridge at Remagen. He earned a battlefield commission, received a Purple Heart, and was awarded a Bronze Star Medal.

During the three years (1946–1948) following his return from service, Spahn won 8, 21, and 15 games, respectively. Taking the average 15 victories for those years as a baseline, Spahn would have won more than 400 games during his career.

94. PETE GRAY: THE ONE-ARMED BALLPLAYER

The story of Pete Gray, St. Louis Browns outfielder, speaks volumes about baseball during World War II. With most big leaguers serving in the armed forces, the Browns brought Gray to the majors in 1945.

Pete Gray had only one arm. He had lost his right arm in a childhood accident and, although a natural right-hander, had taught himself to hit and throw with his left hand. Gray perfected a technique of catching the ball, quickly slipping the glove under the stump of his right arm, retrieving the ball, and throwing it in one rapid continuous motion.

Surprisingly, Gray was an adept bunter. Holding the knob of the bat firmly against his side while sliding his hand up the handle of the bat, he pushed the ball down the lines with good success.

The Browns called up Gray because of his stellar performance in the minor leagues the year before. In 1944, as a member of the Memphis Chicks of the Southern Association, Gray hit .333 and stole 68 bases. He was named the league's most valuable player.

Gray hit .218 in 77 games for the Browns while playing left and center field. He fielded a solid .958. As the season wore on, pitchers found that breaking balls were difficult for Gray to handle. Without a second hand, it was hard for him to check his swing once he had started his bat in motion.

When the war ended and players were released from military service, Gray's major league career ended. In 1946, the Browns sent him to the minors. He played minor league ball until 1949 and barnstormed for a time after that.

Gray's example served as an inspiration for disabled veterans returning from the war. Gray was a frequent visitor to military hospitals and rehabilitation centers, often speaking with amputees.

95. THE WOMEN'S LEAGUE

With the onset of World War II, several major league executives led by Philip K. Wrigley started a women's professional baseball league. The primary motive was to maintain interest in baseball while so many major leaguers were away from the game serving in the armed forces. A secondary objective, at least in Wrigley's mind, was to make productive use of major league ballparks while the existing big league teams were playing on the road. The latter goal never caught on, and the league found most success in non–major league cities in the Midwest, such as South Bend, Indiana, and Rockford, Illinois. During its 1943–1954 existence, the league went through several name changes, but probably its best-known title was the All-American Girls Professional Baseball League.

The women's teams did not originally play regulation baseball, but as the years went by, the rules were gradually adjusted to bring the women's sport closer to the standard game. Initially, the pitcher's mound was only 40 feet from home plate. Pitchers threw underhanded using a ball 12 inches in circumference (the size of a regulation softball). Bases were set at 65 feet apart. From year to year, the size of the baseball shrank until it reached standard baseball size. Meanwhile, the pitching distance was increased to 60 feet, and pitchers were allowed first to throw sidearm (1946) and finally to use a full overhand delivery (1948). Base paths were eventually extended to 85 feet.

As the league was forming, scouts scoured the United States and Canada looking for ballplayers. Tryouts were held in most major cities. Ultimately, 280 ballplayers were invited to a series of final tryouts in Chicago. There, 60 were chosen to be the first women professional ballplayers in the first women's professional league.

The league initially consisted of only four teams: Racine and Kenosha, Wisconsin; Rockford, Illinois; and South Bend, Indiana. Eleven franchises eventually played in 15 cities. Each team consisted of 15 players, a manager, a business manager, and a women's chaperone.

Femininity was stressed, and the league imposed strict standards of conduct. After practice, players were required to attend charm school classes where etiquette, posture, social skills, hygiene, and grooming were taught. A dress code was also imposed: slacks or trousers were never to be worn; lipstick was to be worn at all times; and all players had to have long hair.

On the field, the women played in a "one-piece short-skirted tunic" modeled after other sports uniforms of the day, such as those used in figure skating and tennis. The rest of the ensemble consisted of knee-length socks, satin shorts, and a baseball cap.

Teams played a 108-game schedule that ran from mid-May until the end of September. After a successful first season, additional teams were added. The league continued to thrive after the war ended, and in 1948, the 10-team operation drew almost a million fans.

In 1950, directors decentralized the league establishment, and franchises began operating independently. Publicity, player acquisition, and distribution of talent suffered in the absence of a central controlling authority. At the same time, other forms of recreation and the beginning age of television competed for a shrinking fan base. As attendance declined, financial circumstances also became more difficult until, in 1954, the league ceased operations.

Baseball historians have noted that women's participation in baseball extends far back into the early days of the sport. In 1866, the first women's baseball game was played at Vassar College. For four decades from the 1890s to the 1930s, barnstorming teams known as the Bloomer Girls played to receptive crowds across the country.

Women's League Champions

1943: Racine Belles
1944: Milwaukee Chicks
1945: Rockford Peaches
1946: Racine Belles
1947: Grand Rapids Chicks
1948: Rockford Peaches
1949: Rockford Peaches
1950: Rockford Peaches
1951: South Bend Blue Sox
1952: South Bend Blue Sox
1953: Grand Rapids Chicks
1954: Kalamazoo Lassies

NOTE

1. Because of injury, Williams played only about half of the 1950 season, although he hit 28 home runs.

Chapter Twenty-One

The Legacy of Jackie Robinson

When Jackie Robinson stepped onto a major league diamond, much about baseball—and America—began to change.

96. JACKIE

Americans of less than "a certain age" may find it difficult to understand how different our country was on April 15, 1947. Schools throughout the South were segregated; "white only" and "colored only" labels identified public restrooms and drinking fountains; and the features of some states' political systems included poll taxes and white-only primaries. In the 1948 presidential election, Strom Thurmond of South Carolina ran as a segregationist States' Rights Democrat ("Dixiecrat") and received 39 electoral votes. Issues associated with race were not just "Southern" or regional; de facto discrimination in housing, businesses, and schools was prevalent in cities across the nation. Even the armed forces remained separated by race; it would be another year before President Truman signed the order integrating the military. Seven more years would elapse before *Brown v. Board of Education* declared that separate schools were inherently unequal. Seventeen years would go by before a major civil rights law passed, 18 before the Voting Rights Act was enacted.

What made April 15, 1947—opening day of the baseball season—different from other days in American history was that an African American ballplayer was in the lineup of a major league team. Jackie Robinson was 28 years old when he stepped onto the field as a member of the Brooklyn Dodgers and broke what had come to be known as the "color barrier" in the major leagues.

His presence on the diamond at Ebbetts Field that afternoon did not occur by chance. Dodgers president and general manager Branch Rickey—a mostly unsung hero of the Robinson story—had meticulously planned for the day. Jackie had attended the University of California, Los Angeles, and served as a lieutenant in the army during World War II. Indeed, it was for those reasons and because Robinson was an articulate, nonsmoking, nondrinking, noncarousing, active churchgoer that Rickey chose him.

Convinced after a thorough investigation of Robinson's personal life that Jackie had the qualities he was looking for, Rickey first subjected Robinson to a grueling three-hour cross-examination. More interrogation than interview, Rickey's questions and harangues sought to dramatize the difficulties that Robinson would face—slurs, epithets, and threats from opponents, fans, and some teammates as well. At the end of the session, Rickey felt assured that Robinson could stand up to the abuse and, equally as important, would not retaliate. Indeed, as he told Robinson, Rickey was looking for someone with the "guts not to fight back."

Rickey then began setting the stage for Robinson's entry into the major leagues. Rickey first signed Robinson, who was playing for the Kansas City Monarchs of the Negro League, to a contract with the Dodgers' Montreal franchise in the International League. Robinson played the 1946 season at Montreal, where he won the Most Valuable Player Award.

Opening day 1947 saw Robinson in Brooklyn's starting lineup. As both Robinson and Rickey had anticipated, the pressures were intense. Threats came, along with abuse from fans and opponents. Some players objected strenuously, and the St. Louis Cardinals team threatened to strike. The club backed down when baseball commissioner A. B. "Happy" Chandler announced that he would suspend any player who did so.

Despite the clamorous atmosphere everywhere he played, Robinson had an immediate impact on the Dodgers' success on the diamond. Jackie was a major factor in the team's winning the National League pennant and was voted Rookie of the Year. Two years later, he was selected as the league's Most Valuable Player. Robinson went on to appear in six World Series and six All-Star games before being voted into the Hall of Fame.

Some pundits have noted that when Robinson made the big league club, he was not necessarily the best player in the Negro Leagues, but because of the example he set and the personal qualities he had, he may have been—as Branch Rickey believed—the black player best suited to break the color barrier.[1]

Robinson opened the gate for African Americans in major league baseball, but the path through it remained difficult at first, and the number traveling along it was small. Eleven weeks after Robinson's debut in the majors, on July 15, 1947, Larry Doby broke the color barrier in the American League. Doby appeared in 29 games for the Cleveland Indians that season.

Although his story is less well known than Robinson's, Doby was subjected to the same intense forms of vilification. At the end of the following season, Doby and Satchel Paige, his Cleveland teammate, were the majors' only other black players. In 1953, only six teams had African Americans on their rosters. It was 1959 before every team had at least one black player.

Still, although the numbers were small, the impact of black players on big league teams was immediate—and enormous. Beginning with Brooklyn catcher Roy Campenella's award in 1952 (already his second), African American players won six consecutive Most Valuable Player Awards. Their contributions spurred further progress, although in some areas it came slowly. In 1961, Gene Baker became the first black manager in organized baseball when the Pittsburgh Pirates assigned him to their franchise in Batavia, New York. It was 1975 before Frank Robinson became the first African American to manage a major league team (Cleveland). Meanwhile, Emmett Ashford had become the majors' first black umpire in 1966. Finally, in 1989, Bill White, former ballplayer and broadcaster, was elected president of the National League. As baseball historians have noted, Latinos also owe a debt of gratitude to Robinson; the presence of non-Anglo ballplayers on major league rosters increased significantly after the color barrier was broken.

Robinson's conduct, the visible excellence with which he played the game, and the fact of his participation had consequences far beyond the sport of baseball. A few happened quickly. For example, early in his major league career, complaints that he could not stay with his teammates in the same hotels caused establishments in some cities to begin accepting customers of all races. Other changes were slower in coming, but in the final analysis, Robinson's presence—a black man's presence—in a major league lineup struck a blow against segregation that transcended the game.

On April 15, 1997, the 50th anniversary of the day that Robinson stepped on to a big league diamond, his jersey number 42 was retired on all teams across major league baseball.

NOTE

1. Jackie Robinson was not the first African American to play professional baseball. As early as 1872, an African American named John "Bud" Fowler played second base for a professional team in New Castle, Pennsylvania. For a time in the mid-1880s, the "color line" was briefly relaxed in some leagues, and Fowler and several other black players participated on integrated professional teams. Beginning in 1887, however, blacks were increasingly banned from professional baseball, as segregation became heavier and more pervasive. By about 1898, all of the few remaining African American players in the professional leagues were gone. Until Jackie Robinson, there would be no more.

Chapter Twenty-Two

Pitching

From the time of Alexander Cartwright to the present day, no position in the game of baseball has changed more than that of pitcher.

97. PITCHING: FROM PAST TO PRESENT—TRACING THE CHANGES

The role of pitcher in the modern game is radically different from that envisioned by Alexander Cartwright. Cartwright's rules stated that "the ball must be pitched, not thrown, to the bat." Balls were delivered underhanded with a stiff wrist, much like tossing a horseshoe. The pitcher, or "feeder," threw from inside a prescribed box 45 feet from the plate. The pitcher's box, which frequently changed in shape and size, was part of the game for many years until finally done away with. While the box existed, limits on the pitcher's movements inside it were also revised many times.

For a considerable time, batters could signify whether they wanted the ball thrown to them above or below the waist. Initially, umpires called no strikes; the batter (or "striker") could wait for a pitch that suited him.

The following timeline traces the major changes that have shaped the position and brought it into the modern era. Sources differ slightly regarding the years when some of the changes were introduced—for example, 1881 vs. 1882 for the change from eight vice seven balls constituting a base on balls. The differences are sometimes due, I suspect, to the source's identifying either the year that the change was decided or the year in which it was introduced on the field. Then, too, the leagues in existence at the time did not always implement the changes uniformly. For example, the National League went from seven balls to six balls constituting a walk in 1884; the American Association did not make the same change until 1886. As such, I have attempted to use the most commonly cited dates.

1857: Home plate and the "pitcher's point" were flat, circular iron plates painted or enameled white.

1858: Because batters were becoming too selective, umpires were allowed to call strikes on "good balls" that batters refused to swing at. An effect of the change was to induce pitchers to throw harder but sometimes wilder because there was no penalty for "bad balls."

1863: Umpires were permitted to award first base to batters who received three "bad balls."

1863: Pitchers were required to have both feet on the ground when the ball was released.

1867: The pitcher's box was narrowed to six feet wide and four feet deep, half of the previous size.

1868: All limits on the pitcher's movements inside the pitcher's box were removed; pitchers could take as many steps as they liked.

1868: The shape of home plate was changed from a circle to a 12-inch square. The pitcher's point was also changed from a circle to a square.

1870: Batters were given the right to call for a high or low ball.

1872: Because pitchers were snapping their wrists when they released the ball, that form of delivery was legalized—although pitchers still had to release the ball from below the waist.

1872: Home plate was required to be made of white marble or stone.

1874: The batter's box was introduced.

1875: Pitcher's points were allowed to be made of iron or stone.

1879: Nine balls were required before a walk was awarded.

1880: Eight balls were required before a walk was awarded.

1881: The pitching distance was lengthened from 45 to 50 feet.

1881: Seven balls were required before a walk was awarded. This change was made in 1882 in the American Association and 1884 in the Union Association.

1883: Pitchers were allowed to release the ball up to shoulder level.

1884: Overhand pitching was allowed; almost all prohibitions on a pitcher's motion and delivery were removed.

1884: Six balls were required before a walk was awarded. This change was made in 1886 in the American Association.

1885: The American Association required home plate to be made of white rubber. The National League allowed either rubber or stone.

1886: The National League went back to seven balls required before awarding a walk.

1887: Batters lost the privilege of asking for a pitch above or below the waist. For that year only, a strikeout required four strikes. Pitchers were required to place one foot on the back line of the pitcher's box and not take more than one forward step when delivering the ball. The strike zone was more clearly defined to constitute that from the tops of the shoulders to the bottoms of the knees. The pitcher's box was reduced in size. The National League conformed with the American Association rule requiring home plate to be made of rubber.

1887: Five balls were required before a walk was awarded.

1887: Pitching distance was set at 55 feet 6 inches.

1888: Return to three strikes constituting a strikeout.

1889: Four balls were required before a walk was awarded.

1890: The pitcher's point was required to be made of rubber and was changed from a square to a circle six inches in diameter.

1893: The pitcher's box was done away with. Pitchers were required to deliver the ball with one foot on a rubber slab 12 by 4 inches. The advent of the pitcher's mound was apparently more random and for a time may have varied from park to park. It is possible that for a few years some parks did not have mounds.

1893: The pitching distance was set at 60 feet 6 inches.

1895: The pitcher's rubber slab was changed to the present size: 24 inches long, 6 inches wide.

1900: Home plate was changed from a 12-inch square to a five-sided figure 17 inches across on the flat side facing the pitcher.

1901: For the National League, the first two foul balls were counted as strikes.

1903: For the American League, the first two foul balls were counted as strikes.

1903: The height of the pitcher's mound was limited to 15 inches. Mounds were allowed to vary in height from park to park up to the 15-inch limit.

1920: The spitball and similar pitches were outlawed. Pitchers already in the major leagues with a spitball in their repertoire were "grandfathered." The last spitball pitcher in the big leagues was Burleigh Grimes of the Pittsburgh Pirates. Grimes retired in 1934.

1950: The height of the pitcher's mound was standardized at 15 inches.

1969: The height of the pitcher's mound was lowered to 10 inches.

Relief Pitching

The save rule: To get credit for a save, a relief pitcher must finish a game won by his team (and not be the winning pitcher) and satisfy one of three criteria:

- The relief pitcher must enter the game with the potential tying run on base, at bat, or on deck;
- the relief pitcher must pitch one inning with a lead of three runs or less; or
- the relief pitcher must pitch effectively (in the judgment of the official scorer) for at least three innings.

As many big league managers have stated, "There is no clock in baseball." Unlike other sports, baseball does not permit a coach to sit on a lead and simply let time expire. Because there is no clock, someone has to get the last few outs of the game—and they are almost always the most difficult.

In the early days of the game, relief pitchers were a rarity. That circumstance existed as a result of preference and because, until 1891, substitutes were permitted only in case of injury. A pitcher who was having a bad day simply changed positions with someone else in the field.

Even after the rules were relaxed, bringing in a relief pitcher was the exception and not the norm. For example, during the 1901 season, 87 percent of all games were completed by starting pitchers. In 1904, the Boston team's starting pitchers finished 148 games of its 154-game schedule.

Soon after, however, manager John McGraw of the New York Giants changed the usual game pattern by using starting pitchers in relief on their "off" (i.e., nonstarting) days. That approach became common practice in the big leagues for several decades.

Probably the first bona fide relief pitcher in the majors—a hurler whose primary job was to enter the game in relief—was Firpo Marberry of the Washington Senators. In 1926, Marberry was the first pitcher to record 20 saves in a season. It wasn't until 1965 that Ted Abernathy of the Cubs got as many as 35.

The first modern "closer" was Joe Page, who pitched for the New York Yankees from 1944 to 1950. In 1950, Jim Konstanty of the Philadelphia Phillies appeared in 74 ball games, and during the 1950s the role of the relief pitcher/closer became a recognized position on big league rosters.

The relief pitcher position has continued to evolve and grow over the years.

- In 1982, Rollie Fingers (then pitching for the Milwaukee Brewers) was the first pitcher to save 300 games.
- In 1990, Bobby Thigpen of the Chicago White Sox was the first to save 50 games in a season (he wound up with 57).
- In 1996, Mike Marshall of the Los Angeles Dodgers was the first relief pitcher to appear in 100 or more ball games during a season. That year, Marshall came in from the bull pen a remarkable 106 times.

- In 2006, Trevor Hoffman of the San Diego Padres set the record for saves with 479. By the end of the 2010 season, Hoffman had saved more than 600 games.
- In 2008, Francisco Rodriguez of the Los Angeles Angels set the existing record with 62 saves during the season.
- Yankee closer Mariano Rivera became the all-time save leader in 2011. Rivera has amassed 608 regular season saves during the course of his remarkable career.

The value of the relief pitcher is seen by the fact that most major league teams win 90 percent of the games that they lead going into the eighth inning. Teams with good relief pitchers win as many as 95 percent.

There is, by the way, some question about where the term *bull pen* came from. One account has it that in some early ballparks, relief pitchers often warmed up by Bull Durham tobacco signs. A second possibility comes from an 1877 reference in the *Cincinnati Enquirer* newspaper, describing a roped-in area in foul territory where late-arriving fans were "herded like bulls."

Extra-Inning Coverage about Pitching

- In 1944, Red Barrett of the Boston Braves pitched a complete nine-inning game using just 58 pitches.
- Cleveland Indians pitcher Stan Coveleski once pitched seven consecutive innings without a single pitch being called a ball.
- In 1933, New York Giants pitcher Carl Hubbell pitched an 18-inning shutout without walking a single batter.
- The fastest pitch yet recorded was a 105-mph fastball thrown by Aroldis Chapman of the Cincinnati Reds.
- On April 17, 2012, 49-year-old Jamie Moyer of the Colorado Rockies became the oldest pitcher to win a major league game when the Rockies defeated the San Diego Padres 5–3.

Chapter Twenty-Three

The Reserve Clause

Since the time that teams began paying players to play, a contract provision intended to bind players to a team has been one of the most significant causes of contention between owners and players. Owners have used what is called the *reserve clause* to respond to challenges posed by unstable rosters and escalating player salaries. Because its provisions affect compensation and career opportunity, players have regarded the clause as a threat to their livelihood.

98. MANAGEMENT VS. LABOR

From the earliest days of professional baseball, two interrelated issues caused friction between owners and players: player compensation and what came to be known as the reserve clause. Players mainly saw the two as issues of fairness and limits on their opportunity to market themselves and receive just compensation for their skills. Owners saw high salary costs as a threat to profitability or even franchise viability. As early as 1876–1879, nearly 65 percent of the Boston club's operating expenses went toward player compensation. Owners realized that in a totally "free market," players moving from team to team would make rosters unstable and cause salaries to escalate to the point that they would offset any revenues gained by putting a better ball team on the field.

Over time, the owners' response was the reserve clause: a contract provision that bound a player to a team for a year after his initial contract expired. Devised originally in 1879 by Arthur Soden, owner of the Boston team in the National League, the clause at first protected only a few players on each team but was eventually expanded to encompass the entire roster. The clause essentially stated that the team had the right to renew a player's contract following each season. In effect, the reserve clause gave teams a lifetime option on a player's services. The clause left the player with limited choices: he could accept the contract offer and play for the club; he could "hold out," refuse to play, and hope that the team would eventually make an offer to his liking; or he could quit the game of baseball. The clause permitted clubs to hold salaries down, although even in the early days, major league ballplayers earned two or more times as much as skilled craftsmen in other private sector professions.

Over the years, player unrest caused by dissatisfaction with salaries and the reserve clause erupted periodically. Players' rebellions, a short-lived Players' League, holdouts, and occasional strikes and work stoppages of varying lengths were evidence of the underlying frustrations and turmoil.

The early to mid-1960s saw a turning point in labor relations in major league baseball. Players noted that while baseball salaries remained relatively low, television revenue was flowing into the coffers of team owners, and franchises were expanding in number. In similar circumstances, the compensation of professional football players was increasing more rapidly.

In 1966, Sandy Koufax and Don Drysdale, star pitchers for the Los Angeles Dodgers, refused to play for the salaries initially offered them. Their collective holdout—the first in baseball history—met with considerable success. That lesson, as well as the fact that Koufax and Drysdale had been represented by an agent, was not lost on others throughout the baseball establishment. Soon after, major league players hired attorney Marvin Miller to represent them as executive director of the Major League Baseball Players Association. Under Miller's stewardship, the players initially bargained for increases to the minimum salaries, improved working conditions, and changes in contributions to the player pension fund. (Unlike most unions, the association did not directly help players in individual salary negotiations.)

Several tumultuous years followed that saw additional holdouts, player strikes, and an owner lockout. The low point in labor relations came in 1994 when play was halted on August 12 and the rest of the season, including playoffs and the World Series, was canceled. For major league baseball, it was the first year since 1904 that a World Series had not been played. The main issue in the 1994 confrontation was a salary cap proposal put forward by the owners in return for which time limits on free agent eligibility would be reduced. Neither feature was part of the settlement that finally ended the impasse. (Appendix P provides a list of strikes and work stoppages.)

Over time, the players association and management have reached agreements that increased minimum salaries, gave players the right to be represented by an agent during contract negotiations, and established a formal grievance procedure. As the process eventually evolved, an independent arbitrator would settle salary disputes by choosing between the player's or the team's single offer, using as a guide comparative salaries paid to others with similar playing credentials. The so-called final offer arbitration was made available to players with three years' experience. (An exception allows a specific category of players to request salary arbitration after two years.)

In reserve clause "history," several cases, decisions, and names have achieved lasting notoriety—Curt Flood, "Catfish" Hunter, Peter Seitz, Andy Messersmith, and Dave McNally.

In 1969, Curt Flood, outfielder for the St. Louis Cardinals, refused to be traded to the Philadelphia Phillies. Flood sat out the season and brought an antitrust suit (*Flood v. Kuhn*) against major league baseball. Flood's case went to the Supreme Court, which ruled against him 5–3 in 1972, citing the 1922 exemption from antitrust laws given to baseball.[1] Though he lost, Flood's case set the stage for changes to the reserve clause, salary arbitration, free agency, and collective bargaining that would soon follow.

In 1974, in a case involving Jim "Catfish" Hunter of the Oakland A's, arbitrator Peter Seitz ruled that A's owner Charles Finley had not fulfilled all the provisions of Hunter's contract and, therefore, Hunter was a free agent.

In 1975, pitchers Andy Messersmith of the Los Angeles Dodgers and Dave McNally of the Baltimore Orioles refused the clubs' salary offers and played the year without signed contracts. Following the season, an arbitration panel headed by Peter Seitz declared Messersmith and McNally free agents, a decision later upheld by the courts. The Seitz decision essentially dismantled the reserve clause mechanism that had existed in baseball for almost 100 years.

Worried that the Seitz decision might open the door to mass free agency, in 1976 owners and players reached an agreement modifying the reserve clause system. Under the revised procedures, players became eligible for free agency after six years. Players not under contract after six or more years in the big leagues could request free agency status. Generally, players with three years but less than six years of service could ask for salary arbitration, thus preventing teams from setting their salaries unilaterally. The collective bargaining agreement also set minimum salary levels for each of the first three years of major league service.

The limit on the roster size of big league teams also has reserve clause implications and, of course, directly affects total payroll and player compensation. From the earliest days of the modern era, the major leagues have placed limits on the number of players that each team can carry on its active roster.

For most of the modern era, major league rosters have comprised 25 players. The size was reduced to 23 for a time during the Great Depression, before being restored to 25 in 1939. During the 1946 season, teams were allowed to expand their rosters to provide spaces for veterans returning from World War II. In 1986, owners responded to a dispute with the players' union by reducing rosters to 24 players. Since restored to its former size, the 25-player limit extends from opening day through August 31. On September 1, rosters expand to 40 players through the last day of the regular season.

Interestingly, baseball's first professional club, the Cincinnati Red Stockings, played the entire 70-game or so schedule with a 10-man roster.

NOTE

1. In *Federal Baseball Club of Baltimore, Inc. v. National League of Professional Baseball Clubs*, the Supreme Court unanimously decided that baseball operations did not constitute interstate commerce. Transporting players across state lines, the court ruled, was "mere incident" to business conducted in private ballparks. Baseball was an "amusement"; a schedule of games between independently owned and operated clubs in different cities simply facilitated the "entertainment." Because it was not interstate commerce, antitrust laws did not apply. As of this writing, that 1922 ruling remains in effect.

Chapter Twenty-Four

Running the Business

Over the years, factors such as tradition, owners' arrangements, commissioners' rulings, and, increasingly, collective bargaining agreements have established a framework for conducting the game's business. Rules and deadlines for matters such as waivers, options, and free agency establish a system and provide a structure for transactions associated with staffing and maintaining major league ball clubs. The following section provides information on major features of these key front office operations.

99. FRONT OFFICE OPERATIONS

Roster Composition Limits

From opening day until September 1, major league rosters are capped at 25 players. On September 1 through the remainder of the season, rosters can expand to 40 players. The 25-player limit again applies to division playoffs, league championships, and World Series competitions. Teams must maintain at least 24 players on active rosters during the course of the season.

Trading Timelines

The key date is July 31. From the end of the preceding season through July 31, teams may trade players without going through the waiver process. On and after August 1, players must "clear waivers" before trades can be consummated.

157

The Waiver Process

When a club places a player on waivers (called "requesting waivers"), other teams have two business days to claim the player. If the player is not claimed within that time, the player has "cleared waivers." The team that placed the player on waivers then has several options: it can send the player to the minors; it can trade him to another major league club (even if the normal trading deadline has expired); or it can take no action.

From July 31 through the end of the season, players on the 40-man roster must clear waivers to be traded. If a player does not clear waivers—that is, he is claimed by one or more other clubs—the team that requested the waiver may withdraw the waiver request. If the waiver request is not withdrawn, the transaction proceeds as follows: If only one claim is made, then the player's contract is assigned to the club that made the claim; if more than one team in the same league made a claim, the team lower in the league standings gets the player; if clubs from both leagues made claims, teams in the same league as the club that requested waivers receive preference.

Fifteen-Day Disabled List

There are no limits to the number of players that may be placed on the 15-day disabled list. Players may be transferred to the 60-day disabled list at any time.

Sixty-Day Disabled List

There is no limit on the number of players placed on the list, but it may be used only when the team is carrying the full, 40-player expanded roster. Players on the 60-day list do not count against the 40-player limit. Players placed on the list after August 1 must remain on it through the end of the regular season and playoffs.

Rules Common to Both Disabled Lists

Players may be placed on lists retroactively for a period up to 10 days from the date after the last day they played. With the exception of pitchers, players sent to a minor league team for injury rehabilitation have a maximum of 20 days to rehab. Pitchers are allowed 30 days for injury rehabilitation.

Option Rules

An "optional assignment" designation occurs when a player on the 40-man major league roster is in the minor leagues. Players in this category have a three-season option circumstance. They may be sent down to the minors and returned to the majors an unlimited number of times during those seasons.

The club is charged only one option per season. A player "out of options" is one who is in his fourth professional season (or more) and has been on the 40-man major league roster during three separate seasons. A player "out of options" must clear irrevocable waivers to be returned to the minor leagues.

Designation for Assignment

Designating a player for reassignment allows a team to open up a roster spot for up to 10 days while waiting for the player to clear the waiver process.

Bringing a Player up from the Minors: Recalling vs. Purchasing a Contract

Players are officially "recalled" if they are already on the major league 40-man roster. When players in the major league team's farm system (but not on the 40-man roster) are brought to the major leagues, their contracts are purchased from the minor league franchise. Players whose contracts are purchased must be placed on the big league club's 40-man roster.

Free Agency Status

To be eligible for free agency status, a player must have a minimum of six years of major league service. The process involves several key timelines. An eligible player must file for free agency within 15 days from the first day after the World Series ends. By December 7, the player's former team must offer to arbitrate, or the franchise loses its eligibility to re-sign the player. By December 19, the player must accept the team's offer, or, effective January 9, the former team becomes ineligible to sign the player to a contract.

Free Agency: Special Status

Players may file for free agency when they have played all or parts of seven seasons in the majors or minors and, as of October 15, are not on a team's 40-man roster.

Rule 5 Draft

The Rule 5 draft is a special circumstance that addresses situations associated with young ballplayers. To be eligible for Rule 5 draft, players must

- not be on a major league 40-man roster as of November 20, and
- have been 18 years old or younger when first signed to a professional contract and four Rule 5 drafts have subsequently occurred, or
- have been 19 or older when they first signed a professional contract and three Rule 5 drafts have subsequently occurred.

Salary Arbitration

Players with three years of major league service are eligible for salary arbitration. A special circumstance covers some players with at least two but less than three years in the major leagues. To be eligible, players must be in the top 17 percent of total service in the group of players in the "two but less than three years" category, and at least 86 days of accumulated major league service must have occurred during the preceding season.

Chapter Twenty-Five

Baseball in Song, Verse, and Show Business

It is perhaps the truest measure of how deeply ingrained the game is in our nation's soul: in both prose and poetry, baseball is the most written about of any of America's sports. More films, good and bad, have been made about baseball that any other form of athletics. And although it is unofficial, baseball is the only sport that has an "anthem," for that is indeed what the song "Take Me Out to the Ballgame" has come to be.

100. BASEBALL IN THE ARTS AND ON-SCREEN

Music

"Take Me Out to the Ballgame" is perhaps the most famous piece of music associated with any sport. When the song was introduced in 1908,[1] it became the nation's No. 1 hit record. In recent years, many teams have introduced the custom of singing the song during the "seventh-inning stretch," thanks in large measure to Chicago Cubs announcer Harry Caray, who established the tradition at Wrigley Field.

Except for "Happy Birthday," "Take Me Out to the Ballgame" is regarded as the nation's best-known and most recognized song.

Broadway Musical

Damn Yankees opened on Broadway in 1955 and ran for 1,019 performances. In a modern retelling of the Faust legend, a discouraged Washington Senators fan sells his soul to the devil to enable the team to compete against the

New York Yankees for the American League pennant. The musical has been revived several times over the years and was made into a movie by MGM in 1958.

Verse

If "Take Me Out to the Ballgame" is baseball's national anthem, then surely "Casey at the Bat" is its epic poem. Written by Ernest Thayer, "Casey" was first published in the *San Francisco Examiner* on June 3, 1888. The saga soon gained renown with additional printings and performances on the vaudeville circuit.

The poem tells the tale of Casey's Mudville team, losing, by two runs with two outs in the last inning. When two weak hitters unexpectedly reach base ahead of him, hope springs anew as Mudville's beloved star player, the "mighty Casey," strolls to the plate. So confident that he does not swing at the first two pitches, both called strikes, Casey swings and misses on the third pitch. Casey's strikeout ends the game and sends the crowd home stunned and saddened.

The appeal of the humorous yet poignant verse endures to this day, and the words of the poem's closing stanza are perhaps the most famous of any piece of writing about any sport:

> Oh, somewhere in this favored land the sun is shining bright;
> The band is playing somewhere, and somewhere hearts are light,
> And somewhere men are laughing, and somewhere children shout;
> But there is no joy in Mudville—mighty Casey has struck out.

Appendix Q provides the full text of "Casey at the Bat" and samples from the numerous sequels that have been written over the years.

"Baseball's Sad Lexicon"—better known as "Tinker to Evers to Chance"—is one of those rare items of prose that makes a person or a group immortal. In 1910, a small eight-line poem written by Franklin Pierce Adams made three Chicago Cubs infielders—Joe Tinker, Johnny Evers, and Frank Chance—the most memorable double-play combination in history. Ironically, none of the three initially came to the big leagues in the positions that made them famous. Shortstop Tinker was originally a third baseman; second baseman Evers moved from shortstop; and first baseman Chance began his big league career as a backup catcher.

Double plays were rarer in the era they played; by modern standards, the numbers they turned were not exceptional. Nonetheless, the trio popularized the play and brought fielding into greater focus. Among other things, the three of them are often credited with devising techniques for defending against the bunt and the hit and run. They are thought to have implemented the first known version of the rotation play.

Tinker and Evers fought both on and off the field for much of their major league careers, although they did reconcile in later years. Still, along with Chance during the 1902–1910 period, they sparked the Cubs to four National League pennants and two World Series championships. In 1946, the three of them were inducted simultaneously into the Hall of Fame.

Baseball's Sad Lexicon

These are the saddest of possible words:
"Tinker to Evers to Chance."
A trio of bear cubs, and fleeter than birds,
Tinker to Evers to Chance.
Ruthlessly pricking our gonfalon bubble,
Making a Giant hit into a double—
Words that are heavy with nothing but trouble:
"Tinker to Evers to Chance."

A "gonfalon" is a pennant or a flag, meaning here the National League title. "Hitting into a double" refers to a batter grounding into a double play via shortstop to second to first.

Literature

More books have been written about baseball than about all other major sports combined. Hundreds, if not thousands, of fiction and nonfiction works chronicle the game in all its facets. Lists, necessarily subjective, that purport to identify the "best," the "top 10," or the "top 25" are only slightly fewer in number. The following titles are shown in alphabetical order, and most appear somewhere in the rankings of the major lists. All are notable for their interesting stories and excellent writing.

Babe: The Legend Comes to Life, by Robert W. Creamer
Ball Four, by Jim Bouton
Bang the Drum Slowly, by Mark Harris
Baseball's Great Experiment: Jackie Robinson and His Legacy, by Jules Tygiel
The Boys of Summer, by Roger Kahn
Bums: An Oral History of the Brooklyn Dodgers, by Peter Golenbock
Can't Anybody Here Play This Game? by Jimmy Breslin
The Catcher Was a Spy, by Nicholas Dawidoff
The Celebrant, by Eric Rolfe Greenberg
Cobb: A Biography, by Al Stump
Eight Men Out: The Black Sox and the 1919 World Series, by Eliot Asinof
The Glory of Their Times, by Lawrence Ritter
The Long Season, by Jim Brosnan
Men at Work: The Craft of Baseball, by George F. Will

Moneyball: The Art of Winning an Unfair Game, by Michael Lewis
The Natural, by Bernard Malamud
Pennant Race, by Jim Brosnan
The Southpaw, by Mark Harris
The Summer Game, by Roger Angell
Summer of '49, by David Halberstam
Veeck—As in Wreck, by Bill Veeck
You Know Me, Al, by Ring Lardner

Baseball Movies

Recent compilations show more than 75 feature movies made about baseball. The earliest major film about the sport was *The Pride of the Yankees* (1942). Starring Gary Cooper, the film told the story of Lou Gehrig. The baseball movies that followed over the years have targeted audiences ranging from adults to children and have contained themes stretching from comedy to the paranormal. Many have been quite good; some have been downright awful.

There have been a plethora of "top 10" lists of favorite baseball movies, and the ratings tend to shift over time. Most recent versions contain some combination of the following films.

The Bad News Bears (1976)
Bang the Drum Slowly (1973)
Baseball (1994)
Bull Durham (1988)
Eight Men Out (1988)
Fear Strikes Out (1957)
Field of Dreams (1989)
A League of Their Own (1992)
Major League (1989)
Moneyball (2011)
The Natural (1984)
The Pride of the Yankees (1942)
Sandlot (1993)

Comedy Sketch: "Who's on First?"

In 1999, *Time* magazine named the "Who's on First?" routine, by Bud Abbott and Lou Costello, as the best comedy sketch of the 20th century. The setup of the routine has Costello asking Abbott to name the players on his baseball team. Abbott responds with names like "Who" (the first baseman) and "What" (the second baseman), which cause Costello—not realizing those are the players' names—to become increasingly irate and perplexed.

Baseball routines had long been staples of burlesque entertainment in the mid-1930s when Abbott and Costello began performing "Who's on First?" which they gradually expanded and refined. In 1937, "Who's on First?" became a major hit when they used it in a vaudeville touring production. In 1938, the routine was broadcast for the first time to a national radio audience. Over the years, the skit has been performed for presidents, featured on radio and television, and prominently showcased in two motion pictures.

Although Abbott and Costello performed the routine hundreds of times, they seldom did it exactly the same way; thus, the sketch was fresh and different each time. "Who's on First?" became one of the classic lines in the history of American comedy. A video of "Who's on First?" now plays on screens at baseball's Hall of Fame. The names given in the routine for the players in each position follow:

First base: Who
Second base: What
Third base: I Don't Know
Shortstop: I Don't Give a Darn
Left field: Why
Center field: Because
Pitcher: Tomorrow
Catcher: Today

The name of the shortstop is not given until the end of the sketch. The right fielder is never named, although an interpretation of some versions of the skit could identify him as "Naturally."

NOTE

1. The lyrics were written by Albert von Tilzen and the music by Jack Northworth.

Chapter Twenty-Six

Nicknames

Probably no other sport has players with nicknames richer or more varied than baseball. Beginning with the earliest days of the game, these unique labels painted shorthand images of a player's stature, appearance, demeanor, or reputation.

101. DR. STRANGEGLOVE AND OTHER LABELS

Nothing about the nicknames attached to major league ballplayers is sacred. Through the years, descriptions of players' physiques have been especially colorful. These have included, for example, Jumbo, Blimp, Tubby, Fats, Chub, Porky, and Pudge. The numbers of "Big" are almost countless: Big Ed, Big Bill, Big John, Big Mike, Big *fill-in-the-blank*. At the other extreme is Skinny, Slim, Stick, Twig, and Bones. Stretch, Long, and Lank have identified tall guys, while the more vertically challenged have often been labeled Shorty, Stubby, Flea, or Midget.

Speedy players have been christened Legs, Skates, Deerfoot, Jackrabbit, Bunny, and Road Runner. Players who are, shall we say, less of a threat to steal have been called Twinkletoes, Footsie, Satchelfoot, Piano Legs, and Piano Mover.

In the past, in an age of less political correctness, nicknames were frequently associated with a player's nationality: Dutch, Heinie, Fritz, Swede, Frenchy. The majors have also seen a Mad Russian, a Mad Hungarian, a Big Serb, a Big Finn, a Golden Greek, a Nervous Greek, and one Superjew. Tex, Gator, Jersey, Reb, Rebel, and Dixie tied players to a specific region.

The number of Leftys borders on the infinite. Pug, Schnozz, and Spec have also highlighted a distinguishing characteristic. Hair color has been a major descriptor: Whitey, Blackie, Red, Pinky, Cotton Top . . . and Baldy.

Foodwise, the sport has seen at least one Peanuts, Pretzels, Honey, Sugar, Bananas, Tomatoes, Hot Potato, Apples, Strawberry, Georgia Peach, Jelly, Cheese, Cracker, Oyster, T-Bone, Oats, Cocoa, Buttermilk, Spinach, and Prunes.

Medically speaking, we have had an Earache, a Lumbago, a Gimpy, a Corns, a Bunions, and simply an Old Aches and Pains. Kin folk have included Grandma, Pop, Pops, Uncle Robby, and Uncle Bill.

In terms of creatures great and small, consider Old Hoss, Wild Horse, Mule, Moose, Reindeer, Silver Fox, Jackrabbit, Rabbit, Kangaroo, Pig, Cat, Bunny, Kitten, Bulldog, Mad Dog, Crab, Bullfrog, Penguin, Rooster, Bald Eagle, Grey Eagle, Vulture, Goose, and Ducky.

Dozens of more generic nicknames fill baseball registers. Among the most common have been Babe, Rube, Buzz, Bobo, Shug, Kid, Doc, Buck, Chick, Chip, Skip, Sparky, Mac, Moe, Butch, Spike, Rip, and the ubiquitous Bubba. Dusty almost always identifies a player named Rhodes.

Dr. Strangeglove, by the way, refers to Dick Stuart, a home run–hitting first baseman who played for the Boston Red Sox and Pittsburgh Pirates. It is charitable to say that throughout his career, Stuart's defensive skills were a work in progress. For a time, the license plate on his car read "E-3."[1]

With apologies to fans of any players who may have been omitted, Appendix R includes many of the most famous, most infamous, or unique nicknames from baseball's past and present.

NOTE

1. In baseball scorekeeping, E3 signifies an error committed by the first baseman.

Appendix A: Spring Training Sites

Team	Location
Arizona Diamondbacks	Scottsdale, AZ
Atlanta Braves	Lake Buena Vista, FL
Baltimore Orioles	Sarasota, FL
Boston Red Sox	Fort Meyers, FL
Chicago Cubs	Mesa, AZ
Chicago White Sox	Glendale, AZ
Cincinnati Reds	Goodyear, AZ
Cleveland Indians	Goodyear, AZ
Colorado Rockies	Scottsdale, AZ
Detroit Tigers	Lakeland, FL
Houston Astros	Kissimmee, FL
Kansas City Royals	Surprise, AZ
Los Angeles Angels	Tempe, AZ
Los Angeles Dodgers	Glendale, AZ
Miami Marlins	Jupiter, FL
Milwaukee Brewers	Phoenix, AZ
Minnesota Twins	Ft. Meyers, FL
New York Mets	Port St. Lucie, FL
New York Yankees	Tampa, FL

Oakland A's	Phoenix, AZ
Philadelphia Phillies	Clearwater, FL
Pittsburgh Pirates	Bradenton, FL
San Diego Padres	Peoria, AZ
San Francisco Giants	Scottsdale, AZ
Seattle Mariners	Peoria, AZ
St. Louis Cardinals	Jupiter, FL
Tampa Bay Rays	Charlotte County, FL
Texas Rangers	Surprise, AZ
Toronto Blue Jays	Dunedin, FL
Washington Nationals	Viera, FL

Note. The Grapefruit League is the name collectively given to teams that conduct spring training and play preseason games in Florida. Arizona-based teams compose the Cactus League.

Appendix B: World Series Results

1903: Boston (AL), defeated Pittsburgh (NL) five games to three.

1904: No series.

1905: New York (NL) defeated Philadelphia (AL) four games to one.

1906: Chicago (AL) defeated Chicago (NL) four games to two.

1907: Chicago (NL) defeated Detroit (AL) four games to none (one tie).

1908: Chicago (NL) defeated Detroit (AL) four games to one.

1909: Pittsburgh (NL) defeated Detroit (AL) four games to three.

1910: Philadelphia (AL) defeated Chicago (NL) four games to one.

1911: Philadelphia (AL) defeated New York (NL) four games to two.

1912: Boston (AL) defeated New York (NL) four games to three (one tie).

1913: Philadelphia (AL) defeated New York (NL) four games to one.

1914: Boston (NL) defeated Philadelphia (AL), four games to none.

1915:Boston (AL) defeated Philadelphia (NL) four games to one.

1916: Boston (AL) defeated Brooklyn (NL) four games to one.

1917: Chicago (AL) defeated New York (NL) four games to two.

1918: Boston (AL) defeated Chicago (NL) four games to two.

1919: Cincinnati (NL) defeated Chicago (AL) five games to three.

1920: Cleveland (AL) defeated Brooklyn (NL) five games to two.

1921: New York (NL) defeated New York (AL) five games to three.

1922: New York (NL) defeated New York (AL) four games to none (one tie).

1923: New York (AL) defeated New York (NL) four games to two.

1924: Washington (AL) defeated New York (NL) four games to three.

1925: Pittsburgh (NL) defeated Washington (AL) four games to three.

1926: St. Louis (NL) defeated New York (AL) four games to three.

1927: New York (AL) defeated Pittsburgh (NL) four games to none.

1928: New York (AL) defeated St. Louis (NL) four games to none.
1929: Philadelphia (AL) defeated Chicago (NL) four games to one.
1930: Philadelphia (AL) defeated St. Louis (NL) four games to two.
1931: St. Louis (NL) defeated Philadelphia (AL) four games to three.
1932: New York (AL) defeated Chicago (NL) four games to none.
1933: New York (NL) defeated Washington (AL) four games to one.
1934: St. Louis (NL) defeated Detroit (AL) four games to three.
1935: Detroit (AL) defeated Chicago (NL) four games to two.
1936: New York (AL) defeated New York (NL) four games to two.
1937: New York (AL) defeated New York (NL) four games to one.
1938: New York (AL) defeated Chicago (NL) four games to none.
1939: New York (AL) defeated Cincinnati (NL) four games to none.
1940: Cincinnati (NL) defeated Detroit (AL) four games to three.
1941: New York (AL) defeated Brooklyn (NL) four games to one.
1942: St. Louis (NL) defeated New York (AL) four games to one.
1943: New York (AL) defeated St. Louis (NL) four games to one.
1944: St. Louis (NL) defeated St. Louis (AL) four games to two.
1945: Detroit (AL) defeated Chicago (NL) four games to three.
1946: St. Louis (NL) defeated Boston (AL) four games to three.
1947: New York (AL) defeated Brooklyn (NL) four games to three.
1948: Cleveland (AL) defeated Boston (NL) four games to two.
1949: New York (AL) defeated Brooklyn (NL) four games to one.
1950: New York (AL) defeated Philadelphia (NL) four games to none.
1951: New York (AL) defeated New York (NL) four games to two.
1952: New York (AL) defeated Brooklyn (NL) four games to three.
1953: New York (AL) defeated Brooklyn (NL) four games to two.
1954: New York (NL) defeated Cleveland (AL) four games to none.
1955: Brooklyn (NL) defeated New York (AL) four games to three.
1956: New York (AL) defeated Brooklyn (NL) four games to three.
1957: Milwaukee (NL) defeated New York (AL) four games to three.
1958: New York (AL) defeated Milwaukee (NL) four games to three.
1959: Los Angeles (NL) defeated Chicago (AL) four games to two.
1960: Pittsburgh (NL) defeated New York (AL) four games to three.
1961: New York (AL) defeated Cincinnati (NL) four games to one.
1962: New York (AL) defeated San Francisco (NL) four games to three.
1963: Los Angeles (NL) defeated New York (AL) four games to none.
1964: St. Louis (NL) defeated New York (AL) four games to three.
1965: Los Angeles (NL) defeated Minnesota (AL) four games to three.
1966: Baltimore (AL) defeated Los Angeles (NL) four games to none.
1967: St. Louis (NL) defeated Boston (AL) four games to three.
1968: Detroit (AL) defeated St. Louis (NL) four games to three.
1969: New York (NL) defeated Baltimore (AL) four games to one.
1970: Baltimore (AL) defeated Cincinnati (NL) four games to one.

1971: Pittsburgh (NL) defeated Baltimore (AL) four games to three.
1972: Oakland (AL) defeated Cincinnati (NL) four games to three.
1973: Oakland (AL) defeated New York (NL) four games to three.
1974: Oakland (AL) defeated Los Angeles (NL) four games to one.
1975: Cincinnati (NL) defeated Boston (AL) four games to three.
1976: Cincinnati (NL) defeated New York (AL) four games to none.
1977: New York (AL) defeated Los Angeles (NL) four games to two.
1978: New York (AL) defeated Los Angeles (NL) four games to two.
1979: Pittsburgh (NL) defeated Baltimore (AL) four games to three.
1980: Philadelphia (NL) defeated Kansas City (AL) four games to two.
1981: Los Angeles (NL) defeated New York (AL) four games to two.
1982: St. Louis (NL) defeated Milwaukee (AL) four games to three.
1983: Baltimore (AL) defeated Philadelphia (NL) four games to one.
1984: Detroit (AL) defeated San Diego (NL) four games to one.
1985: Kansas City (AL) defeated St. Louis (NL) four games to three.
1986: New York (NL) defeated Boston (AL) four games to three.
1987: Minnesota (AL) defeated St. Louis (NL) four games to three.
1988: Los Angeles (NL) defeated Oakland (AL) four games to one.
1989: Oakland (AL) defeated San Francisco (NL) four games to none.
1990: Cincinnati (NL) defeated Oakland (AL) four games to none.
1991: Minnesota (AL) defeated Atlanta (NL) four games to three.
1992: Toronto (AL) defeated Atlanta (NL) four games to two.
1993: Toronto (AL) defeated Philadelphia (NL) four games to two.
1994: No series.
1995: Atlanta (NL) defeated Cleveland (AL) four games to two.
1996: New York (AL) defeated Atlanta (NL) four games to two.
1997: Florida (NL) defeated Cleveland (AL) four games to three.
1998: New York (AL) defeated San Diego (NL) four games to none.
1999: New York (AL) defeated Atlanta (NL) four games to none.
2000: New York (AL) defeated New York (NL) four games to one.
2001: Arizona (NL) defeated New York (AL) four games to three.
2002: Anaheim (AL) defeated San Francisco (NL) four games to three.
2003: Florida (NL) defeated New York (AL) four games to two.
2004: Boston (AL) defeated St. Louis (NL) four games to none.
2005: Chicago (AL) defeated Houston (NL) four games to none.
2006: St. Louis (NL) defeated Detroit (AL) four games to one.
2007: Boston (AL) defeated Colorado (NL) four games to none.
2008: Philadelphia (NL) defeated Tampa Bay (AL) four games to one.
2009: New York (AL) defeated Philadelphia (NL) four games to two.
2010: San Francisco (NL) defeated Texas (AL) four games to one.
2011: St. Louis (NL) defeated Texas (AL) four games to three.
Note. AL: American League. NL: National League.

OVERALL WORLD SERIES RECORD—BY TEAM

New York Yankees: 40 appearances—27 wins, 13 losses.
St. Louis Cardinals: 18 appearances—11 wins, 7 losses.
Los Angeles Dodgers: 18 appearances—6 wins, 12 losses. [1]
San Francisco Giants: 18 appearances—6 wins, 12 losses. [2]
Oakland Athletics: 14 appearances—9 wins, 5 losses. [3]
Boston Red Sox: 11 appearances—7 wins, 4 losses.
Detroit Tigers: 10 appearances—4 wins, 6 losses.
Chicago Cubs: 10 appearances—2 wins, 8 losses.
Atlanta Braves: 9 appearances—3 wins, 6 losses. [4]
Cincinnati Reds: 9 appearances—5 wins, 4 losses.
Baltimore Orioles: 7 appearances—3 wins, 4 losses. [5]
Philadelphia Phillies: 7 appearances—2 wins, 5 losses.
Pittsburgh Pirates: 7 appearances—5 wins, 2 losses.
Minnesota Twins: 6 appearances—3 wins, 3 losses. [6]
Chicago White Sox: 5 appearances—3 wins, 2 losses.
Cleveland Indians: 5 appearances—2 wins, 3 losses.
New York Mets: 4 appearances—2 wins, 2 losses.
Miami Marlins: 2 appearances—2 wins, 0 losses. [7]
Kansas City Royals: 2 appearances—1 win, 1 loss.
San Diego Padres: 2 appearances—0 wins, 2 losses.
Toronto Blue Jays: 2 appearances—2 wins, 0 losses.
Texas Rangers: 2 appearances—0 wins, 2 losses.
Arizona Diamondbacks: 1 appearance—1 win, 0 losses.
Los Angeles Angels of Anaheim: 1 appearance—1 win, 0 losses.
Colorado Rockies: 1 appearance—0 wins, 1 loss.
Houston Astros: 1 appearance—0 wins, 1 loss.
Milwaukee Brewers: 1 appearances—0 wins, 1 loss. [8]
Tampa Bay Rays: 1 appearance—0 wins, 1 loss.
Seattle Mariners: 0 appearances.
Washington Nationals: 0 appearances.

WORLD SERIES BONUS POOL

The players' bonus pool is funded with 60 percent of the gate receipts from the first four games of the World Series. The series-winning team gets 35 percent, while the losing team gets 24 percent. Additionally, both league championship losers get 12 percent, while the four division losers get 3 percent. The four second-place teams that failed to qualify for postseason play also receive 1 percent.

There are separate bonus pools for each postseason playoff series. For all three levels of competition—division playoffs, league championships, and World Series—the bonus pool is funded with 60 percent of the gate, using receipts from the first three games of the division series and the first four from the league championships as well as the World Series.

PLAYER SHARES

Shares are voted on by team members who played the entire season. The voting session is chaired by the team's union representative. Players who were not with the team for the entire year may receive a full share, partial share, or no share at all, as determined at the team's meeting. Trainers, clubhouse personnel, and other nonplayers may also be voted full or partial shares. The pool of money is divided according to the number of shares determined by the vote. Thus, individual shares are a function of the size of the bonus pool and the number of shares awarded.

GAME SEQUENCE

World Series competitions use a 2–3–2 format. The first two games are played in the "home team" city (as determined by which league won the season's All-Star Game); the following three are at the visiting team's ballpark; and the final two return to the home city location. The 2–3–2 format is also used for league championship series. In 2001, baseball owners replaced the 2–2–1 format for division-level playoffs with a 2–3 game sequence with the home team hosting games 3, 4, and 5. A return to the 2–2–1 structure will be considered for the 2013 season.

NOTES

1. As the Brooklyn Robins, the franchise lost the World Series in 1916 and 1920. As the Brooklyn Dodgers, the organization won a World Series title in 1955 and lost series competitions in 1941, 1947, 1949, 1952, 1953, and 1956.

2. Five of the franchise's titles (1905, 1921, 1922, 1933, 1954) and eight of its series losses (1911, 1912, 1913, 1917, 1923, 1924, 1936, 1937) were as the New York Giants.

3. Five of the franchise's titles (1910, 1911, 1913, 1929, 1930) and three of its losses (1905, 1914, 1931) came as the Philadelphia Athletics.

4. As the Boston Braves, the franchise won a World Series title in 1914 and lost a series in 1948. When the organization moved to Milwaukee, the Braves won a World Series in 1957 and lost one in 1958.

5. As the St. Louis Browns, the franchise lost the 1944 World Series.

6. As the original Washington Senators, the franchise won the 1924 World Series and lost in 1925 and 1933.

7. The team competed as the Florida Marlins in the 1997 and 2003 World Series.

8. The Brewers competed in the 1982 World Series as an American League team. The franchise transferred to the National League in 1998.

Appendix C: Unassisted Triple Plays

Eric Brunlett, Philadelphia Phillies, 2B, August 23, 2009
Asdrubal Cabrera, Cleveland Indians, 2B, May 12, 2008
Troy Tulowitzki, Colorado Rockies, SS, April 29, 2007
Rafael Furcal, Atlanta Braves, SS, August 18, 2003
Randy Velarde, Oakland Athletics, 2B, May 29, 2000
John Valentin, Boston Red Sox, SS, July 8, 1994
Mickey Morandini, Philadelphia Phillies, 2B, September 20, 1992
Ron Hansen, Washington Senators, SS, July 20, 1968
Johnny Neun, Detroit Tigers, 1B, May 31, 1927
Jimmy Cooney, Chicago Cubs, SS, May 30, 1927
Glenn Wright, Pittsburgh Pirates, SS, May 7, 1925
Ernie Padgett, Boston Braves, SS, October 6, 1923
George Burns, Boston Red Sox, 1B, September 14, 1923
Bill Wambsganss, Cleveland Indians, 2B, October 10, 1920
Neal Ball, Cleveland Indians, SS, July 19, 1909

Note. 1B: first baseman. 2B: second baseman. SS: shortstop.

Appendix D: Perfect Games

Matt Cain, San Francisco Giants
    June 13, 2012, San Francisco 10, Houston 0
Philip Humber, Chicago White Sox
    April 21, 2012, Chicago 4, Seattle 0
Roy Halladay, Philadephia Phillies
    May 29, 2010, Philadelphia 1, Florida 0
Dallas Braden, Oakland Athletics
    May 9, 2010, Oakland 4, Tampa Bay 0
Mark Buehrle, Chicago White Sox
    July 23, 2009, Chicago 5, Tampa Bay 0
Randy Johnson, Arizona Diamondbacks
    May 18, 2004, Arizona 2, Atlanta 0
David Cone, New York Yankees
    July 18, 1999, New York 6, Montreal 0
David Wells, New York Yankees
    May 17, 1998, New York 4, Minnesota 0
Kenny Rogers, Texas Rangers
    July 28, 1994, Texas 4, California 0
Dennis Martinez, Montreal Expos
    July 28, 1991, Montreal 2, Los Angeles 0
Tom Browning, Cincinnati Reds
    September 16, 1988, Cincinnati 1, Los Angeles 0
Mike Witt, California Angels
    September 30, 1984, California 1, Texas 0
Len Barker, Cleveland Indians
    May 15, 1981, Cleveland 3, Toronto 0
Jim "Catfish" Hunter, Oakland A's

May 8, 1968, Oakland 4, Minnesota 0
Sandy Koufax, Los Angeles Dodgers
    September 9, 1965, Los Angeles 1, Chicago 0
Jim Bunning, Philadelphia Phillies
    June 21, 1964, Philadelphia 6, New York 0
Don Larsen, New York Yankees
    October 8, 1956, New York 2, Brooklyn 0[1]
Charles Robertson, Chicago White Sox
    April 30, 1922, Chicago 2, Detroit 0
Addie Joss, Cleveland Bronchos
    October 2, 1908, Cleveland 1, Chicago 0
Cy Young, Boston Americans
    May 5, 1904, Boston 3, Philadelphia 0
Monte Ward, Providence Grays
    June 17, 1880, Providence 5, Buffalo 0
Lee Richmond, Worcester Ruby Legs
    June 12, 1880, Worcester 1, Cleveland 0

OTHER "PERFECT" GAMES

Armando Galarraga, Detroit Tigers, June 2, 2010, Detroit 3, Cleveland 0.
Umpire Jim Joyce mistakenly called Cleveland batter Jason Donald safe at
first on what would have been the 27th and final out of a perfect game.
Replays showed Joyce missed the call. Devastated, Joyce later admitted the
mistake and apologized for it. Galarraga retired the next batter.
    Pedro Martinez, Montreal Expos, June 3, 1995, Montreal 1, San Diego 0.
Martinez pitched nine perfect innings before giving up a hit in the tenth.
    Harvey Haddix, Pittsburgh Pirates, May 26, 1959, Pittsburgh 0, Milwaukee 1. Haddix pitched 12 perfect innings but lost the game. See story 52.
    Ernie Shore, Boston Red Sox, June 23, 1917. See story 54. Some scholars
include Shore's game among the list of perfect games.

NOTE

1. Fifth game of World Series.

Appendix E: Hall of Fame Membership

1936: Ty Cobb, Walter Johnson, Christy Mathewson, Babe Ruth, Honus Wagner

1937: Morgan Bulkeley, Ban Johnson, Nap Lajoie, Connie Mack, John McGraw, Tris Speaker, George Wright, Cy Young

1938: Grover Cleveland Alexander, Alexander Cartwright, Henry Chadwick

1939: Cap Anson, Eddie Collins, Charles Comiskey, Candy Cummings, Buck Ewing, Lou Gehrig, Willie Keeler, Charles Radbourn, George Sisler, Albert Spalding

1942: Rogers Hornsby

1944: Kenesaw Mountain Landis

1945: Roger Bresnahan, Dan Brouthers, Fred Clarke, James Collins, Ed Delahanty, Hugh Duffy, Hugh Jennings, King Kelly, Orator O'Rourke, Wilbert Robinson

1946: Jesse Burkett, Frank Chance, Jack Chesbro, Johnny Evers, Clark Griffith, Tommy McCarthy, Joe McGinnity, Eddie Plank, Joe Tinker, Rube Waddell, Ed Walsh

1947: Mickey Cochrane, Frankie Frisch, Lefty Grove, Carl Hubbell

1948: Herb Pennock, Pie Traynor

1949: Mordecai Brown, Charlie Gehringer, Kid Nichols

1951: Jimmie Foxx, Mel Ott

1952: Harry Heilmann, Paul Waner

1953: Ed Barrow, Chief Bender, Tommy Connolly, Dizzy Dean, Bill Klem, Al Simmons, Bobby Wallace, Harry Wright

1954: Bill Dickey, Rabbit Maranville, Bill Terry

1955: Home Run Baker, Joe DiMaggio, Gabby Hartnett, Ted Lyons, Ray Schalk, Dazzy Vance

1956: Joe Cronin, Hank Greenberg
1957: Sam Crawford, Joe McCarthy
1959: Zack Wheat
1961: Max Carey, Billy Hamilton
1962: Bob Feller, Bill McKechnie, Jackie Robinson, Edd Roush
1963: John Clarkson, Elmer Flick, Sam Rice, Eppa Rixey
1964: Luke Appling, Red Faber, Burleigh Grimes, Miller Huggins, Timothy Keefe, Heinie Manush, John Montgomery Ward
1965: Pud Galvin
1966: Casey Stengel, Ted Williams
1967: Branch Rickey, Red Ruffing, Lloyd Waner
1968: Kiki Cuyler, Goose Goslin, Joe Medwick
1969: Roy Campanella, Stan Coveleski, Waite Hoyt, Stan Musial
1970: Lou Boudreau, Earle Combs, Ford Frick, Jesse Haines
1971: Dave Bancroft, Jake Beckley, Chick Hafey, Harry Hooper, Joseph Kelley, Rube Marquard, Satchel Paige, George Weiss
1972: Yogi Berra, Josh Gibson, Lefty Gomez, Will Harridge, Sandy Koufax, Buck Leonard, Early Wynn, Ross Youngs
1973: Roberto Clemente, Billy Evans, Monte Irvin, George Kelly, Warren Spahn, Mickey Welch
1974: Cool Papa Bell, Jim Bottomley, Jocko Conlan, Whitey Ford, Mickey Mantle, Sam Thomson
1975: Earl Averill, Bucky Harris, Billy Herman, Judy Johnson, Ralph Kiner
1976: Oscar Charleston, Roger Connor, Cal Hubbard, Bob Lemon, Fred Lindstrom, Robin Roberts
1977: Ernie Banks, Martin Dihigo, Pop Lloyd, Al Lopez, Amos Rusie, Joe Sewell
1978: Addie Joss, Larry MacPhail, Eddie Mathews
1979: Warren Giles, Willie Mays, Hack Wilson
1980: Al Kaline, Chuck Klein, Duke Snider, Tom Yawkey
1981: Rube Foster, Bob Gibson, Johnny Mize
1982: Hank Aaron, Happy Chandler, Travis Jackson, Frank Robinson
1983: Walter Alston, George Kell, Juan Marichal, Brooks Robinson
1984: Luis Aparicio, Don Drysdale, Rick Ferrell, Harmon Killebrew, Pee Wee Reese
1985: Lou Brock, Country Slaughter, Arky Vaughan, Hoyt Wilhelm
1986: Bobby Doerr, Ernie Lombardi, Willie McCovey
1987: Ray Dandridge, Catfish Hunter, Billy Williams
1988: Willie Stargell
1989: Al Barlick, Johnny Bench, Red Schoendienst, Carl Yastrzemski
1990: Joe Morgan, Jim Palmer

1991: Rod Carew, Fergie Jenkins, Tony Lazzeri, Gaylord Perry, Bill Veeck

1992: Rollie Fingers, Bill McGowan, Hal Newhouser, Tom Seaver

1993: Reggie Jackson

1994: Steve Carlton, Leo Durocher, Phil Rizzuto

1995: Richie Ashburn, Leon Day, William Hulbert, Mike Schmidt, Vic Willis

1996: Jim Bunning, Bill Foster, Ned Hanlon, Earl Weaver

1997: Nellie Fox, Tommy Lasorda, Phil Niekro, Willie Wells

1998: George Davis, Larry Doby, Lee MacPhail, Bullet Rogan, Don Sutton

1999: George Brett, Orlando Cepeda, Nestor Chylak, Nolan Ryan, Frank Selee, Smokey Williams, Robin Yount

2000: Sparky Anderson, Carlton Fisk, Bid McPhee, Tony Perez, Turkey Stearnes

2001: Bill Mazeroski, Kirby Puckett, Hilton Smith, Dave Winfield

2002: Ozzie Smith

2003: Gary Carter, Eddie Murray

2004: Dennis Eckersley, Paul Molitor

2005: Wade Boggs, Ryne Sandberg

2006: Raymond Brown, Willard Brown, Andy Cooper, Franklin Grant, Pete Hill, Biz Mackey, Effa Manley, Jose Mendez, Alex Pompez, Cum Posey, Louis Santop, Bruce Sutter, Mule Suttles, Ben Taylor, Cristobal Torriente, Solomon White, J. L. Wilkinson, Jud Wilson

2007: Tony Gwynn, Cal Ripken Jr.

2008: Barney Dreyfuss, Goose Gossage, Bowie Kuhn, Walter O'Malley, Billy Southworth, Dick Williams

2009: Joe Gordon, Rickey Henderson, Jim Rice

2010: Andre Dawson, Doug Harvey, Whitey Herzog

2011: Roberto Alomar, Bert Blyleven, Pat Gillick

2012: Barry Larkin, Ron Santo

There are 297 members of the Hall of Fame following the 2012 election. The membership composition consists of 72 pitchers, 16 catchers, 21 first basemen, 20 second basemen, 15 third basemen, 24 shortstops, 21 left fielders, 23 center fielders, 24 right fielders, 20 managers, 9 umpires, and 32 executives. The large 2006 class consists, in part, of 17 selections made by the Special Committee on Negro Leagues.

Appendix F: Major League Ballparks

AMERICAN LEAGUE

Baltimore Orioles

Ballpark: Camden Yards
   Capacity: 45,971
   Dimensions: 333L, 364LC, 410C, 373RC, 318R

Boston Red Sox

Ballpark: Fenway Park
   Capacity: 39,928
   Dimensions: 310L, 379LC, 420C, 380RC, 302R

Chicago White Sox

Ballpark: U.S. Cellular Field
   Capacity: 40,615
   Dimensions: 330L, 377LC, 400C, 372RC, 335R

Cleveland Indians

Ballpark: Progressive Field
   Capacity: 43,405
   Dimensions: 325L, 370LC, 405C, 375RC, 325R

Detroit Tigers

Ballpark: Comerica Park
   Capacity: 40,120

Dimensions: 345L, 382LC, 420C, 365RC, 330R

Houston Astros

Ballpark: Minute Maid Park
   Capacity: 40,950
   Dimensions: 315L, 362LC, 435C, 373RC, 326R

Kansas City Royals

Ballpark: Kauffman Stadium
   Capacity: 38,177
   Dimensions: 330L, 390LC, 410C, 390RC, 330R

Los Angeles Angels

Ballpark: Angel Stadium
   Capacity: 45,050
   Dimensions: 330L, 387LC, 400C, 370RC, 330R

Minnesota Twins

Ballpark: Target Field
   Capacity: 39,504
   Dimensions: 339L, 377LC, 411C, 365RC, 328R

New York Yankees

Ballpark: Yankee Stadium
   Capacity: 52,325
   Dimensions: 318L, 399LC, 408C, 385RC, 314R

Oakland A's

Ballpark: O.co Coliseum
   Capacity: 34,007
   Dimensions: 330L, 375LC, 400C, 375RC, 330R

Seattle Mariners

Ballpark: Safeco Field
   Capacity: 47,447
   Dimensions: 331L, 390LC, 405C, 387RC, 327R

Tampa Bay Rays

Ballpark: Tropicana Field

Capacity: 43,772
Dimensions: 315L, 370LC, 404C, 370RC, 322R

Texas Rangers

Ballpark: Rangers Ballpark in Arlington
  Capacity: 48,911
  Dimensions: 332L, 390LC, 400C, 377RC, 325R

Toronto Blue Jays

Ballpark: Rogers Centre
  Capacity: 50,516
  Dimensions: 328L, 375LC, 400C, 375RC, 328R

NATIONAL LEAGUE

Arizona Diamondbacks

Ballpark: Chase Field
  Capacity: 49,033
  Dimensions: 330L, 413LC, 407C, 374RC, 334R

Atlanta Braves

Ballpark: Turner Field
  Capacity: 50,096
  Dimensions: 335L, 380LC, 400C, 385RC, 330R

Chicago Cubs

Ballpark: Wrigley Field
  Capacity: 41,118
  Dimensions: 355L, 368LC, 400C, 368RC, 353R

Cincinnati Reds

Ballpark: Great American Ballpark
  Capacity: 42,271
  Dimensions: 325L, 379LC, 404C, 370RC, 328R

Colorado Rockies

Ballpark: Coors Field
  Capacity: 50,445

Dimensions: 347L, 390LC, 415C, 375RC, 350R

Los Angeles Dodgers

Ballpark: Dodger Stadium
  Capacity: 56,000
  Dimensions: 330L, 375LC, 400C, 375RC, 330R

Miami Marlins

Ballpark: Marlins Ballpark
  Capacity: 37,000
  Dimensions: 340L, 384LC, 420C, 392RC, 335R

Milwaukee Brewers

Ballpark: Miller Park
  Capacity: 41,900
  Dimensions: 332L, 390LC, 400C, 381RC, 325R

New York Mets

Ballpark: Citi Field
  Capacity: 42,000
  Dimensions: 335L, 379LC, 408C, 383RC, 330R

Philadelphia Phillies

Ballpark: Citizens Bank Park
  Capacity: 43,647
  Dimensions: 330L, 374LC, 401C, 369RC, 329R

Pittsburgh Pirates

Ballpark: PNC Park
  Capacity: 38,496
  Dimensions: 325L, 389LC, 399C, 375RC, 320R

San Diego Padres

Ballpark: Petco Park
  Capacity: 42,500
  Dimensions: 334L, 367LC, 396C, 385RC, 322R

San Francisco Giants

Ballpark: AT&T Park

Capacity: 41,600
Dimensions: 339L, 364LC, 399C, 421RC, 309R

St. Louis Cardinals

Ballpark: Busch Stadium
   Capacity: 46,700
   Dimensions: 336L, 390LC, 400C, 390RC, 335R

Washington Nationals

Ballpark: Nationals Park
   Capacity: 41,222
   Dimensions: 336L, 377LC, 403C, 370RC, 335R

Note. L: left field. LC: left-center field. C: center field. RC: right-center field. R: right field.

Appendix G: Batting Champions

Year	American League	National League
1901	Nap Lajoie, Philadelphia, .426	Jessie Burkett, St. Louis, .376
1902	Ed Delahanty, Washington, .376*	Ginger Beaumont, Pittsburgh, .357
1903	Nap Lajoie, Cleveland, .344	Honus Wagner, Pittsburgh, .355
1904	Nap Lajoie, Cleveland, .376	Honus Wagner, Pittsburgh, .349
1905	Elmer Flick, Cleveland, .308	Cy Seymour, Cincinnati, .377
1906	George Stone, St. Louis, .358	Honus Wagner, Pittsburgh, .339
1907	Ty Cobb, Detroit, .350	Honus Wagner, Pittsburgh, .350
1908	Ty Cobb, Detroit, .324	Honus Wagner, Pittsburgh, .354
1909	Ty Cobb, Detroit, .377	Honus Wagner, Pittsburgh, .339
1910	Ty Cobb, Detroit, .385*	Sherry Magee, Philadelphia, .331
1911	Ty Cobb, Detroit, .420	Honus Wagner, Pittsburgh, .334
1912	Ty Cobb, Detroit, .409	Heinie Zimmerman, Chicago, .372
1913	Ty Cobb, Detroit, .390	Jake Daubert, Brooklyn, 350
1914	Ty Cobb, Detroit, .368	Jake Daubert, Brooklyn, .329
1915	Ty Cobb, Detroit, .369	Larry Doyle, New York, .320
1916	Tris Speaker, Cleveland, .386	Hal Chase, Cincinnati, .339
1917	Ty Cobb, Detroit, .383	Edd Roush, Cincinnati, .341
1918	Ty Cobb, Detroit, .382	Zack Wheat, Brooklyn, .335
1919	Ty Cobb, Detroit, .384	Edd Roush, Cincinnati, .321

1920	George Sisler, St. Louis, .407	Rogers Hornsby, St. Louis, .370
1921	Harry Heilmann, Detroit, .394	Rogers Hornsby, St. Louis, .397
1922	George Sisler, St. Louis, .420	Rogers Hornsby, St. Louis, .401
1923	Harry Heilmann, Detroit, .403	Rogers Hornsby, St. Louis, .384
1924	Babe Ruth, New York, .378	Rogers Hornsby, St. Louis, .424
1925	Harry Heilmann, Detroit, .393	Rogers Hornsby, St. Louis, .403
1926	Heinie Manush, Detroit, .378	Bubbles Hargrave, Cincinnati, .353
1927	Harry Heilmann, Detroit, .398	Paul Waner, Pittsburgh, .380
1928	Goose Goslin, Washington, .379	Rogers Hornsby, Boston, .387
1929	Lew Fonseca, Cleveland, .369	Lefty O'Doul, Philadelphia, .398
1930	Al Simmons, Philadelphia, .381	Bill Terry, New York, .401
1931	Al Simmons, Philadelphia, .390	Chick Hafey, St. Louis, .349
1932	Dale Alexander, Det/Bos, .367	Lefty O'Doul, Brooklyn, .368
1933	Jimmie Foxx, Philadelphia, .356	Chuck Klein, Philadelphia, .368
1934	Lou Gehrig, New York, .363	Paul Waner, Pittsburgh, .362
1935	Buddy Myer, Washington, .349	Arky Vaughan, Pittsburgh, .385
1936	Luke Appling, Chicago, .388	Paul Waner, Pittsburgh, .373
1937	Charlie Gehringer, Detroit, .371	Joe Medwick, St. Louis, .374
1938	Jimmie Foxx, Boston, .349	Ernie Lombardi, Cincinnati, .342
1939	Joe DiMaggio, New York, .381	Johnny Mize, St. Louis, .349
1940	Joe DiMaggio, New York, .352	Debs Garms, Pittsburgh, .355
1941	Ted Williams, Boston, .406	Pete Reiser, Brooklyn, .343
1942	Ted Williams, Boston, .356	Ernie Lombardi, Boston, .330
1943	Luke Appling, Chicago, .328	Stan Musial, St. Louis, .357
1944	Lou Boudreau, Cleveland, .327	Dixie Walker, Brooklyn, .357

1945	Snuffy Stirnweiss, New York, .309	Phil Cavarretta, Chicago, .355
1946	Mickey Vernon, Washington, .353	Stan Musial, St. Louis, .365
1947	Ted Williams, Boston, .343	Harry Walker, StL/Phi, .363
1948	Ted Williams, Boston, .369	Stan Musial, St. Louis, .376
1949	George Kell, Detroit, .343	Jackie Robinson, Brooklyn, .342
1950	Billy Goodman, Boston, .354	Stan Musial, St. Louis, .346
1951	Ferris Fain, Philadelphia, .344	Stan Musial, St. Louis, .355
1952	Ferris Fain, Philadelphia, .327	Stan Musial, St. Louis, .336
1953	Mickey Vernon, Washington, .337	Carl Furillo, Brooklyn, .344
1954	Bobby Avila, Cleveland, .341	Willie Mays, New York, .345
1955	Al Kaline, Detroit, .340	Richie Ashburn, Philadelphia, .338
1956	Mickey Mantle, New York, .353	Hank Aaron, Milwaukee, .328
1957	Ted Williams, Boston, .388	Stan Musial, St. Louis, .351
1958	Ted Williams, Boston, .328	Richie Ashburn, Philadelphia, .350
1959	Harvey Kuenn, Detroit, .353	Hank Aaron, Milwaukee, .355
1960	Pete Runnels, Boston, .320	Dick Groat, Pittsburgh, .325
1961	Norm Cash, Detroit, .361	Roberto Clemente, Pittsburgh, .351
1962	Pete Runnels, Boston, .326	Tommy Davis, Los Angeles, .346
1963	Carl Yastrzemski, Boston, .321	Tommy Davis, Los Angeles, .326
1964	Tony Oliva, Minnesota, .323	Roberto Clemente, Pittsburgh, .339
1965	Tony Oliva, Minnesota, .321	Roberto Clemente, Pittsburgh, .329
1966	Frank Robinson, Baltimore, .316	Matty Alou, Pittsburgh, .342
1967	Carl Yastrzemski, Boston, .326	Roberto Clemente, Pittsburgh, .357
1968	Carl Yastrzemski, Boston, .301	Pete Rose, Cincinnati, .335
1969	Rod Carew, Minnesota, .332	Pete Rose, Cincinnati, .348
1970	Alex Johnson, California, .329	Rico Carty, Atlanta, .366

1971	Tony Oliva, Minnesota, .337	Joe Torre, St. Louis, .363
1972	Rod Carew, Minnesota, .318	Billy Williams, Chicago, .333
1973	Rod Carew, Minnesota, .350	Pete Rose, Cincinnati, .338
1974	Rod Carew, Minnesota, .364	Ralph Garr, Atlanta, .353
1975	Rod Carew, Minnesota, .359	Bill Madlock, Chicago, .354
1976	George Brett, Kansas City, .333	Bill Madlock, Chicago, .339
1977	Rod Carew, Minnesota, .388	Dave Parker, Pittsburgh, .338
1978	Rod Carew, Minnesota, .333	Dave Parker, Pittsburgh, .334
1979	Fred Lynn, Boston, .333	Keith Hernandez, St. Louis, .344
1980	George Brett, Kansas City, .390	Bill Buckner, Chicago, .324
1981	Carney Lansford, Boston, .336	Bill Madlock, Pittsburgh, .341
1982	Willie Wilson, Kansas City, .332	Al Oliver, Montreal, .331
1983	Wade Boggs, Boston, .361	Bill Madlock, Pittsburgh, .323
1984	Don Mattingly, New York, .343	Tony Gwynn, San Diego, .351
1985	Wade Boggs, Boston, .368	Willie McGee, St. Louis, .353
1986	Wade Boggs, Boston, .357	Tim Raines, Montreal, .334
1987	Wade Boggs, Boston, .363	Tony Gwynn, San Diego, .370
1988	Wade Boggs, Boston, .366	Tony Gwynn, San Diego, .313
1989	Kirby Puckett, Minnesota, .339	Tony Gwynn, San Diego, .336
1990	George Brett, Kansas City, .329	Willie McGee, St. Louis, .335
1991	Julio Franco, Texas, .341	Terry Pendleton, Atlanta, .319
1992	Edgar Martinez, Seattle, .343	Gary Sheffield, San Diego, .330
1993	John Olerud, Toronto, .363	Andres Galarraga, Colorado, .370
1994	Paul O'Neill, New York, .359	Tony Gwynn, San Diego, .394
1995	Edgar Martinez, Seattle, .356	Tony Gwynn, San Diego, .368
1996	Alex Rodriguez, Seattle, .358	Tony Gwynn, San Diego, .353
1997	Frank Thomas, Chicago, .347	Tony Gwynn, San Diego, .372

1998	Bernie Williams, New York, .339	Larry Walker, Colorado, .363
1999	Nomar Garciaparra, Boston, .357	Larry Walker, Colorado, .379
2000	Nomar Garciaparra, Boston, .372	Todd Helton, Colorado, .372
2001	Ichiro Suzuki, Seattle, .350	Larry Walker, Colorado, .350
2002	Manny Ramirez, Boston, .349	Barry Bonds, San Francisco, .370
2003	Bill Mueller, Boston, .326	Albert Pujols, St. Louis, .359
2004	Ichiro Suzuki, Seattle, .372	Barry Bonds, San Francisco, .362
2005	Michael Young, Texas, .331	Derrek Lee, Chicago, .335
2006	Joe Mauer, Minnesota, .347	Freddy Sanchez, Pittsburgh, .344
2007	Maglio Ordonez, Detroit, .363	Matt Holliday, Colorado, .340
2008	Joe Mauer, Minnesota, .328	Chipper Jones, Atlanta, .364
2009	Joe Mauer, Minnesota, .365	Hanley Ramirez, Florida, .342
2010	Josh Hamilton, Texas, .359	Carlos Gonzales, Colorado, .336
2011	Miguel Cabrera, Detroit, .344	Jose Reyes, New York, .337

*The 1902 and 1910 titles are disputed. Some scholars award both titles to Nap Lajoie.

ELIGIBILITY

To qualify for a batting title, a hitter must have at least 3.1 plate appearances per team game—a total of 502 for a 162-game season. However, if a player's lead in batting average is such that enough hitless at bats can be added to his total to reach the 502 requirement and the player still has the highest batting average, he is awarded the title. Example: A player with the highest numerical average has only 492 plate appearances. If after 10 additional hitless plate appearances are added (to reach the 502 total), he still has the highest average, he is designated the batting champion.

Appendix H: Home Run Champions

Year	American League	National League
1901	Nap Lajoie, Philadelphia, 14	Sam Crawford, Cincinnati, 16
1902	Socks Seybold, Philadelphia, 16	Tommy Leach, Pittsburgh, 6
1903	Buck Freeman, Boston, 13	Jimmy Sheckard, Brooklyn, 9
1904	Harry Davis, Philadelphia, 10	Harry Lumley, Brooklyn, 9
1905	Harry Davis, Philadelphia, 8	Fred Odwell, Cincinnati, 9
1906	Harry Davis, Philadelphia, 12	Tim Jordan, Brooklyn, 12
1907	Harry Davis, Philadelphia, 8	Dave Brain, Boston, 10
1908	Sam Crawford, Detroit, 7	Tim Jordan, Brooklyn, 12
1909	Ty Cobb, Detroit, 9	Red Murray, New York, 7
1910	Jake Stahl, Boston, 10	Frank Schulte, Boston, 10
		Fred Beck, Chicago, 10
1911	Home Run Baker, Philadelphia, 11	Frank Schulte, Chicago, 21
1912	Home Run Baker, Philadelphia, 10	Heinie Zimmerman, Chicago, 14
	Tris Speaker, Boston, 10	
1913	Home Run Baker, Philadelphia, 12	Gavvy Cravath, Philadelphia, 19
1914	Home Run Baker, Philadelphia, 9	Gavvy Cravath, Philadelphia, 19

1915	Braggo Roth, Chicago/ Cleveland, 7	Gavvy Cravath, Philadelphia, 24
1916	Wally Pipp, New York, 12	Cy Williams, Chicago, 12
		Dave Robertson, New York, 12
1917	Wally Pipp, New York, 9	Gavvy Cravath, Philadelphia, 12
1918	Babe Ruth, Boston, 11	Gavvy Cravath, Philadelphia, 8
	Tilly Walker, Philadelphia, 11	
1919	Babe Ruth, Boston, 29	Gavvy Cravath, Philadelphia, 12
1920	Babe Ruth, New York, 54	Cy Williams, Philadelphia, 13
1921	Babe Ruth, New York, 59	George Kelly, New York, 23
1922	Ken Williams, St. Louis, 39	Rogers Hornsby, St. Louis, 42
1923	Babe Ruth, New York, 41	Cy Williams, Philadelphia, 41
1924	Babe Ruth, New York, 46	Jack Fournier, Brooklyn, 27
1925	Bob Meusel, New York, 33	Rogers Hornsby, St. Louis, 39
1926	Babe Ruth, New York, 47	Hack Wilson, Chicago, 21
1927	Babe Ruth, New York, 60	Cy Williams, Philadelphia, 30
		Hack Wilson, Chicago, 30
1928	Babe Ruth, New York, 54	Hack Wilson, Chicago, 31
		Jim Bottomley, St. Louis, 31
1929	Babe Ruth, New York, 46	Chuck Klein, Philadelphia, 43
1930	Babe Ruth, New York, 49	Hack Wilson, Chicago, 56
1931	Babe Ruth, New York, 46	Chuck Klein, Philadelphia, 31
	Lou Gehrig, New York, 46	
1932	Jimmie Foxx, Philadelphia, 58	Chuck Klein, Philadelphia, 38
		Mel Ott, New York, 38
1933	Jimmie Foxx, Philadelphia, 48	Chuck Klein, Philadelphia, 28
1934	Lou Gehrig, New York, 49	Mel Ott, New York, 35
1935	Hank Greenberg, Detroit, 36	Wally Berger, Boston, 34
	Jimmie Foxx, Philadelphia, 36	
1936	Lou Gehrig, New York, 49	Mel Ott, New York, 33
1937	Joe DiMaggio, New York, 46	Mel Ott, New York, 31
		Joe Medwick, St. Louis, 31

1938	Hank Greenberg, Detroit, 58	Mel Ott, New York, 36
1939	Jimmie Foxx, Boston, 35	Johnny Mize, St. Louis, 28
1940	Hank Greenberg, Detroit, 41	Johnny Mize, St. Louis, 43
1941	Ted Williams, Boston, 37	Dolph Camilli, Brooklyn, 34
1942	Ted Williams, Boston, 36	Mel Ott, New York, 30
1943	Rudy York, Detroit, 34	Bill Nicholson, Chicago, 20
1944	Nick Etten, New York, 22	Bill Nicholson, Chicago, 33
1945	Vern Stephens, St. Louis, 24	Tommy Holmes, Boston, 28
1946	Hank Greenberg, Detroit, 44	Ralph Kiner, Pittsburgh, 23
1947	Ted Williams, Boston, 32	Ralph Kiner, Pittsburgh, 51
		Johnny Mize, New York, 51
1948	Joe DiMaggio, New York, 39	Ralph Kiner, Pittsburgh, 40
		Johnny Mize, New York, 40
1949	Ted Williams, Boston, 43	Ralph Kiner, Pittsburgh, 54
1950	Al Rosen, Cleveland, 37	Ralph Kiner, Pittsburgh, 47
1951	Gus Zernial, Chicago/ Philadelphia, 33	Ralph Kiner, Pittsburgh, 42
1952	Larry Doby, Cleveland, 32	Ralph Kiner, Pittsburgh, 37
		Hank Sauer, Chicago, 37
1953	Al Rosen, Cleveland, 43	Eddie Mathews, Milwaukee, 47
1954	Larry Doby, Cleveland, 32	Ted Kluszewski, Cincinnati, 49
1955	Mickey Mantle, New York, 37	Willie Mays, New York, 51
1956	Mickey Mantle, New York, 52	Duke Snider, Brooklyn, 43
1957	Roy Sievers, Washington, 42	Hank Aaron, Milwaukee, 44
1958	Mickey Mantle, New York, 42	Ernie Banks, Chicago, 47
1959	Harmon Killebrew, Washington, 42	Eddie Mathews, Milwaukee, 46
	Rocky Colavito, Cleveland, 42	
1960	Mickey Mantle, New York, 40	Ernie Banks, Chicago, 41
1961	Roger Maris, New York, 61	Orlando Cepeda, San Francisco, 46
1962	Harmon Killebrew, Minnesota, 48	Willie Mays, San Francisco, 49

1963	Harmon Killebrew, Minnesota, 45	Willie McCovey, San Francisco, 44
		Hank Aaron, Milwaukee, 44
1964	Harmon Killebrew, Minnesota, 49	Willie Mays, San Francisco, 47
1965	Tony Conigliaro, Boston, 32	Willie Mays, San Francisco, 52
1966	Frank Robinson, Baltimore, 49	Hank Aaron, Atlanta, 44
1967	Carl Yastrzemski, Boston, 44 Harmon Killebrew, Minnesota, 44	Hank Aaron, Atlanta, 39
1968	Frank Howard, Washington, 44	Willie McCovey, San Francisco, 36
1969	Harmon Killebrew, Minnesota, 49	Willie McCovey, San Francisco, 45
1970	Frank Howard, Washington, 44	Johnny Bench, Cincinnati, 45
1971	Bill Melton, Chicago, 33	Willie Stargell, Pittsburgh, 48
1972	Dick Allen, Chicago, 37	Johnny Bench, Cincinnati, 40
1973	Reggie Jackson, Oakland, 32	Willie Stargell, Pittsburgh, 44
1974	Dick Allen, Chicago, 32	Mike Schmidt, Philadelphia, 36
1975	Reggie Jackson, Oakland, 36 George Scott, Boston, 36	Mike Schmidt, Philadelphia, 38
1976	Craig Nettles, New York, 32	Mike Schmidt, Philadelphia, 38
1977	Jim Rice, Boston, 39	George Foster, Cincinnati, 52
1978	Jim Rice, Boston, 46	George Foster, Cincinnati, 40
1979	Gorman Thomas, Milwaukee, 45	Dave Kingman, Chicago, 48
1980	Reggie Jackson, New York, 41 Ben Oglivie, Milwaukee, 41	Mike Schmidt, Philadelphia, 48
1981	Bobby Grich, California, 22 Eddie Murray, Baltimore, 22 Dwight Evans, Boston, 22 Tony Armas, Oakland, 22	Mike Schmidt, Philadelphia, 31
1982	Reggie Jackson, California, 39	Dave Kingman, New York, 37

Gorman Thomas, Milwaukee, 39

1983	Jim Rice, Boston, 39	Mike Schmidt, Philadelphia, 40
1984	Tony Armas, Boston, 43	Mike Schmidt, Philadelphia, 36
		Dale Murphy, Atlanta, 36
1985	Darrell Evans, Detroit, 40	Dale Murphy, Atlanta, 37
1986	Jesse Barfield, Toronto, 40	Mike Schmidt, Philadelphia, 37
1987	Mark McGwire, Oakland, 49	Andre Dawson, Chicago, 49
1988	Jose Canseco, Oakland, 42	Darryl Strawberry, New York, 39
1989	Fred McGriff, Toronto, 36	Kevin Mitchell, San Francisco, 47
1990	Cecil Fielder, Detroit, 51	Ryne Sandberg, Chicago, 40
1991	Jose Canseco, Oakland, 44	Howard Johnson, New York, 38
	Cecil Fielder, Detroit, 44	
1992	Juan Gonzalez, Texas, 43	Fred McGriff, San Diego, 35
1993	Juan Gonzalez, Texas, 46	Barry Bonds, San Francisco, 46
1994	Ken Griffey Jr., Seattle, 40	Matt Williams, San Francisco, 43
1995	Albert Belle, Cleveland, 50	Dante Bichette, Colorado, 40
1996	Mark McGwire, Oakland, 52	Andres Galarraga, Colorado, 47
1997	Ken Griffey Jr., Seattle, 56	Larry Walker, Colorado, 49
1998	Ken Griffey Jr., Seattle, 56	Mark McGwire, St. Louis, 70
1999	Ken Griffey Jr., Seattle, 48	Mark McGwire, St. Louis, 65
2000	Troy Glaus, Anaheim, 47	Sammy Sosa, Chicago, 50
2001	Alex Rodriguez, Texas, 52	Barry Bonds, San Francisco, 73
2002	Alex Rodriguez, Texas, 57	Sammy Sosa, Chicago, 49
2003	Alex Rodriguez, Texas, 47	Jim Thome, Philadelphia, 47
2004	Manny Ramirez, Boston, 43	Adrian Beltre, Los Angeles, 48
2005	Alex Rodriguez, New York, 48	Andruw Jones, Atlanta, 51
2006	David Ortiz, Boston, 54	Ryan Howard, Philadelphia, 58
2007	Alex Rodriguez, New York, 54	Prince Fielder, Milwaukee, 50
2008	Miguel Cabrera, Detroit, 37	Ryan Howard, Philadelphia, 48
2009	Carlos Pena, Tampa Bay, 39	Albert Pujols, St. Louis, 47

Mark Teixeira, New York, 39

| 2010 | Jose Bautista, Toronto, 54 | Albert Pujols, St. Louis, 42 |
| 2011 | Jose Bautista, Toronto, 43 | Matt Kemp, Los Angeles, 39 |

Appendix I: Triple Crown Winners

1901: Nap Lajoie, Philadelphia (AL), .426 batting average, 14 home runs, 125 RBI

1909: Ty Cobb, Detroit (AL), .377 batting average, 9 home runs, 107 RBI

1922: Rogers Hornsby, St. Louis (NL), .401 batting average, 42 home runs, 152 RBI

1925: Rogers Hornsby, St. Louis (NL), .403 batting average, 39 home runs, 143 RBI

1933: Chuck Klein, Philadelphia (NL), .368 batting average, 28 home runs, 120 RBI

1933: Jimmie Foxx, Philadelphia (AL), .356 batting average, 48 home runs, 163 RBI

1934: Lou Gehrig, New York (AL), .363 batting average, 49 home runs, 165 RBI

1937: Joe Medwick, St. Louis (NL): .374 batting average, 31 home runs, 154 RBI

1942: Ted Williams, Boston (AL), .356 batting average, 36 home runs, 137 RBI

1947: Ted Williams, Boston (AL), .343 batting average, 32 home runs, 114 RBI

1956: Mickey Mantle, New York (AL), .353 batting average, 52 home runs, 130 RBI

1966: Frank Robinson, Baltimore (AL), .316 batting average, 49 home runs, 122 RBI

1967: Carl Yastrzemski, Boston (AL), .326 batting average, 44 home runs, 121 RBI

Note. AL: American League. NL: National League.

Appendix J: Most Valuable Player Award Winners

Year	American League	National League
1931	Lefty Grove, Philadelphia, P	Frankie Frisch, St. Louis, 2B
1932	Jimmie Foxx, Philadelphia, 1B	Chuck Klein, Philadelphia, OF
1933	Jimmie Foxx, Philadelphia, 1B	Carl Hubbell, New York, P
1934	Mickey Cochrane, Detroit, C	Dizzy Dean, St. Louis, P
1935	Hank Greenberg, Detroit, 1B	Gabby Hartnett, Chicago, C
1936	Lou Gehrig, New York, 1B	Carl Hubbell, New York, P
1937	Charlie Gehringer, Detroit, 2B	Joe Medwick, St. Louis, OF
1938	Jimmie Foxx, Boston, 1B	Ernie Lombardi, Cincinnati, C
1939	Joe DiMaggio, New York, OF	Bucky Walters, Cincinnati, P
1940	Hank Greenberg, Detroit, OF	Frank McCormick, Cincinnati, 1B
1941	Joe DiMaggio, New York, OF	Dolph Camilli, Brooklyn, 1B
1942	Joe Gordon, New York, 2B	Mort Cooper, St. Louis, P
1943	Spud Chandler, New York, P	Stan Musial, St. Louis, OF
1944	Hal Newhouser, Detroit, P	Marty Marion, St. Louis, SS
1945	Hal Newhouser, Detroit, P	Phil Cavarretta, Chicago, 1B
1946	Ted Williams, Boston, OF	Stan Musial, St. Louis, OF
1947	Joe DiMaggio, New York, OF	Bob Elliott, Boston, 3B

1948	Lou Boudreau, Cleveland, SS	Stan Musial, St. Louis, OF
1949	Ted Williams, Boston, OF	Jackie Robinson, Brooklyn, 2B
1950	Phil Rizzuto, New York, SS	Jim Konstanty, Philadelphia, P
1951	Yogi Berra, New York, C	Roy Campanella, Brooklyn, C
1952	Bobby Shantz, Philadelphia, P	Hank Sauer, Chicago, OF
1953	Al Rosen, Cleveland, 3B	Roy Campanella, Brooklyn, C
1954	Yogi Berra, New York, C	Willie Mays, New York, OF
1955	Yogi Berra, New York, C	Roy Campanella, Brooklyn, C
1956	Mickey Mantle, New York, OF	Don Newcombe, Brooklyn, P
1957	Mickey Mantle, New York, OF	Hank Aaron, Milwaukee, OF
1958	Jackie Jensen, Boston, OF	Ernie Banks, Chicago, SS
1959	Nellie Fox, Chicago, 2B	Ernie Banks, Chicago, SS
1960	Roger Maris, New York, OF	Dick Groat, Pittsburgh, SS
1961	Roger Maris, New York, OF	Frank Robinson, Cincinnati, OF
1962	Mickey Mantle, New York, OF	Maury Wills, Los Angeles, SS
1963	Elston Howard, New York, C	Sandy Koufax, Los Angeles, P
1964	Brooks Robinson, Baltimore, 3B	Ken Boyer, St. Louis, 3B
1965	Zoilo Versalles, Minnesota, SS	Willie Mays, San Francisco, OF
1966	Frank Robinson, Baltimore, OF	Roberto Clemente, Pittsburgh, OF
1967	Carl Yastrzemski, Boston, OF	Orlando Cepeda, St. Louis, 1B
1968	Denny McLain, Detroit, P	Bob Gibson, St. Louis, P
1969	Harmon Killebrew, Minnesota, 3B	Willie McCovey, San Francisco, 1B
1970	Boog Powell, Baltimore, 1B	Johnny Bench, Cincinnati, C
1971	Vida Blue, Oakland, P	Joe Torre, St. Louis, 3B
1972	Dick Allen, Chicago, 1B	Johnny Bench, Cincinnati, C
1973	Reggie Jackson, Oakland, OF	Pete Rose, Cincinnati, OF
1974	Jeff Burroughs, Texas, OF	Steve Garvey, Los Angeles, 1B

1975	Fred Lynn, Boston, OF	Joe Morgan, Cincinnati, 2B
1976	Thurman Munson, New York, C	Joe Morgan, Cincinnati, 2B
1977	Rod Carew, Minnesota, 1B	George Foster, Cincinnati, OF
1978	Jim Rice, Boston, OF	Dave Parker, Pittsburgh, OF
1979	Don Baylor, California, DH	Keith Hernandez, St. Louis, 1B Willie Stargell, Pittsburgh, 1B
1980	George Brett, Kansas City, 3B	Mike Schmidt, Philadelphia, 3B
1981	Rollie Fingers, Milwaukee, P	Mike Schmidt, Philadelphia, 3B
1982	Robin Yount, Milwaukee, SS	Dale Murphy, Atlanta, OF
1983	Cal Ripken Jr., Baltimore, SS	Dale Murphy, Atlanta, OF
1984	Willie Hernandez, Detroit, P	Ryne Sandberg, Chicago, 2B
1985	Don Mattingly, New York, 1B	Willie McGee, St. Louis, OF
1986	Roger Clemens, Boston, P	Mike Schmidt, Philadelphia, 3B
1987	George Bell, Toronto, OF	Andre Dawson, Chicago, OF
1988	Jose Canseco, Oakland, OF	Kirk Gibson, Los Angeles, OF
1989	Robin Yount, Milwaukee, OF	Kevin Mitchell, San Francisco, OF
1990	Rickey Henderson, Oakland, OF	Barry Bonds, Pittsburgh, OF
1991	Cal Ripken Jr., Baltimore, SS	Terry Pendleton, Atlanta, 3B
1992	Dennis Eckersley, Oakland, P	Barry Bonds, Pittsburgh, OF
1993	Frank Thomas, Chicago, 1B	Barry Bonds, San Francisco, OF
1994	Frank Thomas, Chicago, 1B	Jeff Bagwell, Houston, 1B
1995	Mo Vaughn, Boston, 1B	Barry Larkin, Cincinnati, SS
1996	Juan Gonzalez, Texas, OF	Ken Caminiti, San Diego, 3B
1997	Ken Griffey Jr., Seattle, OF	Larry Walker, Colorado, OF
1998	Juan Gonzalez, Texas, OF	Sammy Sosa, Chicago, OF
1999	Ivan Rodriguez, Texas, C	Chipper Jones, Atlanta, 3B
2000	Jason Giambi, Oakland, 1B	Jeff Kent, San Francisco, 2B
2001	Ichiro Suzuki, Seattle, OF	Barry Bonds, San Francisco, OF
2002	Miguel Tejada, Oakland, SS	Barry Bonds, San Francisco, OF
2003	Alex Rodriguez, Texas, SS	Barry Bonds, San Francisco, OF

2004	Vladimir Guerrero, Anaheim, OF	Barry Bonds, San Francisco, OF
2005	Alex Rodriguez, New York, 3B	Albert Pujols, St. Louis, 1B
2006	Justin Morneau, Minnesota, 1B	Ryan Howard, Philadelphia, 1B
2007	Alex Rodriguez, New York, 3B	Jimmy Rollins, Philadelphia, SS
2008	Dustin Pedroia, Boston, 2B	Albert Pujols, St. Louis, 1B
2009	Joe Mauer, Minnesota, C	Albert Pujols, St. Louis, 1B
2010	Josh Hamilton, Texas, OF	Joey Votto, Cincinnati, 1B
2011	Justin Verlander, Detroit, P	Ryan Braun, Milwaukee, OF

The first precursor to the Most Valuable Player Award was the Chalmers Award, given 1911–1914. Winners were as follows:

1911	Ty Cobb, Detroit, OF	Frank Schulte, Chicago, OF
1912	Tris Speaker, Boston, OF	Larry Doyle, New York, 2B
1913	Walter Johnson, Washington, P	Jake Daubert, Brooklyn 1B
1914	Eddie Collins, Philadelphia, 1B	Johnny Evers, Boston, 2B

The League Awards were given in the American League from 1922 to 1928 and in the National League from 1924 to 1929.

1922	George Sisler, St. Louis, 1B	
1923	Babe Ruth, New York, OF	
1924	Walter Johnson, Washington, P	Dazzy Vance, Brooklyn, P
1925	Roger Peckinpaugh, Washington, SS	Rogers Hornsby, St. Louis, 2B
1926	George Burns, Cleveland, 1B	Bob O'Farrell, St. Louis, C
1927	Lou Gehrig, New York, 1B	Paul Waner, Pittsburgh, OF
1928	Mickey Cochrane, Philadelphia, C	Jim Bottomley, St. Louis, 1B
1929		Rogers Hornsby, Chicago, 2B

Note. P: pitcher. C: catcher. 1B: first baseman. 2B: second baseman. 3B: third baseman. OF: outfielder. SS: shortstop. DH: designated hitter.

Appendix K: Cy Young Award Winners

From its inception in 1956 through the 1966 season, the Cy Young Award was given to only one pitcher in the major leagues. Winners from those years are shown as follows. Beginning in 1967, Cy Young Awards have been given to a pitcher in each league.

1956: Don Newcombe, Brooklyn (NL)
1957: Warren Spahn, Milwaukee (NL)
1958: Bob Turley, New York (AL)
1959: Early Wynn, Chicago (AL)
1960: Vern Law, Pittsburgh (NL)
1961: Whitey Ford, New York (AL)
1962: Don Drysdale, Los Angeles (NL)
1963: Sandy Koufax, Los Angeles (NL)
1964: Dean Chance, Los Angeles (AL)
1965: Sandy Koufax, Los Angeles (NL)
1966: Sandy Koufax, Los Angeles (NL)

Note. AL: American League. NL: National League.

Year	American League	National League
1967	Jim Lonborg, Boston	Mike McCormick, San Francisco
1968	Denny McLain, Detroit	Bob Gibson, St. Louis
1969	Mike Cueller, Baltimore	Tom Seaver, New York
	Denny McClain, Detroit	
1970	Jim Perry, Minnesota	Bob Gibson, St. Louis

1971	Vida Blue, Oakland	Fergie Jenkins, Chicago
1972	Gaylord Perry, Cleveland	Steve Carlton, Philadelphia
1973	Jim Palmer, Baltimore	Tom Seaver, New York
1974	Catfish Hunter, Oakland	Mike Marshall, Los Angeles
1975	Jim Palmer, Baltimore	Tom Seaver, New York
1976	Jim Palmer, Baltimore	Randy Jones, San Diego
1977	Sparky Lyle, New York	Steve Carlton, Philadelphia
1978	Ron Guidry, New York	Gaylord Perry, San Diego
1979	Mike Flanagan, Baltimore	Bruce Sutter, Chicago
1980	Steve Stone, Baltimore	Steve Carlton, Philadelphia
1981	Rollie Fingers, Milwaukee	Fernando Valenzuela, Los Angeles
1982	Pete Vuckovich, Milwaukee	Steve Carlton, Philadelphia
1983	LaMarr Hoyt, Chicago	John Denny, Philadelphia
1984	Willie Hernandez, Detroit	Rick Sutcliffe, Chicago
1985	Bret Saberhagen, Kansas City	Dwight Gooden, New York
1986	Roger Clemens, Boston	Mike Scott, Houston
1987	Roger Clemens, Boston	Steve Bedrosian, Philadelphia
1988	Frank Viola, Minnesota	Orel Hershiser, Los Angeles
1989	Bret Saberhagen, Kansas City	Mark Davis, San Diego
1990	Bob Welch, Oakland	Doug Drabek, Pittsburgh
1991	Roger Clemens, Boston	Tom Glavine, Atlanta
1992	Dennis Eckersley, Oakland	Greg Maddux, Chicago
1993	Jack McDowell, Chicago	Greg Maddux, Atlanta
1994	David Cone, Kansas City	Greg Maddux, Atlanta
1995	Randy Johnson, Seattle	Greg Maddux, Atlanta
1996	Pat Hentgen, Toronto	John Smoltz, Atlanta
1997	Roger Clemens, Toronto	Pedro Martinez, Montreal
1998	Roger Clemens, Toronto	Tom Glavine, Atlanta
1999	Pedro Martinez, Boston	Randy Johnson, Arizona
2000	Pedro Martinez, Boston	Randy Johnson, Arizona

2001	Roger Clemens, New York	Randy Johnson, Arizona
2002	Barry Zito, Oakland	Randy Johnson, Arizona
2003	Roy Halladay, Toronto	Eric Gagne, Los Angeles
2004	Johan Santana, Minnesota	Roger Clemens, Houston
2005	Bartolo Colon, Los Angeles	Chris Carpenter, St. Louis
2006	Johan Santana, Minnesota	Brandon Webb, Arizona
2007	C.C. Sabathia, Cleveland	Jake Peavy, San Diego
2008	Cliff Lee, Cleveland	Tim Lincecum, San Francisco
2009	Zack Greinke, Kansas City	Tim Lincecum, San Francisco
2010	Felix Hernandez, Seattle	Roy Halladay, Philadelphia
2011	Justin Verlander, Detroit	Clayton Kershaw, Los Angeles

Appendix L: Rookies of the Year

When the Rookie of the Year Award (now officially the Jackie Robinson Award) was introduced in 1947, for that season and the next, only one award was given for both leagues. The winners were Jackie Robinson (Brooklyn Dodgers) in 1947 and Alvin Dark (New York Giants) in 1948. Since 1949, Rookie of the Year Awards have been given to players in both leagues.

Year	American League	National League
1949	Roy Sievers, St. Louis, OF	Don Newcombe, Brooklyn, P
1950	Walt Dropo, Boston, 1B	Sam Jethroe, Boston, OF
1951	Gil McDougald, New York, 3B/2B	Willie Mays, New York, OF
1952	Harry Byrd, Philadelphia, P	Joe Black, Brooklyn, P
1953	Harvey Kuenn, Detroit, SS	Jim Gilliam, Brooklyn, 2B
1954	Bob Grim, New York, P	Wally Moon, St. Louis, OF
1955	Herb Score, Cleveland, P	Bill Virdon, St. Louis, OF
1956	Luis Aparicio, Chicago, SS	Frank Robinson, Cincinnati, OF
1957	Tony Kubek, New York, SS	Jack Sanford, Philadelphia, P
1958	Albie Pearson, Washington, OF	Orlando Cepeda, San Francisco, 1B
1959	Bob Allison, Washington, OF	Willie McCovey, San Francisco, 1B
1960	Ron Hansen, Baltimore, SS	Frank Howard, Los Angeles, OF
1961	Don Schwall, Boston, P	Billy Williams, Chicago, OF

1962	Tom Tresh, New York, SS	Ken Hubbs, Chicago, 2B
1963	Gary Peters, Chicago,P	Pete Rose, Cincinnati, 2B
1964	Tony Oliva, Minnesota, OF	Richie Allen, Philadelphia, 3B
1965	Curt Blefary, Baltimore, OF	Jim Lefebrve, Los Angeles, 2B
1966	Tommie Agee, Chicago, OF	Tommy Helms, Cincinnati, 3B
1967	Rod Carew, Minnesota, 2B	Tom Seaver, New York, P
1968	Stan Bahnsen, New York, P	Johnny Bench, Cincinnati, C
1969	Lou Piniella, Kansas City, OF	Ted Sizemore, Los Angeles, 2B/ SS
1970	Thurman Munson, New York, C	Carl Morton, Montreal, P
1971	Chris Chambliss, Cleveland, 1B	Earl Williams, Atlanta, C/3B/2B
1972	Carlton Fisk, Boston, C	Jon Matlack, New York, P
1973	Al Bumbry, Baltimore, OF	Gary Matthews, San Francisco, OF
1974	Mike Hargrove, Texas, 1B	Bake McBride, St. Louis, OF
1975	Fred Lynn, Boston, OF	John Montefusco, San Francisco, P
1976	Mark Fidrych, Detroit, P	Butch Metzger, San Diego, P
		Pat Zachry, Cincinnati, P
1977	Eddie Murray, Baltimore, 1B	Andre Dawson, Montreal, OF
1978	Lou Whitaker, Detroit, 2B	Bob Horner, Atlanta, 3B
1979	John Castino, Minnesota, 3B	Rick Sutcliffe, Los Angeles, P
	Alfredo Griffin, Toronto, SS	
1980	Joe Charboneau, Cleveland, OF/ DH	Steve Howe, Los Angeles, P
1981	Dave Righetti, New York, P	Fernando Valenzuela, Los Angeles, P
1982	Cal Ripken Jr., Baltimore, SS	Steve Sax, Los Angeles, 2B
1983	Ron Kittle, Chicago, OF	Darryl Strawberry, New York, OF
1984	Alvin Davis, Seattle, 1B	Dwight Gooden, New York, P
1985	Ozzie Guillen, Chicago, SS	Vince Coleman, St. Louis, OF
1986	Jose Canseco, Oakland, OF	Todd Worrell, St. Louis, P
1987	Mark McGwire, Oakland, 1B	Benito Santiago, San Diego, C

1988	Walt Weiss, Oakland, SS	Chris Sabo, Cincinnati, 3B
1989	Gregg Olson, Baltimore, P	Jerome Walton, Chicago, OF
1990	Sandy Alomar Jr., Cleveland, C	Dave Justice, Atlanta, OF
1991	Chuck Knoblauch, Minnesota, 2B	Jeff Bagwell, Houston, OF
1992	Pat Listach, Milwaukee, SS	Eric Karros, Los Angeles, 1B
1993	Tim Salmon, California, OF	Mike Piazza, Los Angeles, C
1994	Bob Hamelin, Kansas City, DH/ 1B	Raul Mondesi, Los Angeles, OF
1995	Marty Cordova, Minnesota, OF	Hideo Nomo, Los Angeles, P
1996	Derek Jeter, New York, SS	Todd Hollandsworth, Los Angeles, OF
1997	Nomar Garciaparra, Boston, SS	Scott Rolen, Philadelphia, 3B
1998	Ben Grieve, Oakland, OF	Kerry Wood, Chicago, P
1999	Carlos Beltran, Kansas City, OF	Scott Williamson, Cincinnati, P
2000	Kazuhiro Sasaki, Seattle, P	Rafael Furcal, Atlanta, SS
2001	Ichiro Suzuki, Seattle, OF	Albert Pujols, St. Louis, OF/3B/ 1B
2002	Eric Hinske, Toronto, 3B	Jason Jennings, Colorado, P
2003	Angel Berroa, Kansas City, SS	Dontrelle Willis, Florida, P
2004	Bobby Crosby, Oakland, SS	Jason Bay, Pittsburgh, OF
2005	Huston Street, Oakland, P	Ryan Howard, Philadelphia, 1B
2006	Justin Verlander, Detroit, P	Hanley Ramirez, Florida, SS
2007	Dustin Pedroia, Boston, 2B	Ryan Braun, Milwaukee, 3B
2008	Evan Longoria, Tampa Bay, 3B	Geovany Soto, Chicago, C
2009	Andrew Bailey, Oakland, P	Chris Coghlan, Florida, OF
2010	Neftali Feliz, Texas, P	Buster Posey, San Francisco, C
2011	Jeremy Hellickson, Tampa Bay, P	Craig Kimbrel, Atlanta, P

Note. P: pitcher. C: catcher. 1B: first baseman. 2B: second baseman. 3B: third baseman. OF: outfielder. SS: shortstop. DH: designated hitter.

Appendix M: Gold Glove Record Holders

First base: Keith Hernandez, St. Louis, New York (National League), 11

Second base: Roberto Alomar, San Diego, Toronto, Baltimore, Cleveland, 10

Third base: Brooks Robinson, Baltimore, 16

Shortstop: Ozzie Smith, San Diego, St. Louis, 13

Outfield: Roberto Clemente, Pittsburgh, 12; Willie Mays, New York (National League), 12

Catcher: Ivan Rodriguez, Texas, Detroit, 13

Pitcher: Greg Maddux, Chicago (National League), Atlanta, Los Angeles (National League), San Diego, 18

Other players who have won 10 or more Gold Gloves include Jim Kaat, pitcher, 16; Omar Vizquel, shortstop, 11; Johnny Bench, catcher, 10; and outfielders Ken Griffey Jr., Andruw Jones, Al Kaline, and Ichiro Suzuki, all with 10. Darin Erstad of the Los Angeles Angels is the only player to have won Gold Gloves as both an outfielder and an infielder (first base). Placido Polanco won two Gold Gloves at second base and one as a third baseman.

Appendix N: Silver Slugger Award Record Holders

First base: Todd Helton, Colorado, 4; Albert Pujols,[1] St. Louis, 4
Second base: Ryne Sandberg, Chicago, 7
Third base: Wade Boggs, Boston, New York (American League), 8
Shortstop: Barry Larkin, Cincinnati, 9
Outfield: Barry Bonds, Pittsburgh, San Francisco, 12
Catcher: Mike Piazza, Los Angeles (National League), Florida, New York (National League), 10
Pitcher: Mike Hampton, Houston, New York (National League), Atlanta, 5
Designated hitter: Edgar Martinez,[2] Seattle, 4; Paul Molitor, Milwaukee, Toronto, Minnesota, 4; David Ortiz, Boston, 4

Alex Rodriguez has 10 awards, 7 as a shortstop for Seattle and Texas and 3 as a third baseman for the New York Yankees.

NOTES

1. Pujols also won awards at third base (1) and in the outfield (1).
2. Martinez also won an award at third base.

Appendix O: Commissioners of Baseball

KENESAW MOUNTAIN LANDIS: 1920–1944

A federal judge and the first and longest-serving commissioner, Landis was appointed to the newly established commissioner's position to restore integrity to the game following the Black Sox scandal. Landis's hard-line approach—banning the players involved for life—and his subsequent actions were credited with rebuilding public confidence in the sport. When appointed to the position, Landis was given the mandate to act in the game's best interests. His decisions over the course of his long tenure established several precedents for future commissioners.

A. B. "HAPPY" CHANDLER: 1945–1951

A former governor and senator from Kentucky, Chandler presided over the integration of the sport. Chandler forcefully upheld the breaking of the "color barrier," strongly supporting the process that brought Jackie Robinson to the major leagues. Chandler is also recalled for establishing the first pension fund for major league players.

FORD FRICK: 1951–1965

A former sportswriter and sportscaster, Frick was president of the National League at the time of his appointment. While in that position, Frick was instrumental in establishing the Hall of Fame. During his tenure as commissioner, he presided over expansions from 8 to 10 teams in each league, oversaw negotiations that led to enhanced television contracts, and instituted the first major league draft. Frick's most controversial decision was to insert an asterisk after Roger Maris's 61 home runs to indicate that Maris had achieved his record in a 162-game season (unlike Babe Ruth's standard of 60, which was accomplished in 154 games.) Years later, the asterisk was removed.

WILLIAM ECKERT: 1965–1968

A surprise compromise choice as commissioner, Eckert was a former lieutenant general in the United States Air Force who brought a strong management and business background to the position. Those credentials were sought by club owners concerned by the uneasy labor and financial environment then affecting the sport. Eckert streamlined business operations and helped stabilize several franchises via lease arrangements and enlarged seating capacities. He was known for promoting the game internationally. Given that his managerial background was the primary reason for his having been chosen for the job, the irony of Eckert's commissionership is that he was forced out by owners for not doing enough to address substantive business issues facing the sport.

BOWIE KUHN: 1969–1984

A lawyer by profession, Kuhn had been legal counsel for major league baseball for almost two decades when he was chosen to replace Eckert. That background likely served him in good stead, for the baseball world was confronted with a variety of contentious legal disputes during his tenure. After successfully negotiating a three-year contract with the players' union soon after taking office, Kuhn later faced thorny problems associated with the Curt Flood case, the end of the reserve clause, and the beginnings of free agency. In 1981, a players' strike shut down baseball for 50 days, the longest work stoppage in the game up to that time. Kuhn was noted for his forceful approach to drug use and other strong measures in response to actions that he considered detrimental to the sport. Kuhn oversaw baseball's expansion from 20 to 26 franchises. With his strong involvement and support, a World Series game was played at night for the first time.

PETER UEBERROTH: 1984–1989

A lifelong sportsman and successful businessman, Ueberroth came to the commissioner's job after his highly lauded performance running the organizing committee for the 1984 Olympic Games in Los Angeles. Ueberroth brought exceptional planning and management skills to the position, successfully ending a dispute with major league umpires and negotiating a new labor agreement with the players' association. His tenure saw increased emphasis on security in major league parks and increasingly lucrative television contracts. Ueberroth expanded the league championship series from a best-of-five to best-of-seven format. Alleged collusion in violation of the collective bargaining agreement regarding the signing of free agents cast a shadow on his time as commissioner.

A. BARTLETT GIAMATTI: 1989

Giamatti came to the commissioner's position as president of the National League. Before that he was a professor at and later president of Yale University. Giamatti's tenure was the shortest of any commissioner; he died of a heart attack after five months in the position. His short term was eventful, however. Giamatti defused the Pete Rose betting scandal by getting Rose to agree to voluntarily—and permanently—withdraw from the game. In his time as National League president and commissioner, Giamatti was known for his efforts to enhance the environment for fans at major league ballparks and for encouraging more minority hirings at all levels and positions in the sport. A former professor of comparative literature, Giamatti wrote essays about baseball that are among the most poignant and insightful writings about the sport.

FAY VINCENT: 1989–1992

Vincent was serving as deputy commissioner of baseball, a new position, when commissioner A. Bartlett Giamatti died of a heart attack. A Yale graduate like Giamatti, Vincent was a lawyer and a media and entertainment executive before being chosen by owners to replace his friend and mentor. Vincent's first major action involved handling decisions associated with the disruption of the World Series in the aftermath of the 1989 San Francisco earthquake. Labor disputes quickly came to the fore, the first and most severe being an owners' lockout that affected the 1990 spring training season and the delay of opening day. Vincent drew the wrath of some owners by banning New York Yankee owner George Steinbrenner (Steinbrenner was later reinstated) for actions that Vincent deemed detrimental to the game. Vincent removed the asterisk from Roger Maris's home run record and presided over expansion to 28 major league franchises.

ALLAN H. "BUD" SELIG: 1992–PRESENT

After Fay Vincent's resignation, Selig served from 1992 to 1998 in an interim status before being formally named commissioner. Selig, who came to the job as owner of the Milwaukee Brewers franchise, presided over baseball during momentous times. The players' strike in 1994 canceled the last third of the season as well as the playoffs and World Series. Division realignments, an expanded playoff format, and the advent of wild card teams have been introduced during his tenure. Expansion to 30 franchises occurred in 1998. A collective bargaining agreement was successfully concluded in 2002. The following year, World Series home-team advantage was assigned to the team from the league that won the season's All-Star Game. More recently, the steroids scandal and extensive changes to the drug-testing regimen have marked Selig's time in office.

Appendix P: Labor Disputes

1972: The first general strike in modern major league history. A 13-day strike (April 1–April 13) caused the season's opening day to be delayed by 10 days. The impasse was broken when agreement was reached on pension fund payments and when owners agreed to add salary arbitration to the collective bargaining agreement.

1981: A strike by players began on June 12, shut down play for almost two months, and caused the cancellation of 713 games. The major issue—free agent compensation—was resolved by a settlement reached on July 31. The compromise agreement allowed teams that lost a "premium" player to free agency to be compensated by choosing from a pool of players left unprotected from all the clubs. Free agency status was restricted to players with six or more years of major league service. Regular season play resumed on August 10 (the All-Star Game was played August 9) in a split-season format. In each division, first-place teams from each half season met in a best-of-five playoff to determine the overall division champion. Most teams played less than 110 games during the season.

1990: In February, owners announced that spring training would not start as scheduled. Donald Fehr, executive director of the Major League Baseball Players Association, expressed the concern that the owners' intention was to introduce a salary cap, thus potentially reducing free agent choices and dampening the potential for multiyear contracts. The lockout wiped out the entire spring training schedule and delayed opening day of the 1990 season by a week (to April 9). A new basic agreement between owners and players, brokered by baseball commissioner Fay Vincent, broke the impasse. The contract increased minimum salaries and established a committee to study revenue sharing.

1994: On August 12, a strike began that ended the season. There were no league champions, and for the first time since 1904, the World Series was not played. The cause was the club owners' proposal for a salary cap. Before the 232-day strike was officially concluded early the following April, more than 900 games had been canceled. While numerous players and teams were affected by the strike, perhaps the most devastating consequence was felt by the Montreal Expos ball club. When play was halted on August 11, the Expos had the best record in major league baseball (74–40) and were leading their division by six full games. Strained by reduced revenues as a result of the shortened 1995 season (among other factors), the franchise never fully recovered.

1995: In a strike-shortened season, teams played only 144 games. The stoppage that halted play the preceding August was not officially resolved until April 2, with opening day set for April 25. The shortened preseason training opportunity initially affected the quality of play throughout both leagues. The termination of the strike was a study in chaos, affected by player-requested injunctions that stretched all the way to the U.S. Court of Appeals and by owners' threats to conduct the season with replacement players. Ironically, play resumed under the conditions of the expired contract in the absence of a formal collective bargaining agreement.

Appendix Q: "Casey at the Bat" and a Sampling of Sequels

The full text of "Casey at the Bat," by Ernest Thayer, as it originally appeared in the *San Francisco Examiner* on June 3, 1888:

> The outlook wasn't brilliant for the Mudville nine that day:
> The score stood four to two, with but one inning more to play
>
> And then when Cooney died at first, and Barrows did the same,
> A sickly silence fell upon the patrons of the game.
>
> Straggling few got up to go in deep despair. The rest
> Clung to that hope which springs eternal in the human breast;
>
> They thought, if only Casey could get but a whack at that—
> We'd put up even money, now, with Casey at the bat.
>
> But Flynn preceded Casey, and did also Jimmy Blake,
> And the former was a lulu and the latter was a cake;
>
> So upon that stricken multitude grim melancholy sat,
> For there seemed but little chance of Casey's getting to the bat.
>
> But Flynn let drive a single, to the wonderment of all,
> And Blake, the much despis-ed, tore the cover off the ball;
>
> And when the dust had lifted, and the men saw what had occurred,
> There was Jimmy safe at second and Flynn a-hugging third.
>
> Then from 5,000 throats and more there rose a lusty yell;

It rumbled through the valley, it rattled in the dell;

It knocked upon the mountain and recoiled upon the flat,
For Casey, mighty Casey, was advancing to the bat.

There was ease in Casey's manner as he stepped into his place;
There was pride in Casey's bearing and a smile on Casey's face.

And when, responding to the cheers, he lightly doffed his hat,
No stranger in the crowd could doubt 'twas Casey at the bat.

Ten thousand eyes were on him as he rubbed his hands with dirt;
Five thousand tongues applauded when he wiped them on his shirt.

Then while the writhing pitcher ground the ball into his hip,
Defiance gleamed in Casey's eye, a sneer curled Casey's lip.

And now the leather-covered sphere came hurtling through the air,
And Casey stood a-watching it in haughty grandeur there

Close by the sturdy batsman the ball unheeded sped-
"That ain't my style," said Casey. "Strike one," the umpire said.

From the benches, black with people, there went up a muffled roar,
Like the beating of the storm-waves on a stern and distant shore.

"Kill him! Kill the umpire!" shouted someone on the stand;
And it's likely they a-killed him had not Casey raised his hand.

With a smile of Christian charity great Casey's visage shone;
He stilled the rising tumult; he bade the game go on;

He signaled to the pitcher, and once more the spheroid flew;
But Casey still ignored it, and the umpire said, "Strike two."

"Fraud!" called the maddened thousands, and echo answered fraud;
But one scornful look from Casey and the audience was awed.

They saw his face grow stern and cold, they saw his muscles strain,
And they knew that Casey wouldn't let that ball go by again.

The sneer is gone from Casey's lip, his teeth are clenched in hate;
He pounds with cruel violence his bat upon the plate.

And now the pitcher holds the ball, and now he lets it go,
And now the air is shattered by the force of Casey's blow.

Oh, somewhere in this favored land the sun is shining bright;
The band is playing somewhere, and somewhere hearts are light,

And somewhere men are laughing, and somewhere children shout;
But there is no joy in Mudville—mighty Casey has struck out.

Over the years, numerous sequels to the "Casey" poem have been written. Some have Casey getting a second chance and returning as a hero. Others have less predictable, more unusual endings. A version variously attributed to sportswriter Grantland Rice or James Wilson casts Casey as a redeemed hero, hitting a bases-loaded home run. The Rice/Wilson poem concludes,

Oh, somewhere in this favored land dark clouds may hide the sun;
And somewhere bands no longer play and children have no fun;

And somewhere over blighted loves there hangs a heavy pall;
But Mudville hearts are happy now—for Casey hit the ball.

Most versions, like the one that follows, seek to preserve the length, tone, names, and rhyming pattern of the original. Like a few others, however, it has a different take on the ending.

Doubleheader at Mudville, by Thomas D. Phillips

So momentous was the discovery, other news was swept away:
Mudville had played a *doubleheader* on that infamous day.

As the blurry microfilm unspooled frame by moldy frame,
No doubt was left in all the world: there had been a second, later, game.

Excited beyond endurance, hearts pounding in each chest,
Experts checked the ag-ed documents that described the final test.

Consumed by the moment's grandeur, too absorbed to chew or chat,
Transfixed in awe at what they read, trembling hands held photostat.

Scholars with redemptive visions hoped for Casey's sake—
That history in its majesty would correct its cruel mistake.

But through the eighth it went as bright fantasies dulled to matte;
No way, it seemed, would Casey get another time at bat.

It was déjà vu all over again; the narrative cast a pall.
Down two going into the ninth again; no chance remained at all.

Cooney and Barrows were out once more and several curses were heard;
To expect Flynn and Blake to reach again just seemed too absurd.

But Flynn's roller died in the grass and as he ran from under his hat—
He narrowly beat the throw to first although he was out of shape and fat.

Then Jimmy Blake strolled to dish, moving at a very slow pace;
He was mired in a terrible slump against a pitcher he'd rather not face.

But Jimmy stepped up and swung and the pitch happened to hit his bat.
The ball banged off the left field wall and he was on second like a cat.

Flynn managed to make it to third and slid in mostly unhurt,
The umpire was on top of the play and called "Safe!" through dust and dirt.

Now Casey—glorious Casey—came up, his club held in furious grip.
None had seen him so determined; there was a snarl upon his lip.

Second chances are rare in life but brave Casey had no dread,
His only worry was for the pitcher's life if the ball flew at this head.

The frightened hurler threw the sphere and Casey smashed it with a roar—
Over the fence, across the street, it shattered a factory door.

Alas alas alas alas the ump yelled the ball was foul;
The crowd went mad with rage but all Casey did was scowl.

Now Casey stood in again, confident in the bellowing throng;
Then suddenly "You're Out!" was called: it seemed obscenely wrong.

The documents told a story as strange as you've ever heard:
They didn't pitch to Casey at the plate—*but they did pick Flynn off third.*

The multitude stood in silence, and some would later claim—
There were tears in Casey's eyes as the team trudged off in shame.

Overcome with grief and shock, for years fans remembered where—
They had been at the moment when dreams broke past repair.

Forever gone was Casey's chance to restore his fabled name,
And shadows still haunt the city from that fateful second game.

Next year the team moved to Tank Town, a shift devoid of grace,
And Mudville stadium was torn down and row houses took its place.

Thus the saga ended, with an outcome unpreferred:
They didn't pitch to Casey at the plate—but they did pick Flynn off third.

Appendix R: Nicknames

No attempt has been made to make the following list all-inclusive; indeed, a list of all of baseball's nicknames would fill a small encyclopedia. Fans who are interested in a more complete menu may wish to examine the *ESPN Baseball Encyclopedia*: "The Science of Hitting: The Batting Register" and "The Science of Pitching: The Pitching Register." Where possible, players are shown as members of the teams for which they played longest or had the most notable connection.

Hank Aaron, OF, Atlanta Braves: "Hammerin' Hank"
Grover Cleveland Alexander, P, Chicago Cubs: "Old Pete"
Walter Alston, M, Los Angeles Dodgers: "Smokey"
Adrian Anson, 1B, Chicago Cubs: "Cap"
Luke Appling, SS, Chicago White Sox: "Old Aches and Pains"
Earl Averill, OF, Cleveland Indians: "Rock"
Frank Baker, 3B, Philadelphia A's: "Home Run"
Ernie Banks, 1B, Chicago Cubs: "Mr. Cub"
Mark Belanger, SS, Baltimore Orioles: "The Blade"
James Bell, OF, Negro Leagues: "Cool Papa"
Charles Bender, P, Philadelphia A's: "Chief"
Lawrence Berra, C, New York Yankees: "Yogi"
Ewell Blackwell, P, Cincinnati Reds: "The Whip"
Jim Bottomley, 1B, St. Louis Cardinals: "Sunny Jim"
Harry Brecheen, P, St. Louis Cardinals: "The Cat"
Roger Bresnahan, C, New York Giants: "The Duke of Tralee"
Mordecai Brown, P, Chicago Cubs: "Three Finger"
Rick Burleson, SS, Boston Red Sox: "Rooster"
Guy Bush, P, Chicago Cubs: "The Mississippi Mudcat"
Joe Bush, P, Philadelphia A's: "Bullet Joe"

Burt Campaneris, SS, Oakland A's: "Campy"
John Candelaria, P, Pittsburgh Pirates: "The Candy Man"
James Carlton, P, Chicago Cubs: "Tex"
Alfonso Carresquel, SS, Chicago White Sox: "Chico"
Orlando Cepeda, 1B, San Francisco Giants: "Baby Bull," "Cha Cha"
Roy Cey, 3B, Los Angeles Dodgers: "The Penguin"
Frank Chance, M/1B, Chicago Cubs: "The Peerless Leader"
Spurgeon Chandler, P, New York Yankees: "Spud"
Hal Chase, 1B, New York Giants: "Prince Hal"
Roger Clemens, P, various AL, NL teams: "Rocket"
Ty Cobb, OF, Detroit Tigers: "The Georgia Peach"
Earle Combs, OF, New York Yankees: "The Kentucky Colonel"
Charles Comiskey, owner, Chicago White Sox: "The Old Roman"
Clint Courtney, C, Washington Senators: "Scrap Iron"
Covelli Crisp, OF, various AL teams: "Co Co"
Hazen Cuyler, OF, various NL teams: "Kiki"
Alvin Dark, SS, New York Giants: "Blackie"
Charles Davis, OF, San Francisco Giants: "Chili"
Jerome Hanna Dean, P, St. Louis Cardinals: "Dizzy"
Paul Dean, P, St. Louis Cardinals: "Daffy"
Dom DiMaggio, CF, Boston Red Sox: "The Little Professor"
Joe DiMaggio, CF, New York Yankees: "Joltin' Joe," "The Yankee Clip-
    per"
William Donovan, P, Detroit Tigers: "Wild Bill"
Joe Dugan, 3B, New York Yankees: "Jumpin' Joe"
Leo Durocher, M, New York Giants: "The Lip"
Lenny Dykstra, OF, New York Mets, Philadelphia Phillies: "Nails"
Johnny Evers, 2B, Chicago Cubs: "The Crab"
Bob Feller, P, Cleveland Indians: "Rapid Robert"
Mark Fidrych, P, Detroit Tigers: "The Bird"
Fred Fitzsimmons, P, New York Giants: "Fat Freddie"
Ed Ford, P, New York Yankees: "Whitey," "The Chairman of the Board"
Jimmie Foxx, OF, Philadelphia A's: "Double X"
Frankie Frisch, 2B, St. Louis Cardinals: "The Fordham Flash"
Carl Furillo, OF, Brooklyn Dodgers: "The Reading Rifle"
Andres Galarraga, 1B, various NL, AL teams: "The Big Cat"
Jim Galvin, P, Pittsburgh Pirates: "Pud," "The Little Steam Engine"
Mike Garcia, P, Cleveland Indians: "The Big Bear"
Lou Gehrig, 1B, New York Yankees: "The Iron Horse"
Charlie Gehringer, 2B, Detroit Tigers: "The Mechanical Man"
Dwight Gooden, P, New York Mets: "Dr. K"
Joe Gordon, 2B, New York Yankees, Cleveland Indians: "Flash"
Rich Gossage, RP, New York Yankees: "Goose"

Jim Grant, P, Cleveland Indians: "Mudcat"
Hank Greenberg, OF, Detroit: "Hammerin' Hank"
Ken Griffey Jr., OF, Cincinnati Reds: "Junior"
Charlie Grimm, 1B, Chicago Cubs: "Jolly Cholly"
Robert Moses Grove, P, Philadelphia Athletics: "Lefty"
George Haas, OF, Philadelphia, Chicago (AL): "Mule"
Stan Hack, 3B, Chicago Cubs: "Smilin' Stan"
Harvey Haddix, P, various NL teams: "The Kitten"
Ken Harrelson, 1B/OF, various AL teams: "Hawk"
Charles Hartnett, C, Chicago Cubs: "Gabby"
Orlando Hernandez, P, New York Yankees, various others: "El Duque"
Al Hrabosky, RP, St. Louis Cardinals: "The Mad Hungarian"
Carl Hubbell, P, New York Giants: "King Carl"
Jim Hunter, P, Oakland A's, New York Yankees: "Catfish"
Joe Jackson, OF, Chicago White Sox: "Shoeless Joe"
Randy Johnson, P, various NL, AL teams: "The Big Unit"
Walter Johnson, P, Washington Senators: "The Big Train"
Sam Jones, P, Boston Red Sox: "Sad Sam"
Willie Jones, 3B, Philadelphia Phillies: "Puddin' Head"
Willie Keeler, OF, various AL, NL teams: "Wee Willie"
Charlie Keller, OF, New York Yankees: "King Kong"
Mike Kelly, OF/C, Chicago White Stockings: "King"
Ellis Kinder, P, Boston Red Sox: "Old Folks"
Tony Lazzeri, 2B, New York Yankees: "Poosh 'Em Up"
Emil Leonard, P, various NL, AL teams: "Dutch"
Harry Lowrey, OF, various NL teams: "Peanuts"
Al Lyle, RP, New York Yankees: "Sparky"
Sal Maglie, P, New York Giants: "The Barber"
Walter James Vincent Maranville, SS, Boston Braves: "Rabbit"
Marty Marion, SS, St. Louis Cardinals: "Slats"
Richard Marquard, P, various NL teams: "Rube"
Johnny Martin, 3B, St. Louis Cardinals" "Pepper," "The Wild Horse of
    the Osage"
Dennis Martinez, P, various AL, NL teams: "El Presidente"
Christy Mathewson, P, New York Giants: "Big Six"
Don Mattingly, 1B, New York Yankees: "Donnie Baseball"
Willie Mays, CF, New York Giants: "The Say Hey Kid"
Willie McCovey, 1B, San Francisco Giants: "Stretch"
Sam McDowell, P, Cleveland Indians: "Sudden Sam"
Joe McGinnity, P, New York Giants: "Iron Man"
Frank McGraw, P, various NL teams: "Tug"
Fred McGriff, 1B, various AL, NL teams: "Crime Dog"
Mark McGwire, 1B, Oakland A's, St. Louis Cardinals: "Big Mac"

Joe Medwick, OF, various NL teams: "Ducky"
Bob Meusel, OF, New York Yankees: "Long Bob"
Wilmer Mizell, P, St. Louis Cardinals: "Vinegar Bend"
John Montefusco, P, various AL, NL teams: "Count"
Stan Musial, OF, St. Louis Cardinals: "Stan the Man"
Hal Newhouser, P, Detroit Tigers: "Prince Hal"
John Odom, P, Oakland A's: "Blue Moon"
David Ortiz, DH, Boston Red Sox: "Big Papi"
Joe Page, P, New York Yankees: "Fireman"
Leroy Paige, P, Negro Leagues, Cleveland Indians: "Satchel"
Dick Radatz, P, various AL, NL teams: "The Monster"
Charles Radbourn, P, Providence Grays: "Old Hoss"
Harold Reese, SS, Brooklyn Dodgers: "Pee Wee"
Allie Reynolds, P, New York Yankees: "The Superchief"
James Rhodes, OF, New York Giants: "Dusty"
Phil Rizzuto, SS, New York Yankees: "Scooter"
Alex Rodriguez, 3B, New York Yankees: "A-Rod"
Francisco Rodriguez, P, variou AL, NL teams: "K-Rod"
Elwin Roe, P, Brooklyn Dodgers: "Preacher"
Pete Rose, IF/OF, Cincinnati Reds: "Charlie Hustle"
Lynwood Rowe, P, Detroit Tigers: "Schoolboy"
Harold Ruel, C, various AL teams: "Muddy"
George Herman Ruth, OF, New York Yankees: "Babe," "The Bambino,"
    "The Sultan of Swat"
Nolan Ryan, P, Texas Rangers: "The Ryan Express"
Tom Seaver, P, various NL, AL teams: "Tom Terrific"
Francis Shea, P, New York, Washington (AL): "Spec"
Al Simmons, OF, various AL, NL teams: "Bucketfoot Al"
Harry Simpson, OF, various AL, NL teams: "Suitcase"
Bill Skowron, 1B, New York Yankees: "Moose"
Enos Slaughter, OF, St. Louis Cardinals: "Country"
Ozzie Smith, SS, St. Louis Cardinals: "The Wizard of Oz"
Edwin Snider, OF, Brooklyn Dodgers: "Duke," "The Silver Fox"
Sammy Sosa, OF, Chicago Cubs: "Slammin' Sammy"
Tris Speaker, OF, Boston Red Sox: "Spoke," "The Grey Eagle"
Willie Stargell, OF, Pittsburgh Pirates: "Pops"
Casey Stengel, M, New York Yankees: "The Ol' Perfessor"
George Stirnweiss, 2B, New York Yankees: "Snuffy"
Dick Stuart, 1B, Boston Red Sox: "Dr. Strangeglove"
Frank Thomas, 1B/DH, Chicago White Sox: "The Big Hurt"
Marv Throneberry, 1B, various AL, NL teams: "Marvelous Marv"
Paul Trout, P, Detroit Tigers: "Dizzy"
Virgil Trucks, P, Detroit Tigers: "Fire"

Clarence Vance, P, Brooklyn Dodgers: "Dazzy"
Joseph Vaughn, SS, Pittsburgh Pirates: "Arky"
George Waddell, P, various NL, AL teams: "Rube"
Honus Wagner, SS, Pittsburgh Pirates: "The Flying Dutchman"
Fred Walker, OF, Brooklyn Dodgers: "Dixie," "The People's Cherce"
Harry Walker, OF, St. Louis Cardinals: "Harry the Hat"
William Walters, P, various NL teams: "Bucky"
Lloyd Waner, OF, Pittsburgh Pirates: "Little Poison"
Paul Waner, OF, Pittsburgh Pirates: "Big Poison"
Lon Warneke, P, various NL teams: "The Arkansas Hummingbird"
David Wells, P, various AL, NL teams: "Boomer"
Steven Wendell, P, various NL teams: "Turk"
Lou Whitaker, 2B, Detroit Tigers: "Sweet Lou"
Mitch Williams, P, various NL, AL teams: "Wild Thing"
Ted Williams, OF, Boston Red Sox: "The Thumper," "The Splendid
    Splinter," "Teddy Ball Game"
Walt Williams, OF, Chicago White Sox: "No Neck"
William Wilson, OF, New York Mets: "Mookie"
Joe Wood, P, Boston Red Sox: "Smokey Joe"
Jim Wynn, OF, Houston Astros: "The Toy Cannon"
Carl Yastrzemski, OF, Boston Red Sox: "Yaz"
Denton Young, P, various AL, NL teams: "Cy"
Gus Zernial, OF, various AL teams: "Ozark Ike"
Don Zimmer, IF, various NL, AL teams: "Popeye"

EXTRA-INNINGS COVERAGE

From the hundreds of other lesser-known major league nicknames, the following 150 are among the most fascinating:

Bob Addy, OF, various NL teams: "Magnet"
Grady Adkins, P, Chicago White Sox: "Butcher Boy"
John Anderson, OF, various AL, NL teams: "Honest John"
Hank Arft, 1B, St. Louis Browns: "Bow Wow"
Morrie Arnovich, OF, Philadelphia Phillies: "Snooker"
Eldon Auker, P, Detroit Tigers: "Submarine"
Bruce Barmes, OF, Washington Senators: "Squeaky"
Dick Barnett, P, Philadelphia Phillies: "Kewpie Dick"
Bill Barrett, OF, Chicago White Sox: "Whispering Bill"
Eddie Basinski, IF, Brooklyn Dodgers: "Bazooka"
Harry Bay, OF, Cleveland: "Deerfoot"
Desmond Beatty, OF, New York Giants: "Desperate"

Walter Beck, P, Philadelphia Phillies: "Boom Boom"
William Bell, P, Pittsburgh Pirates: "Ding Dong"
Joe Benes, IF, St. Louis Cardinals: "Bananas"
Bill Bernhard, P, Cleveland: "Strawberry Bill"
Joe Berry, P, Philadelphia A's: "Jittery Joe"
Carson Bigbee, OF, Pittsburgh Pirates: "Skeeter"
Emil Bildilli, P, St. Louis Browns: "Hill Billy"
Clarence Blethen, P, various NL teams: "Climax"
Henry Boyle, P, various NL teams: "Handsome Henry"
Sig Boskie, C, Boston Braves: "Chops"
Marv Breuer, P, New York Yankees: "Baby Face"
Frank Brower, OF, Washington Senators: "Turkeyfoot"
Eddie Brown, OF, Boston Braves: "Glass Arm Eddie"
Ollie Brown, OF, various NL, AL teams: "Downtown"
Tommy Brown, IF/OF, Brooklyn Dodgers: "Buckshot"
William Burns, P, various NL, AL teams: "Sleepy Bill"
Larry Burright, IF, New York Mets: "Possum"
John Butler, IF, Brooklyn Dodgers: "Trolley Line"
Hardin Cathey, P, Washington Senators: "Lil Abner"
Elton Chamberlain, P, Cincinnati Reds: "Icebox"
Mike Chartuk, OF, various AL teams: "Shotgun"
Jack Chesbro, P, New York (AL): "Happy Jack"
Walter Christensen, OF, Cincinnati Reds: "Cuckoo"
Phil Collins, P, Philadelphia Phillies: "Fidgety Phil"
Harry Craft, OF, Cincinnati Reds: "Wildfire"
Clifford Cravath, OF, Philadelphia Phillies: "Cactus"
Jack Daniels, OF, St. Louis Browns: "Sour Mash Jack"
Pompeyo Davalillo, SS, Washington Senators: "YoYo"
Curt Davis, P, Brooklyn Dodgers: "Coonskin"
Bob Deluba, P, St. Louis Cardinals: "Ach"
Walt Dickson, P, various NL teams: "Hickory"
Bill Dietrick, P, Chicago White Sox: "Bullfrog"
Bill Doak, P, St. Louis Cardinals: "Spittin' Bill"
Jack Doyle, IF, New York Giants: "Dirty Jack"
Larry Doyle, 2B, New York Giants: "Laughing Larry"
Clem Dreisewerd, P, Boston Red Sox: "Steamboat"
George Dumont, P, Philadelphia Phillies: "Pea Soup"
Jim Dwyer, OF, Baltimore Orioles: "Pig Pen"
Mike Epstein, 1B, Washington Senators: "Superjew"
Robert Fausett, 3B, Cincinnati Reds: "Leakey"
Dave Ferris, P, Boston Red Sox: "Boo"
James Galloway, IF, St. Louis Cardinals: "Bad News"
Ralph Garr, OF, Atlanta Braves: "Road Runner"

Jim Gentile, 1B, Baltimore Orioles: "Diamond Jim"
Charles Getzien, P, various NL teams: "Pretzels"
Jack Gilbert, OF, various NL teams: "Jackrabbit"
Tommy Giordano, 2B, Philadelphia A's: "T-Bone"
Vernon Gomez, P, New York Yankees: "Goofy"
George Gore, OF, various NL teams: "Piano Legs"
Elijah Green, IF, Boston Red Sox: "Pumpsie"
Jim Hamby, C, New York Giants: "Cracker"
Luke Hamlin, P, Brooklyn Dodgers: "Hot Potato"
Roy Harrell, P, St. Louis Cardinals: "Cowboy"
George Hennessey, P, various NL teams: "Three Star"
Tommy Henrich, OF, New York Yankees: "The Clutch"
Johnny Hopp, OF/1B, various NL, AL teams: "Hippity"
Gene Host, P, various AL teams: "Twinkles"
Frank House, C, Detroit Tigers: "Pig"
Frank Howard, OF, Washington Senators: "Hondo"
Bill Howerton, OF, various NL teams: "Hopalong"
Ben Hunt, P, various AL, NL teams: "High Pockets"
Hal Ireland, IF, Philadelphia Phillies: "Grump"
Frank Isbell, IF, Chicago White Sox: "Bald Eagle"
Randy Jackson, 3B, Chicago Cubs: "Handsome Ransom"
Travis Jackson, SS, New York Giants: "Stonewall"
William Jacobson, OF, St. Louis Browns: "Baby Doll"
Al Javery, P, Boston Braves: "Bear Tracks"
Hughie Jennings, IF, various AL, NL teams: "Ee-yah"
Davy Jones, OF, various AL, NL teams: "Kangaroo"
Oscar Jones, P, Brooklyn Dodgers: "Flip Flop"
Sam Jones, P, various AL, NL teams: "Toothpick"
Sheldon Jones, P, New York Giants: "Available"
Sherman Jones, P, various NL teams: "Roadblock"
Vernon Jones, IF, St. Louis Cardinals: "Nippy"
Jake Kafora, C, Pittsburgh Pirates: "Tomatoes"
Harry Kane, P, various AL, NL teams: "Klondike"
Bill Keisten, IF, various AL, NL teams: "Wagon Tongue"
Jimmy Kennan, P, various AL, NL teams: "Sparkplug"
Bill Killefer, C, various NL teams: "Reindeer Bill"
Ed Killian, P, Detroit Tigers: "Seacap," "Twilight Ed"
Bill McGhee, IF/OF, Philadelphia A's: "Fibber"
John McGraw, M, New York Giants: "Little Napoleon"
Lloyd Merriman, OF, Cincinnati Reds: "Citation"
Doggie Miller, C/OF, various NL teams: "Foghorn"
George Moolic, C/OF, Cincinnati Reds: "Prunes"
Gene Moore, P, various NL teams: "Blue Goose"

Tom Morgan, P, various AL teams: "Plowboy"
Hugh Mulcahy, P, Philadelphia Phillies: "Losing Pitcher"
Johnny Murphy, P, New York Yankees: "Grandma"
Sam Nahem, P, various NL teams: "Subway Sam"
Julio Navarro, P, various AL teams: "Whiplash"
Al Nixon, OF, Boston Braves: "Humpty Dumpty"
Lou Novikoff, OF, Chicago Cubs: "The Mad Russian"
John O'Brien, 2B, various NL teams: "Chewing Gum"
Federico Olivo, P, Milwaukee Braves: "Chi Chi"
Andy Pafko, OF, various NL teams: "Handy Andy"
Milt Pappas, P, various AL, NL teams: "Gimpy"
Roy Parmelee, P, New York Giants: "Tarzan"
Freddie Patek, SS, Kansas City Royals: "The Flea"
Bill Phillips, P, Cincinnati Reds: "Whoa Bill"
Dick Porter, OF, Cleveland: "Twitches," "Wiggles"
Joe Prescko, P, St. Louis Cardinals: "Baby Joe"
Hub Pruitt, P, various AL, NL teams: "Schucks"
Jim Ray, P, Houston Astros: "Sting"
Phil Regan, P, various AL, NL teams: "The Vulture"
Jim Rivera, OF, Chicago White Sox: "Jungle Jim"
Wilbert Robinson, C, various NL, AL teams: "Uncle Robby"
Dick Rudolph, P, Boston Braves: "Baldy"
Allan Russell, P, various AL teams: "Rubberarm"
Ray Schalk, C, Chicago White Sox: "Cracker"
John Schmitz, P, various AL, NL teams: "Bear Tracks"
George Selkirk, OF, New York Yankees: "Twinkletoes"
Jim Shaw, P, Washington Senators: "Grunting Jim"
Anthony Shines, 1B, Montreal Expos: "Razor"
Lou Skizaz, OF, various AL teams: "The Nervous Greek"
Bob Smith, P, various AL, NL teams: "Riverboat"
Frank Smith, P, various AL, NL teams: "Piano Mover"
Lonnie Smith, OF, various AL, NL teams: "Skates"
Willie Smith, OF, Chicago Cubs: "Wonderful Willie"
Archie Stemmel, P, Cincinnati Reds: "Lumbago"
Allen Stout, P, various NL teams: "Fish Hook"
Charles Street, C, various AL, NL teams: "Gabby," "Old Sarge"
Tom Sturdivant, P, various AL teams: "Snake"
Ed Summers, P, Detroit Tigers: "Kickapoo Ed"
Wayne Terwilliger, IF, various NL, AL teams: "Twig"
Jim Tobin, P, Boston (NL): "Abba Dabba"
Bill Tremel, P, Chicago Cubs: "Mumbles"
Bob Turley, P, New York Yankees: "Bullet Bob"
Jim Turner, P, various AL, NL teams: "Milkman Jim"

Guy Tutwiler, IF, Detroit Tigers: "King Tut"
Jake Wade, P, various AL teams: "Whistling Jake"
Frank Welch, OF, Philadelphia Phillies: "Bugger"
Charlie Wilson, IF, St. Louis Cardinals: "Swamp Baby"
Rollie Zeider, IF, various AL, NL teams: "Bunions"
Bill Zuber, P, various AL teams: "Goober"

Note. P: pitcher. RP: relief pitcher. C: catcher. 1B: first baseman. 2B: second baseman. 3B: third baseman. IF: infielder. CF: center fielder. OF: outfielder. SS: shortstop. DH: designated hitter. M: manager. AL: American League. NL: National League.

Notes

Throughout the book, I have relied primarily on the *ESPN Baseball Encyclopedia* for career- and season-specific material. ESPN's volume is only one of many equally fine references that chronicle the sport in extraordinary detail. The various editions of the *Bill James Historical Baseball Abstract*, the *Baseball America Almanac*, and others also provide comprehensive information.

Indeed, one of the reasons for baseball's broad appeal may be the easy accessibility to the sport's defining stories and milestones. In this most statistically oriented sport, the numbers associated with key accomplishments are typically not much in dispute, and the few that are generally date back to the early days of the game.

Because of the common agreement on major facts and their ready availability, the comments that follow supplement the associated stories or provide perspective regarding them.

CHAPTERS 1–2: STORIES 1–8

Among the best descriptions of baseball during the sport's sunrise moments are those found in Geoffrey C. Ward and Ken Burns's *Baseball: An Illustrated History*, Benjamin G. Rader's *Baseball: A History of America's Game* (2nd ed.), and George Will's *Men at Work: The Craft of Baseball*. The famous quote by Red Smith regarding the magic of 90 feet between bases is in Will's *Men at Work* (p. 259). David Nemec and Gary Flatow's *Great Baseball Feats, Facts, and Firsts 2010* contains a valuable chronology of the sport's early days (pp. 4–13). I am especially grateful to Freddy Berowski, reference librarian, A. Bartlett Giamatti Research Library, National Baseball Hall of Fame and Museum, for providing information regarding the development of the relay throw, cutoff play, and wheel play.

CHAPTER 8: STORY 57

The National Baseball Hall of Fame research staff confirms that it is Schilling's sock from the October 24 game that is on loan to them.

CHAPTER 14: STORY 81

Although published before the most recent new parks were opened, the books cited in the bibliography are superbly researched and photographed and are delights to read. Josh Leventhal's book also contains pictures and information on minor league and Negro League ballparks. Websites for each of the major league teams contain up-to-the minute stadium information.

CHAPTER 15: STORIES 82–85

Rader's *Baseball: A History of America's Game* traces the introduction and evolution of specialized gear particularly well. Ward and Burns's *Baseball: An Illustrated History* is also an excellent source.

CHAPTER 16: STORY 87

Among other works, Nemec and Flatow's *Great Baseball Feats, Facts, and Firsts* does a superb job of highlighting special accomplishments and unique individual and team records, such as those described in this story. Douglas B. Lyons's *Baseball: A Geek's Guide* is a source for interesting and sometimes off-the-beaten-path tidbits of information. Both references provide sources for this story and others throughout the book.

CHAPTER 19: STORY 90

As noted in the story, Canseco's book drew public attention to steroid use by major league ballplayers. Although overblown in places, the book warrants a look by readers interested in exploring the issue from the beginning of its time in the spotlight. In contrast, the Fainura-Wade and Williams book *Game of Shadows* provides an exhaustively researched chronicle of the BAL-CO–Barry Bonds episode.

CHAPTER 20: THE IMPACT OF WORLD WAR II

President Roosevelt's "green light letter" for continuing major league baseball during the war is discussed in Rader's *Baseball: A History of America's Game* (p. 171) and quoted by Ward and Burns's *Baseball: An Illustrated History* (pp. 276–77). A photo of the letter appears in Verducci's *Sports Illustrated: The Baseball Book* (p. 113).

CHAPTER 22: STORY 97

I am especially grateful to Bill Francis and his research colleagues at the National Baseball Hall of Fame and Museum for information regarding changes to pitching rules over the years.

CHAPTER 23: STORY 98

The full cite for *Federal Baseball Club of Baltimore, Inc. v. National League of Professional Baseball Clubs* is 259 U.S. 200 (1922). The court's unanimous decision that the Sherman Antitrust Act did not apply to baseball was written by Chief Justice Oliver Wendell Holmes. The case was argued on April 19, 1922, and decided on May 19, 1922.

CHAPTER 25: STORY 100

The most charming illustrated version of "Casey at the Bat" that I have seen is by Christopher Bing (Scholastics, Inc., 2000). Among many other sources, "Baseball's Sad Lexicon" can be found in Lyons's *Baseball: A Geek's Guide*

(p. 228). *Abbott and Costello: Sixty Years of "Who's on First"*, by Stephen Cox and John Loflin (Nashville, TN: Cumberland House Publishing, 1997) is one of several sources that provide information on the classic routine.

CHAPTER 26: STORY 101

Nicknames were selected from player information contained in the *ESPN Baseball Encyclopedia*. The interesting tidbit about Dick Stuart's "E-3" license plate is in Lyons's *Baseball: A Geek's Guide* (p. 289).

BIBLIOGRAPHY

The bibliography contains separate segments that correspond with major subject areas in the book. Readers interested in further exploring facets of the game's history may wish to consider the references identified in those sections—including the Hall of Fame, the All-Star Game, the Negro Leagues, ballparks, the Black Sox scandal, the steroids era, the impact of World War II, and the legacy of Jackie Robinson.

Bibliography

GENERAL REFERENCES

Brown, Gerry, and Michael Morrison, eds. *ESPN: Sports Almanac 2009*. New York: ESPN Books, 2009.

Dickson, Paul. *The Unwritten Rules of Baseball: The Etiquette, Conventional Wisdom, and Axiomatic Codes of Our National Pastime*. New York: Harper, 2009.

Formosa, Dan, and Paul Hamburger. *Baseball Field Guide: An In-Depth Illustrated Guide to the Complete Rules of Baseball*. Cambridge, MA: Da Capo Press, 2008.

Gillette, Gary, Pete Palmer, and Peter Gammons, eds. *The ESPN Baseball Encyclopedia*, 5th ed. New York: Sterling, 2008.

James, Bill. *The New Bill James Historical Baseball Abstract*. New York: Free Press, 2001.

Lingo, Will, ed. *Baseball America 2012 Almanac*. Durham, NC: Baseball America, 2011.

Lyons, Douglas B. *Baseball: A Geek's Guide*. New York: Barnes & Noble, 2007.

Nemec, David, Scott Flatow, and Dave Zeman. *Great Baseball Feats, Facts, and Firsts*. New York: Signet, 2011.

Rader, Benjamin G. *Baseball: A History of America's Game*, 2nd ed. Urbana: University of Illinois Press, 2002.

Southworth, Harold S. *Baseball's Greatest Moments*. Hopatcong, NJ: Republic Books, 1999.

Thorn, John. *Baseball in the Garden of Eden: The Secret History of the Early Game*. New York: Simon & Schuster, 2011.

Vecsey, George. *Baseball: A History of America's Favorite Game*. New York: Modern Library, 2008.

Verducci, Tom, ed. *Sports Illustrated: The Baseball Book*. New York: Sports Illustrated, 2011.

Ward, Geoffrey C., Ken Burns, and Kevin Baker. *Baseball: An Illustrated History*. New York: Knopf, 2010.

Will, George. *Men at Work: The Craft of Baseball*. New York: Macmillan, 1990.

Zoss, Joel. *Greatest Moments in Baseball*. New York, Exeter, 1987.

Zoss, Joel, and John S. Bowman. *Diamonds in the Rough: The Untold History of Baseball*, rev. ed. Lincoln, NE: Bison Books, 2004.

HALL OF FAME

General

Blount, Roy, Jr. *The Baseball Hall of Fame 50th Anniversary Book.* New York: Simon & Schuster, 1990.

Sugar, Bert R. *Bert Sugar's Baseball Hall of Fame: A Living History of America's Greatest Game.* New York: Running Press, 2009.

Babe Ruth

Creamer Robert W. *Babe: The Legend Comes to Life.* New York: Simon & Schuster, 1974.

Montville, Leigh. *The Big Bam: The Life and Times of Babe Ruth.* Norwall, MA: Anchor Press, 2007.

Pirone, Dorothy Ruth, and Chris Martens. *My Dad, the Babe: Growing Up with an American Hero.* Boston: Quinlan Press, 1988.

Smelser, Marshall. *The Life That Ruth Built: A Biography.* Lincoln, NE: Bison Books, 1993.

Wagenheim, Kas. *Babe Ruth: His Life and Legend.* New York: Holt, 1974.

Walter Johnson

Kavanagh, Jack. *Walter Johnson: A Life.* Lanham, MD: Taylor Trade, 1995.

Thomas, Henry W. *Walter Johnson: Baseball's Big Train.* Lincoln, NE: Bison Books, 1998.

Ty Cobb

Cobb, Ty, and Al Stump. *My Life in Baseball: The True Record.* Lincoln, NE: Bison Books, 1993.

Rhodes, Don. *Ty Cobb: Safe at Home.* Guilford, CT: Lyons Press, 2008.

Stump, Al. *Cobb: A Biography.* New York: Algonquin Books, 1996.

Honus Wagner

DeValeria, Dennis. *Honus Wagner: A Biography.* Pittsburgh: University of Pittsburgh Press, 1998.

Hittner, Arthur D. *Honus Wagner: The Life of Baseball's "Flying Dutchman."* Jefferson, NC: McFarland, 2003.

Christy Mathewson

Hartley, Michael. *Christy Mathewson.* Jefferson, NC: McFarland, 2004.

Robinson, Ray. *Matty: An American Hero.* New York: Oxford University Press, 1994.

Seib, Philip. *The Player: Christy Mathewson, Baseball, and the American Century.* Cambridge, MA: Da Capo Press, 2004.

ALL-STAR GAME

Freedman, Lew. *The Day All the Stars Came Out: Major League Baseball's First All-Star Game, 1933.* Jefferson, NC: McFarland, 2010.

Nurse, Ammie L. *Baseball's All-Star Game Reference Guide 1933–2007: 78 Games in 74 Years.* Tucson, AZ: Wheatmark, 2007.

Vincent, David, and David W. Vincent. *The Midsummer Classic: The Complete History of Baseball's All-Star Game.* Lincoln, NE: Bison Books, 2001.

NEGRO LEAGUES

Clark, Dick, and Larry Lester. *The Negro League Book: Limited Edition.* Cooperstown, NY: Society for American Baseball Research, 1994.
Heaphy, Leslie A. *The Negro Leagues, 1869–1960.* Jefferson, NC: McFarland, 2002.

ELYSIAN FIELDS: THE BALLPARKS

Enders, Eric. *Ballparks: Then and Now.* San Diego: Thunder Bay Press, 2007.
Gershman, Michael. *Diamonds: The Stories of the Ballparks.* New York: Houghton Mifflin, 1993.
Leventhal, Josh. *Take Me Out to the Ballpark: An Illustrated History of Baseball Parks Past and Present.* New York: Black Dog & Leventhal, 2011.
Ritter, Lawrence S. *Lost Ballparks: A Celebration of Baseball's Legendary Fields.* New York: Studio, 1992.

BLACK SOX SCANDAL

Asinof, Eliot. *Eight Men Out: The Black Sox and the 1919 World Series.* New York: Holt, 1977.
Gropman, Donald. *Say It Ain't So, Joe! The True Story of Shoeless Joe Jackson and the 1919 World Series.* New York: Little, Brown, 1979.

STEROIDS ERA

Canseco, Jose. *Juiced: Wild Times, Rampant 'Roids, Smash Hits, and How Baseball Got Big.* New York: Morrow, 2005.
Fainura-Wada, Mark, and Lance Williams. *Game of Shadows: Barry Bonds, BALCO, and the Steroids Scandal that Rocked Professional Sports.* New York: Gotham, 2006.

IMPACT OF WORLD WAR II

General

Bullock, Steven R. *Playing for Their Nation: Baseball and the American Military during World War II.* Lincoln: University of Nebraska Press, 2004.
Mead, William B. *Baseball Goes to War.* New York: Broadcast Interview Source, 1998.
———. *Even the Browns: Baseball during World War II.* Mineola, NY: Dover, 2010.

Ted Williams

Linn, Ed. *Hitter: The Life and Turmoils of Ted Williams.* New York: Harcourt, 1993.
Nowlin, Bill. *Ted Williams at War.* Burlington, MA: Rounder Books, 2007.
Seidel, Michael. *Ted Williams: A Baseball Life.* Chicago: Contemporary Books, 1991.
Williams, Ted, and John Underwood. *My Turn at Bat: The Story of My Life.* New York: Simon & Schuster, 1969.

Bob Feller

Feller, Bob, and Bill Gilbert. *Now Pitching, Bob Feller.* New York: Citadel, 1990.
Sickels, John. *Bob Feller: Ace of the Greatest Generation.* Dulles, VA: Potomac Books, 2004.

Warren Spahn

Shapiro, Milton. *The Warren Spahn Story.* Chicago: Messner, 1963.
Silverman, Al. *Warren Spahn, Immortal Southpaw.* New York: Sports Magazine Library, 1961.

Pete Gray: The One-Armed Ballplayer

Kashatus, William C. *One-Armed Wonder: Pete Gray, Wartime Baseball, and the American Dream.* Jefferson, NC: McFarland, 2001.
Nicholson, William G. *Pete Gray: One-Armed Major Leaguer.* New York: Prentice Hall, 1976.

Women's League

Browne, Lois. *Girls of Summer: The Real Story of the All-American Girls Professional Baseball League.* New York: HarperCollins, 1993.
Gilbert, Sarah. *A League of Their Own.* New York: Warner Books, 1992.

THE LEGACY OF JACKIE ROBINSON

Chalbert, John. *Rickey and Robinson: The Preacher, the Player, and America's Game.* Wheeling, IL: Harlan Davidson, 2000.
Rampersad, Arnold. *Jackie Robinson: A Biography.* New York: Knopf, 1997.
Robinson, Jackie, and Alfred Duckett. *I Never Had It Made: An Autobiography of Jackie Robinson.* New York: HarperCollins, 1972.
Simon, Scott. *Jackie Robinson and the Integration of Baseball.* Hoboken, NJ: Wiley, 2002.
Tygiel, Jules. *Baseball's Great Experiment: Jackie Robinson and His Legacy.* New York: Oxford University Press, 2008.
Wilson, John R. M. *Jackie Robinson and the American Dilemma.* New York: Prentice Hall, 2009.

Note. Interested readers are invited to peruse the list of baseball's best literature shown in chapter 25. The nonfiction works on the extended list all contain meaningful slices of the game's history.

Index

About the Author

Thomas D. Phillips teaches baseball history and speaks about the sport to a variety of audiences. His writings about baseball have appeared in *Elysian Fields Quarterly: The Baseball Review*, *Spitball: The Baseball Literary Journal*, and other publications. During a 36-year military career, he played and coached baseball at several locations around the globe. He is a four-time gold medal winner in interservice athletics. During his military service, Phillips led an isolated unit through a terrorist episode, served as director of the Air Force Military Personnel Readiness Center during Operation Desert Storm, and led some of the first American troops into Sarajevo, Bosnia-Herzegovina. Phillips's writings about military affairs and national defense have appeared in several national and international publications. He is the author of a memoir, *A Pilgrim in Unholy Places: Stories of a Mustang Colonel*, and a military history, *Battlefields of Nebraska.*

CPSIA information can be obtained at www.ICGtesting.com
Printed in the USA
BVOW011319140812

297786BV00001B/2/P